2500

THE ROOTS OF BEGIN'S SUCCESS

The Roots of Begin's Success

THE 1981 ISRAELI ELECTIONS

Edited by DAN CASPI, ABRAHAM DISKIN
and EMANUEL GUTMANN

CROOM HELM
London & Canberra
ST. MARTIN'S PRESS
New York

© 1984 D. Caspi, A. Diskin and E. Gutmann
Croom Helm Ltd, Provident House, Burrell Row,
Beckenham, Kent BR3 1AT
Croom Helm Australia, PO Box 391, Manuka,
ACT 2603, Australia

British Library Cataloguing in Publication Data
The Roots of Begin's success.
    1. Israel--History
    2. Israel--Politics and government
    I. Gutmann, E.   II. Caspi, D.
    III. Diskin, A.
    956.94'054   DS126.4
    ISBN 0-7099-1146-7

Library of Congress Cataloging in Publication Data
Main entry under title:

The Roots of Begin's success.

    1. Israel. Keneset--Elections, 1981--Addresses,
essays, lectures. 2. Begin, Menachem, 1913-
--Addresses, essays, lectures. I. Gutmann, Emanuel,
1924-   . II. Caspi, Dan. III. Diskin, Avraham.
JQ1825.P365R66   1984   324.95694'054   83-3120
ISBN 0-312-69309-5 (St. Martin's Press)

Printed and bound in Great Britain

CONTENTS

PREFACE

Israel's political system has undergone a fundamental change, one which extends far beyond the coalitionary shifts which followed the 1977 elections and was reaffirmed in 1981. At least up until the early 1970s, Israel had had a "dominant party" system in which Mapai, although never achieving an outright majority, maintained its position by virtue of its relatively large electoral lead.

During the long years of Mapai dominance, election analysts were primarily concerned with accounting for the fact that despite a fourfold population increase and a concomitantly vast change and diversity in the socio-economic make-up of the voting public, aggregate voting behavior remained remarkably constant for over twenty years.

At this stage, however, it appears that Israel is approaching a roughly balanced version of a two-party (or party-bloc) system. The last two election results emphasize the general impression of a more dramatic change in the electoral preferences of the Israeli voter which occured during the time of relatively slow demographic change.

The present book is apparently a by-product of the 1981 elections. While each of its eleven chapters attempts in its own way to place these elections within a broader context; they share a common objective: comprehension of the electoral results as the outcome of deep-rooted, long-range trends within the Israeli political system. The 1977 elections can no longer be viewed as an one-time episode: A combination of three factors — ethnicity, age and religious observance — which caused the rise of the Likud, remains responsible for the relatively stable basis for the new "dominant party." The electoral upheaval of 1977 is attributed to the so-called ethnic vote, referring in this context, to Sephardic (Oriental) Jews, i.e. those who immigrated to Israel primarily from Muslim, Arabic-speaking countries in North-Africa and the Middle East, as well as their descendants. By the mid-1970s, this sector accounted for just over half of the Israeli Jewish population.

In other words, the electoral success of Likud in 1981, and particularly of its prominent leader Mr. Menachem Begin is a result of the diffuse support that was reassured among the Sephardim, young people and the religiously inclined. This support assisted Mr. Begin to reverse the public opinion within a relatively short period of six months prior the 1981 election and efficiently serves him in facing frequent political crisis.

Aronson and Yanai open the volume by emphasizing both the institutional and structural aspect of the political map, including severe problems of leadership, which prepared the ground for the Likud's retention of power in 1981.

The next four articles sought a different basis for these results, primarily in terms of characteristics of the two major parties. In his first article, Diskin utilizes aggregate data, enabling him to reassess long-range intensification of the ethnic vote, which favors the Likud. Gonen adopts a similar strategy with aggregate data, ecologically describing the growth of Likud popularity among low-income Sephardic immigrants since 1965. The ethnic vote for the Likud progressed centrifugally over the years, from the poorer quarters of the major cities to immigrant housing projects on the outskirts of older cities and still later in the so-called development towns. Peres and Shemer remain faithful to survey data and continue analysis of the ethnic vote, projecting a deterministic picture. In two different ways, Peres and Shemer arrive at the same conclusion as Diskin, observing a clear-cut differentiation in the ethnic vote between the two major parties, intensification of which will apparently ensure the Likud's retaining power for a long period of time. In his second paper, Diskin also uses survey data, examining the evident voter volatility and polarization between the two major political camps. He reveals that supporters of the Likud and Alignment are not diametrically opposed in thier values and policy positions, although their respective party loyalties are considerable.

Friedman and Landau refer to other parts of the political map: Friedman explains the sharp drop in electoral support for the National Religious Party (NRP), while Landau considers the Arab vote, which had reversed its trend of the last two decades, possibly in a one-time deviation. Friedman's argument is that the mediating role between religious electors and the governmental system of the NRP, unlike that of the ultra-Orthodox Agudat Israel Party, has largely become superfluous. Landau challenges the conservative trend of the Arab voters, noting that more than one-third traditionally voted for the radical Communist Party, which ran as the Hadash list in the 1981 elections, while nearly another third abstain, many in order to express their reservations regarding the Zionist political establishment.

The vital link between election outcomes and policy-making is debated in the next two articles. Peri first defines four types of legitimate wars and then demonstrates the gradual shift from the *preventive war* conception of the Labor-led governments to that of *war as an instrument for attaining national objectives* of the Likud government, as exemplified by the recent war in Lebanon. Radian, who has likwise undertaken a historical analysis, refers to another crucial field of policy-making, comparing tax policy initiatives during the period 1955–1981.

The comparative approach also guided the last two articles, which refer specifically to the propaganda campaign. Caspi historically verifies the extent of voter exposure to party propaganda. Changes in propaganda style, particularly the professionalization trend in managing and running the campaign, have induced parallel changes in voters' "uses and gratifications"; more than ever before, past campaigns, voters tend to be more exposed to the party propaganda for enter-tainment reasons and less for information-seeking. Weimann deals specifically with the very blatant use of pre-election polls which significantly penetrated the Israeli politics in the last years. His long-range content analysis of the press reports reveals a considerable growth in quantity and qualita-tive coverage which may justify the name of his article: "Every Day is Election Day."

The editors are indebted to the many people who offered their assistance and advice. Particularly earnest gratitude is expressed to the Konrad Adenauer Stiftung of Bonn (Federal Republic of Germany— and its active and efficient representa-tive in Israel, Mr. Norbert Chauvistre, for their most generous support, enabling the planning and publishing of this book and providing funds for the research of its three editors. Special thanks go to Charlotte Goldfarb of the Hebrew University's Authority for Research and Development for her kind and endless patience and to the devoted linguistic consultant, Mr. Zvi Ofer, who survived the editors' caprices.

Jerusalem, 3 Sivan 5743   D.C.
                                                                      A.D.
                                                                      E.G.

1

CRITICAL ASPECTS OF THE ELECTIONS AND THEIR IMPLICATIONS

Shlomo Aronson* and Nathan Yanai**

The 1981 elections marked the completion of a realigning electoral era in Israel[1], beginning with the creation of a competitive two-party (bloc) system in the 1973 elections, producing the first change of the leading ruling party (in a system of coalition government) in the 1977 elections and reaffirming this change in the 1981 elections. A successful challenge by the Alignment to the maiden regime of the Likud, in 1981, might have turned it into a mere *ad hoc* deviation from an historic dominant party system. A resurgence of the 1977 voters' coalition was responsible for the outcome of the election, yet, the striking mid-term fluctuation in voters' attitudes demonstrated the volatility and the potential mobility of Israeli electorate (Diskin 1983).

The purpose of this article is to provide a framework for discussion of major structural and behavioral aspects in the 1981 elections, their origins and consequences.

Two-Bloc Dominance in the Knesset

Fragmentation in the Israeli multi-party system was significantly arrested in the 1981 election. The two main Knesset factions (blocs) combined gained the largest number of seats (95 out of 120) and the number of lists which acquired representation in the Knesset (10) is the smallest in the history of Israel's parliament.

*Associate Professor of Political Science, The Hebrew University of Jerusalem.
**Lecturer, Israel Studies and Political Science, The University of Haifa.

Table 1: **Combined Number of Seats Gained by the Two Largest Knesset Factions**

1949	1951	1955	1959	1961	1965	1969	1973	1977	1981
65	65	55	64	59	71	82	90	77	95

Table 2: **Number of Lists Acquiring Representation***

1949	1951	1955	1959	1961	1965	1969	1973	1977	1981
12	15	12	12	11	13	13	11	12	10

The number of Knesset factions usually increased in mid-term as a result of party splits.

The challenge from the new political center to the two major blocs was successfully contained: Shinui gained only two seats as against the fifteen gained in the 1977 elections by its parent political movement — the defunct Democratic Movement for Change; A new electoray entry — Moshe Dayan's Telem — also gained only two seats. The radical left returned to the Knesset with curtailed representation: Sheli did not succeed in passing the one percent threshold required for representation; the Citizens' Rights Movement (CRM)[2] returned again with a single seat, and the Communist List (Rakah) lost one of its five seats. The new radical right (Techiya) gained only three seats and failed to seriously erode the electoral support of the Likud. The first legitimate electoral appeal to the ethnic-oriental communities (Tami) did not fail altogether but gained only three seats. The religious parties lost considerable support: The National Religious Party (NRP) — half of its representation (six out of twelve seats) and Agudat Israel/Poalei Agudat Israel — one out of five seats.

The structural change from a highly fragmented multi-party system, with a dominant party at its center (the Alignment) into a moderate and competitive multi-party system with a two-bloc- dominance took place in an electoral system of almost pure proportional representation.[3] The change thus lacks constitutional safeguards and is entirely dependent on the voters, who are left with an electoral system which is capable of accurately reflecting their multi-party choice.

Electoral Weakness and Coalition Strength of Intermediary ("Third") Parties

The close outcome of the two-bloc electoral competition producing no majority bloc and almost equal Knesset representation (the Likud — 48 seats; the Alignment — 47) vested coalition-making power in the hands of the intermediary (third) parties, despite the decrease in their Knesset representation. This situation actually passed the decision from the voters (close to eighty percent of whom supported one of the two blocs) to the minor coalitionary factions. The almost equal representation of the two blocs, which turned into a virtual parity (with the immediate entry of the CRM's single-member Knesset faction into the Alignment), diffused the well-established traditional claim of the largest faction to head the coalition government. In this parliamentary situation the intermediary parties, primarily the religious ones, decided to maintain the pre-election coalition headed by the Likud, the bloc with the largest popular vote. Tami, and the former members of the defunct Telem faction followed suit. (Midterm defections of two members of the Likud to the Alignment turned the latter into the largest Knesset faction, albeit without any immediate coalitionary consequence).

Despite the narrow margin of the coalition government elected by the new Knesset, the latter actually demonstrated expansion of the "coalitionary circle," i.e., the availability of Knesset factions to participate in a given coalition. With the exception of Hadash, the communist list, which lacks potential major allies in the Knesset, no other faction excluded itself from coalitionary politics; all at least indicated their preference for a coalition possibility and a pragmatic bargaining position for participation in it. This new coalitionary attitude, contrary to exclusive protest policies prevalent among radical partis in the past, is the product of the new competitive two-bloc dominance in the Israeli party system and its attendant political and social polarization.

Coalitionary Advantage and Change in Coalitionary Attitude

The condition of virtual parity in representation exposed and highlighted the coalitionary advantage of the Likud over the Labor Alignment which resulted in reinstatement of the pre-election coalitionary alliances. The major coalition parties, the Likud and the NRP, actually appealed to the voters to reinstate their coalition government while the Alignment was unable to propose a tangible alternative, and could not win enough votes to enable exclusion of the religious parties from the government.

The alliance between the Likud and the religious parties was not only the outcome of policy agreements and concessions, but also of a meaningful change in coalitionary attitudes on the part of the principal ruling bloc, the Likud, towards government by coalition and to coalitionary partership.[4] Mapai*, under the prolonged leadership of David Ben-Gurion, in its bid for a majority position among the voters, challenged the very legitimacy of the coalition rule and campaigned against the disproportionate power of minor coalitionary parties, describing them, at times, as "extortionist" and "fraction-like-parties." Mapai competed openly for the potential constituencies of its coalitionary partners, strove to limit their capacity to transform a coalitionary position into an electoral advantage and did not hesitate to initiate coalition crises in order to redefine rules of coalitionary discipline, reject demands and challenge the ruling legitimacy of a coalitionary party.[5]

In a stable dominant party system, the actual scope and significance of electoral competition is sharply reduced. It does not relate primarily to the mandate of the dominant party to rule but rather to the make-up of the rest of the coalition and consequently the terms or cost of the coalitionary agreement. In comparison, in a competitive party system — electoral competition relates primarily to the mandate of the leading ruling party and not only to its relative strategic position versus the coalition and the consequential costs of the coalitionary agreement. In the former system, there is no

*The former principal party in the Israel Labor Party and (Labor) Alignment (between it and Mapam).

overbearing incentive to forge a durable, overt, coalitionary alliance prior to the election. In the latter — it may be advisable to do so in the absence of a good prospect to win a majority in a proportional-representation electoral system. In the former system — the dominant party may compete and confront its coalitionary partners with minimal risks; in the latter system — such an attitude is risky indeed. For example: Ben-Gurion was able to pursue long-term (although not endless) politics of confrontation within the coalition government at minimal cost, while Rabin's punitive action against a coalitionary partner (the NRP) in 1977, within a competitive party system, contributed to a change of coalitionary orientation in that party. Mapai's coalitionary attitudes were compatible with its position and interests as a dominant party and with its general reformist approach defined by Ben-Gurion — to the party system and the structure of the government. The Likud's attitudes are compatible with its position and interests in a competitive party system and with its general accommodating approach to the existing party system and structure of government.

The Likud, under the leadership of Menachem Begin, introduced three changes in Mapai's traditional coalitionary attitude (defined by Ben-Gurion):

a) Acceptance of the coalition as a fully legitimate and positive form of government relating to the coalitionary alliance as desirable rather than forced.

b) Seeking a wide coalitionary agreement, based on maximal ideological understanding, as a basis for durable alliances rather than a more restrictive agreement aiming at limited partnership.

c) A calculatedly generous approach towards allocation of coalitionary rewards, approximating the utilitarian rule: maximum compensation to most coalition participants within the limitations of the system of government, viz: the rule of Law, the consent of the parliament and management of conflicting inter-party positions.

Unlike Mapai, the Likud was cooperative and forthcoming in accommodating the needs of coalitionary parties. Mapai strove to allocate what may be termed particularistic rewards, while the Likud was prepared to allocate universalistic ones as well. Mapai was prepared to partially finance independent religious institutions and responded to the integrating needs of the religious section of the population; e.g. the institution of kosher kitchens in the army and governmental institutions. It was reluctant, however, to accept any universalistic demand which would limit the freedom of choice of the secular sector beyond the acceptable *status quo ante* originating in traditional custom and rule of government of the Ottoman and British regimes in Palestine. Mapai was prepared to legislate a Sabbath law only on the basis of existing practices and arrangements, which the religious parties refused to sanction by law. The Likud, in contrast, accepted a demand to cancel El Al flights on the Sabbath; i.e. — to terminate a well-established practice. The Likud acquiesced to universalistic religious legislative demands to amend and limit the abortion law and to legislate the Anatomy and Pathology law.

The Centripetal Trend and the Left

Since 1965, the Labor movement has undergone a realigning process which culminated in the formation of the Israel Labor Party in 1968 and its alignment with Mapam in 1969. The radical left inside and outside Mapam, the major leftist party within the Zionist Labor Movement, challenged this process by attempting to force Mapam out of the Alignment and by forming competing parties (Ya'ad and Sheli).[6]

The fall of the Labor government in the 1977 elections precipitated a change of orientation in the radical left: centrifugal pressures, which failed to produce any encouraging results, where replaced by a new centripetal trend which put an end (at least temporarily) to the perennial debate within Mapam on the future of the Alignment, brought leading members of Sheli to join Mapam and led to the organization of a radical party club (*Hug* 77) within the ILP itself.

The electoral defeat of the Alignment in the 1977 election created both a sense of alarm and of opportunity among the diffused groups of the radical left: alarm over the ascendancy of the Likud and opportunity created by the apparent political weakening of the established Labor movement and its susceptibility to a "movement-type" message in its search for a new ideological and political definition following the traumatic electoral defeat. The convergence of the change in the radical left and the post-election search within the Labor movement set the stage for a new opening towards the left within the Alignment, which legitimized the new role of radical spokesmen and "clubs" therein.

This opening to the left, characteristic of European Labor parties in opposition[7] may also be viewed as a defensive reaction of the radical left in Israel to centripetal pressures emerging within a pure P.R. electoral system. This reaction is generally more typical of a restraining electoral system — a single member district or high threshold for representation. The Israel electoral system's vulnerability to fragmentation obviously allows for resumption of the old schism between radical and moderate wings in the Labor movement.

The new orientation did not weaken the radical left; it may even have strengthened it somewhat as had occurred previously in Great Britain and West Germany.[8] It did, however, create a coalitionary obstacle and a new political dilemma for the leadership of the Alignment, leading to the adoption of an anti-clerical stand, as well as a change in the traditional moderate hawkish image. Both these stands drove a wedge between the Labor movement and the religious parties, including the labor-dominated NRP.

The absence of Alignment prospects for a coalition government, despite the sharp increase in its Knesset representation, invited the appearance of counter-pressures designed to curtail the opening to the left, rehabilitate the traditional moderate hawkish posture and rebuild bridges to the religious parties. Such change was also advocated for the purpose of rectifying political alienation among Sephardic voters who were found to maintain a hawkish approach and a special affinity to religious tradition (Shamir & Arian 1982).

The Centripetal Trend and the Religious Parties

The NRP was victimized by both the centripetal electoral trend (defection to the Likud) and deviation therefrom (the formation of the Sephardic-oriented list, Tami, and the nationalistic Techiya). In the 1981 election, the NRP lost half its Knesset representation. Nevertheless, the parliamentary impasse and the new coalitionary orientation of the Likud enabled the NRP and the other minor coalitionary parties to score unprecedented coalitionary gains. This proved to be a double-edged sword, however, exposing the traditional constituencies of the NRP to the indirect wooing of the Likud in a dramatic two-bloc contest. A dominant party system with built-in tension between the leading party (Mapai — Labor Party and the minor coalitionary parties was indeed electorally safer for the NRP.

Under the continued threat of voter defection, the NRP was left with three electoral strategies, in addition to the possibility of another independent run. (The possible return of party leaders who defected to Tami and Techiya in 1981 may be a decisive factor in ruling out these options.):

a)   Renewal of the United Religious Front with the Aguda parties, as in the elections to the First Knesset in 1949. This would accentuate anew the particularistic appeal of these parties to the religious constituencies, while still exposing the more open and nationalistically-oriented constituency of the NRP to the appeal of the pro-religious Likud. Furthermore, the NRP's electoral losses in 1981 and the existence of a safe onstituency for Agudath Israel may defeat any effort to devise a scheme for composing a joint list.

b)   Forming an "electoral front" with the Likud as an expansion of the inter-party alliance in the coalition government. Such an option may reaffirm the electoral position of the NRP at the cost of diffused party identity and curtailed party independence. Furthermore, it may expose the party to possible defection in an opposite direction — i.e., towards the Alignment. The Likud may indeed initiate such a list, as it would provide some insurance against a break in the coalitionary alliance and would enhance its consensus image and ruling legitimacy.

c)   Any serious consideration given to this possibility may produce the third electoral option — a possible split between the two major NRP factions and their respective alignment with the dominant Knesset blocs. In such an eventuality, the more nationalistically oriented "Young" faction (*Zeirim*) would align itself with the Likud, while the more socially-oriented *Lamifne* faction would join the Labor camp. The first faction was the political parent of Gush Emunim, while the second represents Hapoel Hamizrahi — the religious labor federation which belongs to the unionist section of the Labor-dominated Histadrut — the General Federation of Labor — and participates in its Health Fund (*Kupat Holim*).

The 1981 elections left the NRP with critical tests of unity and purpose: Is there a basis for continued co-existence of its long-time embattled factions? What is the true nature of its nationalist approach: subscribing to the principle of a Greater Israel largely as a religious commitment or as a firm, active secular political orientation as well. The NRP, if capable of maintaining its unity and independence, would probably continue to press for a government of national unity which — apart from other considerations — represents the best chance for maintaining its particular intermediary role and qualifying its support for the Likud government.

The Centripetal Trend at the Cost of Political and Social Polarization

The centripetal trend produced a two-bloc dominance at the cost of political and social polarization. This phenomenon was expressed in the 1981 election by a mutual challenge of legitimacy by both the Likud and the Alignment, and the convergence of cumulative ethnic, social — communal and partisan — electoral tensions.

The two political camps were conscious of the critical significance of the 1981 election, which would decide the shape of the party system and the government for years to come: restoration of Labor dominance or conclusion and stabilization of the process of realignment. This consciousness intensified the inter-party conflict, created political over-participation in certain sectors of Israeli society, developed patterns of politics of de-legitimization and contributed to a temporary surge in partisan identification in a political system already characterized by processes leading to its gradual demise. Indeed, partisan identification in the 1981 elections was fed, to a large extent, by secondary group identifications which led groups of voters to mobilize in support of the party (bloc) in the defense of their vital interests and/or the symbolic components of their national, cultural, religious, social and communal identity.

The emergence of two-bloc dominance, which is the closest approximation to a two-party sysfem in a proportional representation electoral system, may be viewed as a positive systemic development, despite the absence of a majority parliamentary bloc and the need for coalition government. However, the new system emerged at the cost of political and social polarization; hence its long-term contribution to the stability of the system is predicated on the adaptation of the two blocs to the requirements and risks of a competitive party system, namely, the acceptance of a change in government as a permanent, legitimate expectation, the movement of the two blocs towards the political center and the end to politics of de-legitimacy.

The competitive parliamentary status of the opposition bloc and the increasing importance of critical dividing issues, (among them the issue of annexation of Judea and Samaria) encouraged both blocs to pursue the mutual challenge of legitimacy beyond the election campaign. Nevertheless, it is still feasible to foresee conditions for the possible formation of a provisional, *ad hoc* grand coalition in Israel,[9] including a parliamentary deadlock without a majority support for an early election, or a state of national emergency and an acute crisis of confidence in government without recourse to immediate change. The intermediary parties, chiefly the NRP, hold the key to such a possibility. The NRP has been committed to the establishment of a government of national unity since the 1977 elections; it actually pressed for the formation of such a government, to no avail, after the 1981 elections. The Likud officially accepted this demand without having to face and evaluate its consequences, while, the Alignment leadership remains divided. For the NRP, such a government presents the best strategy for highlighting its unifying national role and for obtaining a dual coalitionary option. Such a government, like its predecessor (1967–1970), may also serve the interests of the Labor opposition, as its very formation may undermine the legitimacy and stability of the Likud government, create bridges to the minor coalitionary parties (especially the NRP), and pave the way for a change in the initial coalition government.

A Challenge to the Supremacy of the Veteran Elite Groups

The outcome of the 1977 and especially the 1981 elections may be viewed as a successful political and social assertion of new claimant groups in response to the loss of effectiveness or "leadership fatigue" of the historic political elite.[10] The new — like the old — political elite groups acquired their prominence through or within the framework of a political party.

The historic political elite, associated with the Labor Alignment, comprised leading members of the ruling bureaucracies (state, municipal, and Zionist organization), members of the collective (kibbutz) and the cooperative (moshav) settlement movements and the principal activists of the Histadrut establishment. The new, challenging elite, associated with the Likud parties, comprises either veteran groups which were rejected or those which formed during the prolonged Labor regime:

a) rejected veteran groups — the former members of the "Irgun" and the "Stern Group," settlers of the old farmers' villages (Moshavot), and veteran urban "citizen" and business groups; b) new immigrants of Sephardic origin (from Arab states who developed independent leadership position in municipal government or labor workers' committees; and c) new economic groups which intensified their political involvement only during the closing phase of the Labor regime.

Loss of political effectiveness or "leadership fatigue" of the political labor elite was demonstrable in five areas:

a)   Lack of capacity to manage a durable and stifling internal leadership conflict within the Labor Party: this conflict acquired some degree of legitimacy in the new democratized, competitive system of nomination for the Prime Minister (since 1974), which contrasted markedly with the prevalent party caucus method of nomination for high office during the Mapai founders' era (Yanai 1981).[11] Labor failed to disengage effectively from each of the three nominating contests between Rabin and Peres and reestablish a unified leadership behind the party standard-bearer. The winner-take-all outcome of the wide-open nominating contest for the Prime Minister's post collided with the structure of party bodies and the party list of candidates within an electoral system of proportional representation; thus, after the deciding vote, the party was still left with the task of allocating representation in party organizations and lists in accordance with sectional make-up and in relation to the outcome of the critical nominating contest. In doing so, the party actually widened and institutionalized the divisive nominating contests after its nominal resolution.

b) Lack of immediate and demonstrable skill and capability for renewal in the areas of leadership recruitment and public service in the face of a score of incidents of corruption in high office among members of the ruling Labor elite.

c) The aforementioned two failures undermined the leadership legitimacy of the ruling labor elite even among some of its traditional constituencies, namely urban, educated upper middle classes of European origin, who were successfully mobilized in the 1977 elections in support of a new entry, the Democratic Movement for Change — a short-lived citizen's type "good government" political party, which attempted, in vain, to offer an alternative to the Labor political leadership within the veteran elite.

d) Cumulative alienation between the Alignment and the non-European communities, which followed the loss of leadership legitimacy, skill and unity.

e) Labor's crisis of leadership was coupled with partial withdrawal from the universalistic concept of statehood (*Mamlachtiut*) which was developed by Mapai under the leadership of Ben-Gurion. This concept and its demonstrable enforcement in key areas of state government (e.g. the army) enhanced the ruling legitimacy of Mapai and turned it, in some respects, into the party most identified with the state.

The loss of leadership efficacy of the Labor ruling elite may be explained in part by changes which have occurred in Israeli society as a whole and the ruling elite itself:[12] the former underwent a process of change from a communal, elitist and ideologically-oriented society to a modern, mass, and pragmatically-oriented democracy; the latter — from a mobilizing, pioneer elite to a responsive, routine political elite.

The End of a Dominant Party Position

Mapai, whose leadership led the critical transition from community (the *Yishuv*) to state, acquired a dominant position in the early years of independence.[13] While it did not succeed in obtaining a majority among voters, its Knesset representation was more than double that of its closest competition; it was in fact, the sole contender to head the government coalition until the mid-seventies (since 1968 — as the Labor Party), and its hegemony was widely accepted as the principal national leadership.

This process was accompanied by de-legitimization of the opposition parties of the Zionist left (Mapam) and the right (Herut). Mapam adopted a pro-Soviet orientation which, for close to a decade, isolated a vital part of the Labor pre-state elite in the areas of defense and settlement. Herut was founded by the commanders of the Irgun — the anti-British Jewish underground which operated outside the elected communal bodies and defied their authority. Prior to its formation, upon the foundation of the state, the leaders of Herut were involved in a violent confrontation with the provisional government (the Altalena Affair) which underscored historic animosities and prevented national reconciliation at an opportune time. For at least 17 years, this confrontation postponed the full integration of Herut in the mainstream of Israeli politics, which was marked later by the formation of a joint bloc with the Liberal Party (Gahal) in 1965 and culminated in the formation of a larger bloc (the Likud) in 1973, with its eventual rise to power in 1977.

The pre-state political debate was actually decided in favor of Mapai, the leading party in the leadership of the *Yishuv* and the Zionist organization. The U.N. partition resolution and the ensuing establishment of the State of Israel justified in retrospect the political course taken by the Zionist bodies during the final years of the British Mandatory regime. The alternative political schemes devised and advocated by other parties were either proved erroneous or rendered irrelevant.* The crises of transition to statehood and the initial tasks of state and nation building were managed successfully under the primary leadership of Mapai.[14] Furthermore, during the final years of the *Yishuv* and the early years of the state, the Israeli political leadership was able to establish virtually autonomous authority in the areas of defense and foreign policy. This authority was fortified by successive achievements: The 1947 U.N. General Assembly Resolution, the founding of the State of Israel, the War of Independence, the obtaining of international recognition and the development of bilateral relations with the principal powers, the Sinai Campaign. The specific authority granted to the legitimate political leadership (primarily, to Prime Minister Ben-Gurion) was demonstrated and reached its peak in the case of the Sinai Campaign — which was sanctioned by Ben-Gurion alone, planned by his principal aides in the army and the defense ministry (Dayan and Peres) and presented for ratification of government ministers prior to commencement of operations. This authority was accepted for some time by both veteran and new segments of the Israeli society. It was acceptable to veteran goups and immigrants of European origin, who recognized its functionality under a state of siege and conditions of crisis. Following the Holocaust, these groups had lost their firm orientation toward the external world and were prepared to let a successful leadership redefine the place of the new State in a perilous world and provide for its very existence. It was acceptable to the new immigrants from Arab States, who were accustomed in their countries of origin to political passiveness and as new immigrants were in-

*Mapam — bi-national state; Ahdut ha-avoda — international mandate for a short transitional period to create conditions for the foundation of a state in the entire land of Israel; Herut — immediate establishment of the state in Greater Israel; Liberal leaders — postponement of statehood until resolution of the Arab-Jewish conflict.

clined to accept the authority of an effective existing leadership.

Several developments eroded the dominance of Mapai and its successor party, Labor, within the context of the aforementioned processes of change — which began in the early fifties — from an elitist, ideologically oriented political community towards an open, pragmatically-oriented volatile mass democracy and from mobilizing pioneer elite to a responsive routine ruling elite: The inner leadership conflict in Mapai and the consequent demise of Ben-Gurion's leadership, the impacts of the Lavon Affair, the Six-Day and the Yom Kippur wars, the political development of new immigrants' communities and the belated impact of the Holocaust (Aronson 1978).

The public posture and partisan leadership of Ben-Gurion were severely undermined during the divisive Lavon Affair 1960 — 1961.[15] His leadership in government lost some of its effectiveness in the following years and he was challenged by members of his cabinet on policy matters (e.g. Golda Meir's challenge to Ben-Gurion's policy regarding Germany). Both contributed to his eventual resignation in 1963, which did not evoke much protest among his associate veteran leaders; under the unanimously-accepted, conciliatory leadership of Levi Eshkol, they willingly assumed responsibility for the leadership of the party and the State. Eshkol and the veteran successors emerged victorious in their eventual open rift with Ben-Gurion in the party (although it led to a party split and Ben-Gurion's exit) and in the general election of 1965, but found it difficult to maintain their authority in government and failed the critical test of leadership in the area of defense in the crisis preceding the Six-Day-War. Removal of the Prime Minister (Eshkol) from his concurrent position as Defense Minister, the appointment of an external choice (Dayan) to his post and the institution of a government of national unity, under vocal public pressure and effective partisan manipulation, put an end to Mapai's exclusive role in this area since 1949. The maiden participation of Herut (in the framework of Gahal) in the government terminated Mapai's long-time coalitionary ban against this party and enabled its leadership to play a legitimate and a vital role in the resolution of a critical internal and external crisis.

The Six-Day-War reopened a major national issue — the question of Israel's boundaries and the associated aspiration for greater Israel — which was considered largely settled following the War of Independence. Herut joined the new debate as a legitimate partner whose persistent nationalist views formerly considered risky and irrelevant, suddenly acquired new relevance in the post-war circumstances when Israel actually controlled the West Bank of Jordan.

The Lavon Affair undermined the moral legitimacy of Mapai's rule; the Six-Day-War — its leadership legitimacy in the critical area of defense. However, several developments mitigated the potentially devastating political consequences of the pre-war crisis: the sweeping military victory; the 1968 party merger (Mapai, Ahdut Ha'avoda and Rafi) which gave birth to the Israel Labor Party and the inclusion of Dayan therein. Following the war, Dayan presented the strongest potential challenge to the established veteran leaders; in doing so, he actually preempted the central political role of the nationalist opposition (Gahal) until after the Yom Kippur War, which put an end to Dayan's independent electoral promise. Ultimately, Golda Meir succeeded the deceased leader, Eshkol, who was identified with the pre-war leadership failure. Meir was better suited to conform to present a politically safe posture, combining a moderate ideological stand with a current hawkish approach. During the post-war period, Labor actually institutionalized its leadership divisions in the party and the government and sanctioned a pluralistic and complex ideological and policy position, as compared with the clear, simplistic, ideological and policy positions of Herut and Gahal (subsequently, the Likud).

The outbreak of the Yom Kippur War in October 1973 shattered Israeli expectations. The sudden coordinated Egyptian-Syrian surprise attack and the early military reversals cast a shadow on the performance of the government and the army. The eventual impressive military gains and the prospect of a diplomatic process (the separation of forces agreement and the convening of the Geneva Conference) aided Labor in maintaining its position in government with only minimal electoral losses (December 1973). However, continued party discontent coupled, with a poor state of health and advancing age, led the Prime Minister to resign. Dayan followed suit. Meir's successor, Itzhak Rabin, established his leadership claim in the army, having served as chief-of-staff during the 1967 war; he belonged to a new generation of party leaders which came to the fore after the resignation of Dayan and the by-passing of Allon — the immediate potential successors of the veteran leaders. The national trauma induced by the war, the accepted notion of leadership misconduct (directed primarily against Dayan and Meir), and the removal of Dayan (the powerful potential successor or challenger of the veteran leaders) created favorable conditions for the assertion of a new political claim by a legitimized leadership of the Likud, headed by a veteran leader, Menachem Begin. Following the Six-Day-War, the Likud succeeded in recruiting ex-military heroes to its ranks (Weizman and Sharon).

During the early years of statehood, Mapai — and to a lesser extent, other parties as well — exchanged services (or appeared to do so due to their leadership position in public bureaucracies), including "identification services," for electoral support and political passiveness. The role of the party in the absorption of immigration and the allocation of services was eventually inhibited due to the relatively rapid development of governmental civil service, legislation which standardized and nationalized key social services (employment, education, social security, vocational training) and the political education of the new immigrants' constituencies, including development of politically competent local government. Mapai played a leading role in this last development, nurturing the recruitment of leaders for local offices in these new constituencies, who became the settlers and the builders of new townships and settlements developed by the State and the Jewish Agency. Mapai was successful in organizing large groups of new immigrants within the party, gradually incorporating their representatives (mostly appointed, some elected) in party national bodies and allocating symbolic representation in the party Knesset faction and subsequently even in the government. Mapai's integrationist approach to organization was followed by other parties, contributing to the eventual emergence of a claim for uninhibited political participation of these groups in the political process and at all levels of political leadership.

The initial attitudes of political, cultural and psychological patronage towards the new immigrants, including large numbers of immigrants from Arab states, gradually collided with the integrationist policies and responsive attitude and strategy of the ruling veteran elite. This group developed an electoral dependence on immigrants' constituencies and strove to stabilize and structure its association with them. The failure to entirely resolve this contradiction (patronage and responsiveness versus representation and participation) set the stage for political rebellion against the ruling elite when it lost its leadership efficacy and legitimacy.

Another phenomenon which may have contributed to the cumulative challenge to the authority and moral legitimacy of the veteran Israeli leadership is the belated impact of the Holocaust, crystallizing at the beginning in the late 1960's and early 1970's among Israelis of European descent, particularly among survivors and their families, including the second generation (Kav-Venaki & Nadler 1981). The organized *Yishuv* viewed the Holocaust as the ultimate expression of hatred of Jews by a cruel world — which produced this disaster without perceiving itself as particularly in debt to the Jewish people after it. The *Yishuv* felt traumatically helpless in face of the Holocaust and did not blame its leaders for what had happened. Instead, it drew a political conclusion which fortified an earlier ideological commitment: to hasten the foundation of the State of Israel as a haven for the Jewish people and a home for the surviving refugees. The Zionist leadership and the organized *Yishuv* offered a realistic approach and demonstrated considerable political skill in obtaining these goals. The Kastner Trial (Rosenfeld 1955) marked the first major attempt to cast doubt on the policies and conduct of the established Zionist leadership during the Holocaust. Herut and those educated in its parent organization, the Revisionist Movement, charged that Mapai's Realpolitik — its methods of political maneuvering and seeking compromises rather than confrontation — actually fostered the uninterrupted continuation of the Holocaust. The same methods, they claimed, eventually led to loss of territorial rights in the Land of Israel and created a threat to the very existence of the Jewish community therein (Aronson 1981; Ben-Elissar 1978).

Such an argument could not have taken root among Holocaust survivors unless the State itself became self-evident to them. The strength of the State and its capacity for overt and covert operations were projected backward on a period in which it had not yet come into being. The memory of the Holocaust, reconstructed in the Eichmann trial in Jerusalem (1961) accorded a concrete dimension to the Arab threats to annihilate the State of Israel. This relation was already detectable in the War of Independence. (One of the participants in this war, a young woman, wrote: "I saw Arabs and shot the Nazis."). The crisis of the Six-Day War, beginning with an Arab blockade and open threats to the very existence of the State, again produced an acute sense of confrontation with the threat of a new Holocaust. The Yom Kippur War (1973), which followed a six-year lull in the aftermath of the Six-Day War, intensified the impact of conscious memory of traumatic Jewish history, with the Holocaust at its center.

The belated impact of the Holocaust was produced by the convergence of a new reconstructed memory thereof shared by the entire Israeli society,[16] the formulation of an historical national conclusion which tended to favor a strategy of confrontation in face of a possible Holocaust and the re-emergence of an imminent physical peril to the national existence in Israel. This syndrome, which may have led to opposing extreme personal attitudes, seemed to feed a national mood of defiance and threatened to depict a willingness for compromise on "ultimate national rights" as defeatist, risky and futile. In general, during the 1970's and early 1980's this syndrome helped to produce a positive response to the hawkish appeal of authoritative leadership by a nationalist movement. It converged with the particular fear of the Israeli non-European communities. Although these communities, spared from the Holocaust, feared a possible new encounter with the Arabs under previous humiliating conditions and were conscious of the fate of a defeated nation and rebellious individuals in their countries of origin. They may have shared such values with the Arabs.

The Election Campaign: Social Tensions and Party Competition

Religious tension and communal-ethnic tension are undoubtedly the most severe social tensions in the Jewish Israeli society. The former originates in an uncompromising philosophical approach and in excluding cultural and social practices while the latter is rooted in social, economic and cultural gaps between Jews of Oriental (Sephardic) and European (Ashkenazic) descent, although devoid of any serious ideological definition.

Religious tension led to an historic separate partisan organization, while until 1981, the ethnic-communal tension did not lead to any appreciable attempt to form a separate party during the era of statehood. Furthermore, the general oriental communal associations that had engaged in political and electoral tasks in the *Yishuv* era lost their electoral appeal and failed to organize the new immigrants after the founding of the State.[17] Following a poor showing in elections to the First and Second Knesset, these associations ceased their electoral activities and their elected representatives joined existing parties.

The parties of the religious section presented only limited integrative claims and did not share a utopia of complete social and cultural integration in a new heterogeneous, pluralistic Israeli society. Their demands for integration in State institutions (e.g. kosher kitchens etc.,) were largely accepted without creating unmanageable crises during the prolonged Labor-dominated regime. In contrast, the oriental communities presented fuller integrative claims and protested existing gaps between the utopia of integration and its lagging implementation. The absence of a separate party organization may have hampered the response to the particularistic needs of the oriental communities, but it also prevented the creation of an organizational barrier to processes of political integration.

The salience of the communal-ethnic tension was expressed by three developments in the 1981 election:
1) The appearance of an ethnic-oriental party Tami, under the leadership of Aharon Abuhatzeira, a leading member of the most aristocratic rabbinical family within the Moroccan

Jewish community. Abuhatzeira split from the NRP, while serving as party representative in the cabinet, in the wake of a prolonged personal ordeal involving charges of corruption which brought him twice to court. (He was acquitted in his first trial, held prior to the elections and subsequently convicted on several counts in a second one, which took place after the elections).

Tami scored only modest gains in the elections and did not sense the much discussed potential for a separatist ethnic protest vote. Its gain was largely confined to voters of North African origin and was based on personal and local alliances. Nevertheless, Tami marked a departure from traditional electoral politics in Israel in presenting a direct ethnic appeal by legitimate political leaders who were elected to high office by existing history parties including a cabinet minister and a NRP member of the Knesset, as well as a former Labor cabinet member. This group of leaders managed to obtain substantial financial support for their independent run, mostly acquired from donors abroad, thereby limiting their dependence on the veteran party establishment.

2) The Likud increased its leading share of the non-European ethnic vote. About two-thirds of Likud voters were of oriental descent, while about 70% of the Alignment voters were of European descent (Smith 1981). The ethnic protest vote was thus largely channeled to an existing historic, non-ethnic party (bloc).

3) Communal-ethnic tension became a major campaign issue (in the closing phase of the campaign) for the first time in the history of the State, thus contributing to social polarization and two-bloc dominance in the Knesset. This phenomenon violated the venerable national goal of integration (*Mizug galuyot* — integrating the various ethnic communities in Israel) and produced a critical moral, social and political problem for the Labor movement, despite its past integrationist policies and equalitarian ideology.

The eruption and exposure of communal-ethnic tension in the 1981 election took place against the background of both a significant achievement and a relative failure of the processes of political integration in the Israeli society. (Peres 1976; Smooha 1978). New immigrants of oriental descent mastered the rules of the partisan game and rose — within one generation — to a dominant position in local municipal government outside of large veteran cities.[18] They have gained control over party branches in new development towns, acquired important positions in sovereign national party bodies (The Central Committee and Convention) and have also attained a major position in the Histadrut's (General Federation of Labor) establishment and the workers' committees.

These massive gains on the local level and the awareness of social, economic and political gaps, together with a new sense of political integration in the Israeli society (Peres 1976; Smooha 1978). New immigrants of non-European descent incentive for a belated attempt to form a communal-ethnic party and a claim for participation in the national leadership beyond the symbolic, appointed representation traditionally accorded to these groups in the historic parties. David Levy of the Likud, who rose from a local position of partisan and unionist leadership to head of Likud faction in the Histadrut and who gained a pivotal position in the government and the national leadership of the party (Herut and the Likud), is the most successful example of the new generation of formerly ethnic-local leaders who seek national recognition and national leadership.

In summary, the very processes of political integration paradoxically created pressure for the formation of an independent communal-ethnic party. This development threatened to replace the prospect of gradual increased integration and a new position of power within the historic parties with immediate assertion and manipulation of independent political power. These pressures threatened to constitute an organizational and ideological barrier to political and social integration. The ethnic voters did not lend much support to direct, separatist ethnic electoral appeal in the 1981 election, (although they do keep its potential alive); instead, they asserted themselves integratively, channeling the bulk of the protest vote to an historic, heterogeneous bloc.

The Election Campaign: The Leader's Role

The personalization of politics in democratic societies, including Israel, tends to increase the autonomy of politics — especially that of electoral politics as an independent area of social behavior. Elections turn into a democratic ritual with the political leader at their center, providing an immediate and manipulative basis for a new or renewed political-electoral identification. The leaders' political and communicative style and personality may serve as significant factors in determining the characteristics of the campaign and — to a lesser extent — the outcome, even in a viable party system.

The key party leaders — Menachem Begin of the Likud and Shimon Peres of the Alignment — played a major role in the 1981 elections. In the contest between them, Mr. Begin's image enjoyed four advantages in his appeal to the potential constituencies of the Likud:

a)   As a representative of the political tradition and historical rights of his movement (Herut) and as the legitimate, acclaimed consensual standard-bearer of the Likud bloc, its parties, leaders and constituencies.

b)   An incumbent, responsible government leader, along with the residual image of a defiant, anti-establishment figure — the former head of an anti-British underground (the Irgun) and the leader of the former perennial radical opposition party.

c)   The Prime Minister who achieved the first peace treaty between Israel and an Arab State (Egypt) and as a world statesman: a member of the Camp David "Leadership Club," together with Presidents Carter and Sadat, and a Nobel Peace Prize Laureate.

d)   A leader with an authoritative image and a populist political style. Begin responded effectively to the psychological needs of large groups of voters, especially immigrants from Arab states — groups which were victimized by social, economic and cultural gaps and were highly exposed to the destabilizing impacts of national tensions (primary among them — the problem of security), while alienated from the old ruling political elite. These groups found comfort in authoritative and communicative leadership. In comparison, the leader of the Labor Alignment, Mr. Peres, appeared before the potential constituencies of his movement as a routine leader presiding over a party (the Labor Party) torn by prolonged inner conflict and incapable of disengaging from the continuous three-round contest between himself and Rabin. Peres lost the first two rounds in the nominations. contest; in 1977, however, the Rabin family's entanglements with foreign currency regulations worked in Peres's favor, forcing Rabin to give up the nomination he had narrowly won. Peres handily won the 1981 nomination over Rabin but failed to assert strong personal leadership. He had to put up with divided party leadership in a system of centralized and permanent party structure, which curbs the leader's prerogatives in party appointments and appropriates representation rights to the losing faction in a nominating contest.

Following the 1977 electoral defeat, Peres succeeded in maintaining the unity of the Alignment, *inter alia,* by moving the Labor Party to the left. As an opposition leader, he adopted an assertive — partisan strategy against the Likud government, while seeking an extended political-diplomatic role outside the government beyond past traditions, as in his talks with the Egyptian President and other foreign leaders during the official peace negotiations, for example. Nevertheless, in the electoral campaign, Peres was not able to rid himself of the controversial partisan posture he had acquired as an opposition leader. His elitist style appealed primarily to veteran voting blocs of European descent and alienated the non-European constituencies. These obstacles impaired Peres' attempt to highlight his impressive past governmental achievements, including his role in the Sinai Campaign, the establishment of the military and aviation industries and the Entebbe rescue operation.

Menachem Begin was undoubtedly a dominant figure in the 1981 election. His awakening from political dormancy only a few months before the election was an important contributing factor to the Likud's success in turning a mid-term poor showing in public surveys into a pre-election lead and narrow electoral victory.

It may therefore be appropriate to comment briefly on Begin's political personality in historical perspective. Begin's political philosophy, similar to that of his mentor, Zeev Jabotinsky, combines elements of nationalism and liberalism. His interpretation of events and general political approach has strong historical, legal and emotional undertones. He manifests a constant awareness of events and lessons of Jewish and world history, primarily the Holocaust, which appears to permeate everything he says or does. From the lessons of history he derives a collection of absolute rights and obligations. Unlike Jabotinsky, who was influenced by the optimistic approach of the upper European bourgeoisie, Begin, as a young political leader in the Jewish community of Poland, was close to the apocalyptic outlook of the lower middle classes with their acute apprehension of the perils of the modern world. Begin, the Zionist activist, was particularly anxious over the potential holocaust for the Jews in Europe. His apocalyptic outlook and belief in the absolute rights of the Jewish people in the Land of Israel led him to advocate direct action against the British Mandatory regime in Palestine.

As a commander of the Irgun, the Jewish underground, Begin pursued such a course of action in defiance of the authority and policies of the elected bodies of the *Yishuv.* After a crisis of adaptation to the regular political process in the new State and a transient phase of confrontation with its legitimate leaders, Begin developed into an avid and able parliamentarian and a radical though patient opposition leader who wasted no opportunity to gain political legitimacy and assert his leadership in the non-labor grouping of the Israeli party system and electorate. The foundation of Gahal (1965), the National Unity Government (1967) and the Likud (1973) served as critical stations along this path. Ascending to power in a belated and somewhat unexpected turn of events in 1977, Begin's inclination for direct action, whether political or military, based on clearly and sharply defined national rights, converged during his first term in office with his eagerness to establish a reputation of a statesman. Both contributed to the Camp David agreement and the peace treaty with Egypt (the same inclination contributed in 1982 to the invasion of Lebanon in face of adverse, threatening conditions — the PLO's menacing build-up in southern Lebanon).

36   *Shlomo Aronson and Nathan Yanai*

Begin's forceful articulation of national rights and apprehensions and his call for direct action or hawkish policies of national self-help in the area of security — contrasted with what may have appeared as Labor's inclusive policies of delay and compromise — appealed to large segments of the Israeli society. This message contributed to electoral success when directed at a pluralistic immigrants' society burdened by cumulative national and social tensions and alienated — to some extent — from the external world.

The New Realignment — A Stable Phenomenon?

The outcome of the 1981 elections justifies our observation concerning completion of a new realigning era, while between-elections public opinion surveys exposed the potential volatility of Israeli voters in an electoral system (P.R.) which reflects their choice accurately. The success of the Likud at remaining in power in the face of a potent challenge to its electoral supremacy and ruling legitimacy enhanced the potential impact of incumbency and the inclination of the new voters' alignment to perpetuate itself. An effective use of governmental powers in the areas of appointments and appropriations, combined with pursual of the joint ruling interests of the Likud and continuation of the new permissive coalitionary strategy may contribute to the maintenance of the Likud regime. However, the acquisition of a stable ruling identity is certain to expose the Likud to new expectations and protestations, especially in the economic field. The rebellious mood of the voters during mid-term economic crises demonstrated the vulnerability of the ruling party, even among voters of oriental descent. In sum, the Likud was successful in building a new voters' coalition and party coalition in government, both of which tend to perpetuate themselves provided the new leading party in government, like its long-time predecessor (Mapai and the Labor Party), continues to demonstrate effective control and resourceful leadership in government. Failure to manage internal and external crises may rock the coalition government and change voters' allegiances.

The stability of the Likud regime is also a function of the condition and posture of the major opposition bloc: the capacity of the Alignment to resolve a prolonged leadership crisis effectively, move towards the political center, restore cooperation with the religious parties and manage the crisis of alienation among ethnic — communal voters. Activity in these areas would aid the Alignment in improving its electoral position and in reestablishing the prospect of an alternative coalition government.

NOTES

1) Campbell's classification of presidential elections (1966) has been applied in the discussion of the 1973 and 1977 Israeli elections. Regarding the 1973 election, A. Arian correctly observed that the concept of "realigning electoral era" is more suitable than the concept of "critical election" for the discussion of electoral changes in a dominant party system (Arian 1975, 1977).

2) The leftist identity of the Civil Rights Movement (Ratz), under the leadership of Shulamit Aloni, was emphasized only in the 1981 elections; prior to that time, it appeared as a radical party, primarily professing secular and feminist protest policies.

3) On the transition from multipolar competition to two, three or four-party competition see: Sartory (1976: 346—346).

4) On coalition making in Israel see: Selikter (1975), Diskin (1975), Nachmias (1973, 1975) and Felsenthal (1974).

5) On the coalitionary attitude of Mapai see: Yanai (1982: 80—86). During the Mapai regime, the religious sector adopted a defensive attitude designed to protest vital interests. See Don-Yehiya and Liebman (1972:83).

6) Personal differences among the founding leaders of Ya'ad led to its dismantling prior to any electoral run; Sheli acquired one or two Knesset seats until the 1981 election, in which it failed to acquire any representation at all.

7) The position of the left was strengthened in the opposition British Labor Party, while the French Socialist Party fostered a cooperative attitude towards the Communists.

8) On the radical left in West Germany see: Loewenberg (1972: 165—168).

9) On the grand coalition in Germany see: Sartori (1976: 299), Institut für Zeitgeschichte (1973: 588—592).

10) On the Israeli political elite see: Gutmann and Landau (1977: 192—228); On the make-up and the recruitment process of the the pre-state elite see: Horowitz and Lissak (1980), Lissak (1981).

11)   On the nomination of the Prime Minister and Cabinet, see Yanai (1981: 41–79).
12)   For a discussion of the factors contributing to the Alignment's electoral defeat, see: Aronson (1979), Aronoff (1979), Arian (1979), Shapiro (1979).
13)   See: Gutman and Landau (1977: 128–130), Horowitz and Lissak (1980), Medding (1972: 299–307), Arian and Barnes (1974), Yanai, Ibid, pp. 13–66.
14)   See: Yanai, Ibid, pp. 13–66.
15)   See: Aronson, ibid., pp. 1–80; Yanai, Ibid, pp. 111–151.
16)   Abba Eban, who can hardly be suspected of hawkishness, described Israel's 1967 pre-war boundaries as "Auschwitz borders."
17)   The Sephardi List gained four seats in the first Knesset and two in the Second; the Yemenite List — one seat in each.
18)   By 1965, 44% of all elected local officials were already of non Ashkenazic descent See: Weiss (1970:66).

BIBLIOGRAPHY

Arian, A.
1973   *The Choosing People.* Tel Aviv: Massada (Hebrew).

1975   "Where the 1973 Elections Critical?" in: Arian, A. (ed.), *The Elections in Israel — 1973.* Jerusalem: Academic Press.

1979   "Conclusion." in: Penniman, H.R. (ed.), *Israel at the Polls — The Knesset Election of 1973.* American Enterprise Institute for Public Policy Research, pp. 283-302.
    and Barness, S.M.
1974   "The Dominant Party System: A Neglected Model of Democratic Stability." *Journal of Politics* 36, pp. 592-614.

Aronoff, M.J.
1979   "The Decline of the Israeli Labor Party: Causes and Significance." in: Penniman 1979, *op. cit.,* pp. 115-146.

Aronson, S.
1978   *Conflict and Bargaining in the Middle East.* Baltimore and London: Johns Hopkins University Press.

1981 "The Impact of the Holocaust on Israel's Domestic Order and Foreign Policy." Paper presented at the Fourth Annual Conference of the International Society of Political Psychology (ISPP), Mannheim, June 26, 1981.

Ben-Elissar, E.
1978 *The Extermination Plot: The Foreign Policy of the Third Reich and the Jews.* Jerusalem: Edanim (Hebrew).

Campbell, A.
1966 "A Classification of the Presidential Elections." in: Campbell, A., Converse, P. Miller, W. and Stokes, D. *Elections and the Political Order.* New York: Wiley, pp. 63-77.

Caspi, D.
1972 "Floating Vote and Floating Voters in Israeli Elections." *Medina Umimshal* (State and Government) 1, 3, pp. 81-98 (Hebrew).

Diskin, A.
1975 "The Composition of Coalitions in Israel and their Examination through the Typology of the Party System." *Medina Mimshal Vihasim Benleumiyyim* (State, Government and International Relations) 8, pp. 130-160 (Hebrew).

1983 "Polarization and Volatility among Voters in Elections for the Tenth Knesset " (this volume).

Don-Yehiya, E.
1975 "Religion and Coalition: The National Religious Party and Coalition Formation in Israel." in: Arian 1975, pp. 255-284.

1980 "Stability and Change in a Camp Party — the NRP and the Youth Revolt." *Medina, Mimshal Vihasim Benleumiyyim* (State, Government and International Relations) 14, pp. 25-52 (Hebrew).

 and Liebman, C.S.
1972 "Separation of Religion and State: Slogan and Content." *Molad* 83, pp. 25-26 (Hebrew).

Eisenstadt, S.N.
1980 "Civility in Israel: Beyond the Shtetl." *Forum* 38, pp. 19-23.

Felsenthal, D.
1974   "The Relation between Number of Ministers and
          Coalition Structure." *Netivei Irgun* 1-2, pp.
          26-34 (Hebrew).
Gutmann, E. and Landau, J.M.
1977   "The Israeli Political Elite: Its Characteristics
          and Composition." in: Lissak, M. and Gutmann,
          E. (eds.), *The Israeli Political System.* Tel Aviv:
          Am Oved (Hebrew).
Horowitz, D. and Lissak, M.
1980   *The Origins of the Israeli Polity.* Chicago: Uni-
          versity of Chicago Press.
Institut für Zeitgeschichte
1973   *Deutsche Geschichte seit dem ersten Weltkrieg.*
          Stuttgart: Deutsche Verlags-Anstalt.
Ishai, Y.
1980   "Factionalism in the National Religious Party."
          in Arian, A. (ed.), *The Elections in Israel — 1977.*
          Jerusalem: Academic Press, pp. 57-74.
Kav-Venaki, S. and Nadler, A.
1981   "Trans-Generational Effects of Massive Psychic
          Traumatization: Psychological Characteristics of
          Children of Holocaust Survivors in Israel."
          Paper presented at the Fourth Annual Conference
          of the International Society of Political Psycho-
          logy (ISPP), Mannheim, June 26, 1981.
Lissak, M.
1981   *The Elites of the Jewish Community in Palestine.*
          Tel Aviv: Am Oved (Hebrew).
Loewenberg, G.
1972   *Parlamentarismus im politischen System der
          Bundesrepublik Deutschland.* Tübingen: Rainer
          Wunderlich.
Medding, P.Y.
1972   *Mapai in Israel.* Cambridge: Cambridge University
          Press.
Nachmias, D.
1973   "A Note on Coalition Payoffs in a Dominant
          Party System: Israel." *Political Studies* 21, 3,
          pp. 301-305.

1975   "Coalition, Myth and Reality." in: Arian 1975, pp. 225-284.

Peres, Y.
1976   *Ethnic Relations in Israel.* Tel Aviv: Sifriyat Poalim (Hebrew).

Rosenfeld, S.
1955   *Criminal Case No. 124.* Tel Aviv: Karni (Hebrew).

Sartori, G.
1976   *Parties and Party Systems.* Cambridge: Cambridge University Press.

Selikter, O.
1975   "Coalition Theories and Coalition Formation." *Medina Mimshal Vihasim Benleumiyyim* (State, Government and International Relations) 8, pp. 117-129 (Hebrew).

Shapiro, Y.
1975   "The End of a Dominant Party System." in: Arian 1975, pp. 23-38.

Shamir, M. and Arian, A.
1982   "The Ethnic Vote in Israel's 1981 Elections." *Medina Mimshal Vihasim Benleumiyyim* (State, Government and International Relations) **19-20**, pp. 117-129. (Hebrew).

Smith, H.
1981   "Ethnic Polarization Transformed into Party Polarization." *Maariv*, February 9, 1982 (Hebrew).

Smooha, S.
1978   *Israel: Pluralism and Conflict.* Berkeley and Los Angeles: University of California Press.

Weiss, S.
1970   *Typology of Elected Local Officials and Stability of Local Governments in Israel.* Jerusalem: Akademon. (Hebrew).

Yanai, N.
1981   *Party Leadership in Israel: Maintenance and Change.* The Modern Middle East Series Vol. 13, Middle East Institute, Columbia University. Ramat Gan: Turtledove.

1982   *Political Crises in Israel: Ben-Gurion's Era.* Jerusalem: Keter. (Hebrew).

2

THE JEWISH ETHNIC VOTE:
AN AGGREGATIVE PERSPECTIVE*

*Avraham Diskin***

Introduction

The ethnic vote was one of the most noteworthy aspects of the 1981 Knesset elections. The tendency among Sephardim to support the right-wing parties has been analyzed repeatedly since the early 1960s (Lissak 1969). However, this phenomenon — together with the parallel tendency among Ashkenazim to support the Alignment — became much more salient in the 1981 elections, as evidenced by virtually all articles in the present volume.

The term "Sephardim" generally refers to Jews who immigrated to Israel from Asia and Africa, most of whom arrived in the 1950s — the victims of persecution in various Arab countries following the 1948 War of Independence. The second generation of this ethnic group (i.e. young people born in Israel) is believed to support the Likud and its predecessors (Gahal and the Herut Party) even more devotedly than the parents' generation. "Ashkenazim," in turn, are primarily Jews who came to Israel from Europe and North America (especially those of Eastern European origin), the older generation of whom is known to be rather consistent in its support of the Alignment.

Ashkenazim were always considered to be the main component of Israeli society's higher social strata, while Sephardim

*Data for this article were accumulated with the assistance of Prof. Y. Haitovsky of the Hebrew University. The same data base has been used by Prof. Haitovsky and myself in another study focusing upon the development of a new model of election-night forecasting. I also express my gratitude to Mr. Stephen Levitt for his kind assistance.
**Senior Lecturer in Political Science, the Hebrew University of Jerusalem.

were judged to be at the opposite extreme, regardless of the set of social indicators employed, e.g. education, occupation, economic status, self-identification. etc. The differences between Sephardic and Ashkenazic Jews in their social status, origin, cultural background and political affiliation inspired a series of studies which attempted to explain the correlations among these features (Peres 1971; Yatziv 1979). Note that such attempts have recently lost some of their validity, owing to the increase in correlation between party identification and ethnicity and the concomitant decrease between the former and other variables (e.g. ideological position, social qualities, etc.).

One article which demonstrates the lack of polarization between Likud and Alignment supporters is included in this volume (Diskin 1983). An even better example of these new difficulties may be found in a new study by Shamir and Arian (1982), which compares five different theoretical explanations of the ethnic vote in Israel. Most amazing among their findings is the low Pearson correlation between the *combination* of all these factors and voting for the Likud and the Alignment (R = 0.34). Lower correlations were found when Sephardic and Ashkenazic voter populations were examined separately (0.30 and 0.32, respectively). Since the correlation between ethnicity alone and voting for these two parties was higher in 1981 (and even in 1977 — see Table 1), it appears inappropriate to attempt to explain the phenomenon in terms of a limited set of variables. Furthermore, even the combination of all well-known theories does not appear sufficiently powerful to provide a full explanation of the extent of the 1981 ethnic vote. Thus, the objective of the present paper is not to suggest any new explanation of the ethnic vote in Israel but rather to supply some aggregative evidence of various aspects thereof — supplementing those elaborated upon in Gonen 1983 (this volume). The second part of this study compares correlations between different demographic variables and support for the two major lists, the third presents some hypotheses on the connection between the 1981 floating vote and the ethnic vote, while the fourth demonstrates the possible directions of the 1981 floating vote in selected neighborhoods in Israel's three largest cities.

Aggregative Analysis of Social Variables and Voting Behavior

Most analyses of the Jewish ethnic vote in Israel were based upon data which had been accumulated in public opinion polls. Only a few writers based their conclusions upon aggregative data, i.e. upon investigation of the characteristics of Knesset polling stations or examination of the social and electoral characteristics of specific neighborhoods (Matras 1965; Kies 1969; Diskin 1980; Gonen 1983). None of these studies focused upon the floating vote (i.e. upon the gains and losses of the parties at specific polling stations), nor did any investigate the correlation between voting and demographic characteristics of polling stations. Our findings, which are therefore unique in this respect, are based upon data accumulated as follows: Firstly, each of the 4,397 polling regions of the 1981 elections was compared with the 3,850 polling regions of the 1977 elections. The analysis focused only upon those 2,324 stations which were defined as "identical" for both elections, i.e. those regions whose geographical borders and population did not change significantly (0% and 15%, respectively). Secondly, different social qualities characterizing "statistical regions" (which are larger than "polling regions") were correlated with polling stations. We were thus able to calculate the gains and losses of each party in the 1981 elections for all "identical" stations. Moreover, any social characteristic — such as country of origin, nationality, age distribution, etc. — could be simultaneously estimated for most identical polling regions.

Table 1 depicts the Pearson linear coefficient of correlation which links "political results" — in this case the performance of the Likud and the Alignment in 1977 and 1981 elections and the gains and losses of both parties in 1981 — and selected demographic variables. Gains and losses are referred to as "b − a" in succeeding tables and should be regarded as an aggregative indicator of "individual party floating vote."

Many of the social variables examined were not represented in Table 1 as they either resembled others or were insignificant.

The most prominent finding depicted in Table 1 is the superiority of the first variable (percentage of Jews born in Asia and Africa) over all others. In other words, the correlation between this variable and each of the "political results"

Table 1: Pearson Correlations Between Likud and Alignment Performance (1977 and 1981) and Selected Demographic Variables

Variable	N	Likud			Alignment		
		% in 1977 (a)	% in 1981 b)	gains/losses 1981 (b–a)	% in 1977 (a)	% in 1981 b)	gains/losses 1981 (b–a)
% of Jews born in Asia & Africa	2,108	+0.58	+0.66	+0.36	−0.32	−0.50	−0.53
% of Jews born in North Africa	1,967	+0.31	+0.39	+0.27	−0.16	−0.34	−0.46
% of Jews born in Europe & America	291	−0.39	−0.40	−0.15	+0.26	+0.38	+0.39
% of non-Jews	485**	−0.42	−0.42	−0.09	−0.33	−0.20	+0.17
% of persons under 30	2,249	−0.07	−0.03	+0.08	−0.17	−0.25	−0.24

N is different for each row because of insufficient information regarding demographic variables in certain polling regions.

**Only polling regions with non-Jewish (Arab) voters were included.*

investigated is higher than the correlation of those results and any other demographic variable.

It is astonishing to note that the general "Asia-Africa" variable is superior to the "North African" (second) one, as Likud support among Jews of North African origin is known to be more prominent than that of Sephardim in general. The apparently contradictory phenomenon depicted in Table 1 resulted from both statistical and unique political factors: for example, the percentage of "second generation" youngsters of African origin who are not yet eligible to vote is much higher than the equivalent percentage among "second generation" Asian Jews (Central Bureau of Statistics, 1982). The new Tami Party, which did not participate in the 1977 elections and won three seats in 1981, was almost exclusively supported by North African Jewish voters.

From a socio-political point of view, the most significant phenomenon is the evident intensification of identification between well-defined social groups and the two major lists. Older voters, Arabs and Ashkenazim have always preferred the Alignment (and its predecessors) — tendencies which became more intense in 1981 in comparison to 1977. A parallel development occurred among Sephardim and young people in general, who tended to prefer the Likud to the Alignment in 1981 more than they had previously. This trend of intensification is well-demonstrated not only by the more significant correlations in column (b) of Table 1 — in comparison with column (a) — but also by the directions of all correlations in the (a — b) columns. For example: the higher the percentage of Asian and African-born Jews in a polling region, the higher the gain for the Likud and the lower the gain (or the greater the loss) for the Alignment in 1981. Given the veteran, well-known tendencies of Sephardic voters, the results most certainly point to a clear intensification.

It is interesting to measure the extent of overlap among the various demographic-political correlations. In some cases, such overlap is obvious: the higher the percentage of Sephardim, the lower the percentage of Ashkenazim; the higher the percentage of Ashkenazim, the older the population; the higher the percentage of North African Jews, the higher the percentage of Asian-African Jews in general, etc. In other instances, however, they are not as evident. We have conducted a series of regression analyses in order to investigate such possibilities more thoroughly. Two demonstrations of the results are presented in Table 2:

Table 2: Regression Indicator for Gains and Losses by the Likud and the Alignment as a Function of Selected Demographic Variables

Dependent Variable: Likud gains/losses — 1981 (b—a)

Independent Variables	Multiple R	Simple R	Change in Multiple R Square
% of Jews born in Asia and Africa	0.36	0.36	0.13
% of persons under 30	0.38	0.08	0.01
% of non-Jews	0.38	− 0.09	0.00

Dependent Variable: Alignment gains/losses

Independent Variables	Multiple R	Simple R	Change in Multiple R Square
% of Jews born in Asia and Africa	0.53	−0.53	0.28
% of persons under 30	0.53	0.17	0.00
% of non-Jews	0.53	0.24	0.00

The cases presented in Table 2 indicate an obvious overlap among the three correlations calculated for each party. The "gain" to our explanation of the Likud's and Alignment's "floating vote" is virtually nil — in terms of the square multiple R — when we add the "non-Jews" and "under 30" variables to the "Asia-Africa" variable. In other words, the superiority of the prominent variable in Table 1 is even more salient in Table 2.

Overlap was also clear in regressions calculated for other sets of variables, although it did not always reach the extent noted in Table 2. In any case, the prominence of the "Asia-Africa" variable was proved most impressive in all regressions we have conducted.

Ethnic Vote and Floating Vote in the 1977 and 1981 Elections

In a two-party system, when a single variable — such as Jewish ethnicity — is so strongly correlated with the changes in electoral power of both parties, we would expect a clear direct floating vote between these two parties in both directions, according to the different values of this prominent "explanatory" variable prevailing in various sub-populations. The data presented in Tables 3 and 4 might even strengthen such expectations in the Israeli case. Nevertheless, we should bear in mind that Israel is not a two-party system; in spite of the unprecedented successes of the two major lists, the small parties could have played a major role in the floating vote developments of 1981.

Table 3: The Ethnic Vote and Likud Gains and Losses
at Identical Polling Stations

	N	Total	Gains and Losses (b – a)				
			less than −15.1%	−0.1% to −15.1%	0.0% to +5.0%	+5.1% to 15.0%	more than +15.1%
% of Jews born in Asia and Africa							
0.0– 9.9	676	100	0.52	51.63	36.09	11.24	0.44
10.0–19.9	490	100	0.82	41.02	37.76	19.39	1.02
20.0–29.9	459	100	1.31	25.05	36.38	29.85	7.41
30.0–39.9	365	100	1.64	19.18	23.84	42.47	12.88
40.0+	118	100	1.69	15.25	10.17	55.08	17.80

Table 4: The Ethnic Vote and Alignment Gains and Losses
at Identical Polling Stations

	N	Total	Gains and Losses (b – a)				
			less than −15.1%	−0.1% to −15.1%	0.0% to +5.0%	+5.1% to 15.0%	more than +15.1%
% of Jews born in Asia and Africa							
0.0– 9.9	676	100	0.00	3.99	8.88	31.21	55.92
10.0–19.9	490	100	0.00	4.69	11.84	33.67	49.80
20.0–29.9	459	100	1.31	10.89	20.70	50.76	16.33
30.0–39.9	365	100	1.92	23.01	38.36	30.13	6.58
40.0+	118	100	0.85	35.39	40.68	18.64	4.24

The correlation between ethnicity and support for the Likud and the Alignment was not as strong in 1977 as it was in 1981 (see Table 1). Nevertheless, a direct floating vote between the Alignment and the Likud was in evidence — especially among Sephardic voters. Our hypotheses regarding the 1977 floating vote are displayed graphically in Figure 1.

Figure 1: Directions of Floating Vote in 1977

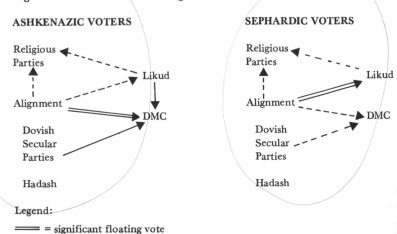

ASHKENAZIC VOTERS

SEPHARDIC VOTERS

Legend:

═══ = significant floating vote
─── = considerable floating vote
---- = slight floating vote

In 1981, when the correlation between ethnicity and support for the Likud and the Alignment increased significantly, it appears that there was no significant direct movement of votes between the two major parties. Possible directions of the 1981 floating vote are shown in Figure 2.

Figure 2: Directions of Floating Vote in 1981

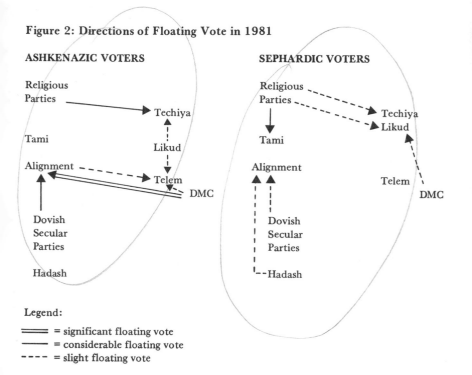

Legend:
═════ = significant floating vote
───── = considerable floating vote
▬ ▬ ▬ = slight floating vote

The hypotheses depicted in Figure 2 suggest how gains of Ashkenazic votes for the Alignment accompanied by losses for the Likud could have occurred *without* any direct floating vote between these two parties. It is also suggested that the Sephardic floating vote of 1981 was *not* between the two major lists. This series of hypotheses should be examined through an analysis of changes in electoral power among the minor lists in different sub-populations, carried out in parallel to investigation of such changes within the Likud and the Alignment.

The 1977 and 1981 Floating Vote in Selected Neighborhoods

In order to examine the set of hypotheses suggested above, we have focused upon electoral results in eight different neighborhoods of Israel's three largest cities. Four of these neighborhoods are considered affluent, with an Ashkenazic population of 70% or more, while the other four are known to be poor, with a Sephardic population of at least 70%. Table 5 indicates support for the various parties in each of these neighborhoods in the 1973 elections.

Table 5: Results of the 1973 Elections in Selected Neighborhoods
(% of total valid vote)

	Hadash (Communists)	Dovish Secular Parties	Alignment	Religious Parties	Likud
Entire Country	3.4	7.2	39.6	12.1	30.2
Affluent Ashkenazic Neighborhoods					
Rehavia (Jerusalem)	0.1	19.5	32.1	14.2	31.3
Beit Hakerem (Jerusalem)	0.1	11.8	31.4	14.1	35.7
Ramat Aviv (Tel Aviv)	0.3	18.2	42.6	3.7	33.1
Ahuza (Haifa)	0.1	21.3	35.4	6.4	35.7
Poor Sephardic Neighborhoods					
Morasha (Jerusalem)	0.9	2.4	24.3	16.9	42.4
New Gonen (Jerusalem)	0.2	6.1	27.5	12.3	48.6
Hatikva (Tel Aviv)	0.3	2.0	18.4	17.3	55.6
Wadi Salib (Haifa)	1.9	3.8	28.6	17.9	39.3

In the Sephardic neighborhoods, the Likud maintains an obvious superiority over the Alignment. The situation in Ashkenazic neighborhoods is not as clear, however: the Likud's power in these areas exceeds its nationwide mean support, while that of the Alignment is weaker. This results from the fact that the Likud is a virtually invisible party in Jewish rural (and Arab) settlements, where the Alignment is most powerful: at kibbutzim, for example, whose population constitutes 3% of the electorate, support for the Alignment often exceeds 90%.

Another prominent phenomenon depicted in Table 5 is the clearly Ashkenazic nature of the dovish secular parties. The religious parties tend to be slightly more popular in the poor neighborhoods. The Communist Party is very weak in all investigated neighborhoods, as its main support comes from Arab voters: in Nazareth (Israel.s largest Arab city), for example, Hadash received 58.2% of all valid votes in 1973.

Strong tendencies towards ethnic voting among supporters of virtually all of Israel's political parties were apparently in evidence in 1973 and even earlier (see, *inter alia*, Arian 1972). We now proceed to examine how these tendencies developed in 1977 and 1981. The net gains and losses of the parties in the investigated Ashkenazic and Sephardic neighborhoods are represented in Tables 7 and 8, respectively and may be compared with the general developments depicted in Table 6.

One prominent finding emerging from this study is the intensified tendency of the Likud towards becoming a Sephardic-supported party. The Likud lost power in the affluent Ashkenazic neighborhoods, while increasing its support among poor Sephardim. This phenomenon was most obvious in 1977 but repeated itself in a more moderate fashion in 1981 as well. In fact, the net nationwide gain of the Likud in 1981 was even higher than in 1977. This is not

Table 6: Overall Gains and Losses of Different Parties — 1977 and 1981 (% of total valid vote)

	Hadash	Dovish Secular Parties	DMC/ Shinui	Align- ment	Religious Parties	Tami	Telem	Likud	Techiya
1977	+1.2	−3.2	+11.6	−15.0	+1.8	—	—	+3.2	—
1981	−1.2	−1.6	−10.9	+12.0	−4.4	+2.3	+1.6	+3.7	+1.6

Table 7: Gains and Losses of the Main Parties in Affluent Ashkenazic Neighborhoods — 1977 and 1981 (%)

	Hadash	Dovish Secular Parties	DMC/ Shinui	Align- ment	Religious Parties	Tami	Telem	Likud	Techiya
Rehavia (Jerusalem)									
1977	+0.1	−10.8	+24.8	−12.2	+4.4	—	—	−5.3	—
1981	+0.1	−3.4	−21.4	+20.5	−2.9	+1.3	+1.8	−0.8	+4.7
Beit Hakerem (Jerusalem)									
1977	+0.1	−6.7	+19.4	−13.7	+6.4	—	—	−2.4	—
1981	+0.0	−2.0	−17.2	+17.1	−0.5	+0.9	+1.7	−3.4	+4.5
Ramat Aviv (Tel Aviv)									
1977	+0.2	−9.5	+29.1	−16.5	+0.7	—	—	−4.8	—
1981	−0.2	−2.7	−25.9	+26.7	−1.3	+0.5	+2.9	−2.0	+3.9
Ahuza (Haifa)									
1977	+0.1	−15.0	+38.4	−15.2	+1.6	—	—	−10.7	—
1981	−0.1	−0.7	−33.7	+26.3	−2.1	+0.2	+3.1	+3.1	+4.4

Table 8: Gains and Losses of the Main Parties in Poor Sephardic Neighborhoods — 1977 and 1981 (%)

	Hadash	Dovish Secular Parties	DMC/ Shinui	Align- ment	Religious Parties	Tami	Telem	Likud	Techiya
Morasha (Jerusalem)									
1977	+1.3	+0.3	+1.6	−11.4	+3.3	—	—	+14.4	—
1981	−2.1	−2.3	−1.0	+0.8	−12.1	+11.7	+0.4	+1.0	+0.9
New Gonen (Jerusalem)									
1977	0.0	−2.9	+6.9	−12.8	+1.9	—	—	+8.1	—
1981	+0.1	−1.3	−6.2	+7.4	−5.7	+2.6	+1.4	+0.8	+2.3
Hatikva (Tel Aviv)									
1977	+0.1	−0.8	+1.5	−9.3	+0.4	—	—	+10.0	—
1981	−0.2	0.5	−1.3	+3.9	−5.2	+1.6	+0.8	+1.1	+1.1
Wadi Salib (Haifa)									
1977	+1.8	−2.1	+2.2	−15.6	+2.2	—	—	13.6	—
1981	−1.5	−.08	−1.2	+4.6	−12.3	+8.0	+0.7	+4.9	+0.7

represented in Tables 7 and 8, which relate to large cities only, as the Likud's greatest achievements in 1981 were in the new peripheral cities dominated by a Sephardic majority (Gonen 1983).

The Alignment lost nearly half its power in 1977 in both Sephardic and Ashkenazic neighborhoods. However, in 1981, it gained more votes in the rich neighborhoods than it had lost in the previous general elections. On the other hand, its gains in poor areas in 1981 were quite low in comparison to the losses of 1977. Thus, the Alignment's tendency to become an Ashkenazic party was not intensified in 1977, although the trend was in evidence nonetheless in 1981. Once again, the full extent of the 1981 development is not shown in the tables, which do not account for smaller cities and towns.

It appears that the floating vote in 1977 in the poor neighborhoods was direct — from the Alignment to the Likud. Otherwise we could not explain why the only prominent electoral changes in such constituencies were the significant losses of the former and the remarkable gain of the latter. Developments were different in the affluent areas: the main loser was the Alignment and the party gaining but its votes and others was the DMC. Thus the DMC was clearly almost a "pure" Ashkenazic party. The same may be said about secular dovish parties, which lost many of their supporters to the DMC.

In 1981, the Shinui movement, which succeeded the DMC, was heavily defeated in the Ashkenazic constituencies, as were other secular dovish parties. The greater the defeat of these parties, the greater the success of the Alignment. Thus, the main direction of floating vote in the large cities was of Ashkenazic voters who defected from the DMC and other secular parties to support the Alignment. Another direction of the secular Ashkenazic floating vote was towards Telem — the new party of the late Moshe Dayan.

The religious parties increased their power almost everywhere in 1977 but suffered humiliating defeat in 1981. The NRP gained only six seats — half its traditional representation in the Kneset. Poalei Agudat Israel, represented in all Knessets since the First in 1949, failed to gain even a single seat in the Tenth Knesset. In Ashkenazic areas, the 1981 losses of the religious parties were accompanied by the success of the new

Techiya Party. The more serious decline in religious party power in poor Sephardic neighborhoods was matched by the new Tami Party's gains. It is most plausible that the floating vote among religious voters is well depicted by these facts. In any event, it is obvious that Techiya backing was primarily Ashkenazic, while Tami was supported almost exclusively by Sephardim. The traditional religious parties tended to become slightly more Ashkenazic than they had been prior to 1981.

Conclusion

For many years, various scholars had predicted an ultimately inevitable victory for Israel's right-wing parties, owing to the continuous increase in proportion of Asian-African Jews in the electorate and the well-known characteristics of ethnic voting in Israel. In 1961, in fact — when Begin's Herut was a neglected opposition party which attained only 13.8% of the valid vote — people born in Asia and Africa and their Israel-born children constituted 37.5% of the voting population (Central Bureau of Statistics 1982, p. 56). In 1981, when the governing Likud increased its electoral power and gained 37.1% of the valid vote, the percentage of first and second generation Asian and African Jews increased by only 0.1%. Thus it is obvious that the veteran tendencies of eithnic voting constituted only a minor factor in the upheaval of 1977 and the repeated success of the Likud in 1981. The *intensification* of the ethnic vote phenomenon is highly evident according to the aggregate data, as is the fact that in 1981, this development was more influential than ever before — not only upon the Likud but upon virtually all of Israel's political parties.

Nevertheless, two questions remain unsolved:
a) What are the full reasons for this intensification?
b) What developments are to be expected in the future?

We may have to wait until the next electoral campaign to accumulate sufficient data for answering these questions satisfactorily.

BIBLIOGRAPHY

Arian, A. (ed.)
1972   *The Elections in Israel. 1969.* Jerusalem: Academic Press.
Central Bureau of Statistics.
1981   "Results of Elections to the Tenth Knesset, June 30, 1981." Special Series no. 680, Jerusalem (Hebrew).

1982   *Statistical Abstract of Israel 1981* (No. 32). Jerusalem.
Diskin, A.
1980   *Das Politische System Israels: eine raumlich-zeitliche Untersuchung. 1949-1978.* Cologne and Vienna: Bohlau.

1983   "Polarization and Volatility Among Voters in Elections for the Tenth Knesset" (this volume).
Gonen, A.
1983   "A Geographical Analysis of the Elections in Jewish Urban Communities" (this volume).
Kies, N.E.
1969   "Constituency, Support and the Israeli Party System." Unpublished Ph.D. dissertation, M.I.T.
Lissak, M.
1969   *Social Mobility in Israel.* Jerusalem: Israel Universities Press.
Matras, J.
1965   *Social Change in Israel.* Chicago: Aldine.
Peres, Y.
1971   "Ethnic Relations in Israel." *American Journal of Sociology* 76, 6, pp. 1021-1047.
Shamir, M. & Arian, A.
1982   "The Ethnic Vote in Israel's 1981 Elections." *Medina Mimshal Vihasim Benleumiyyim* (State, Government and International Relations) 19-20, pp. 88-105 (Hebrew).
Yatziv, G.
1979   "The Social Basis of Party Identification: The Israeli Example." Jerusalem: The Hebrew University (Hebrew).

3

A GEOGRAPHICAL ANALYSIS OF THE ELECTIONS IN JEWISH URBAN COMMUNITIES

Amiram Gonen *

Introduction

The 1977 change in Israeli government — in which the Likud, rather than the Alignment, formed the coalition — is to be interpreted as an abrupt change reflecting a long and continuous electoral process whereby the share of the former list (or its component parties) in the electorate increased at the expense of the latter. In the 1965 elections, the Alignment components — Labour (Mapai), Mapam and Rafi — won 51.3% of the vote, as compared with 21.3% for the Gahal list, forerunner of the Likud. In the 1981 elections, however, the Alignment's proportion decreased to 36.8% and the Likud's rose to 37.1%.

This chapter examines some of the broad geographical patterns characterizing the electoral competition between the two major blocs currently active on the Israel political scene. Such patterns often indicate correlations between a population's socio-economic processes and characteristics and its electoral behavior — all of which constitute the core of electoral geography (Taylor & Johnston 1979). Population characteristics may be measured directly in each of the geographical units under consideration (Butler & Stokes 1969; Cox 1971; Garrahan 1977); alternatively, they may be inferred through a typology of these units (Johnston 1982). This chapter will employ both methods. We emphasise, however, that such geographical investigation pertains to the aggregate ecological level alone; hence no conclusions should be drawn therefrom regarding the electoral behavior of

Professor of Geography, the Hebrew University of Jerusalem.

59

individuals. This is especially true with regard to correlations between individual behavior and aggregate level population characteristics, which could lead to what is generally termed "ecological fallacy." (Alker 1969, Robinson 1950).

Our investigation pertains solely to the urban Jewish population. The electoral behavior of Israel's Arab population is of a distinct character and demands separate examination. Furthermore, rural Jewish communities are characterized by a high degree of politicization in both economic and social life, as most such communities have political affiliations. Hence electoral competition between the two major political blocs likewise assumes a distinct pattern in rural communities, differing from that of urban areas and meriting separate inquiry as well.

Available statistics enable us to follow the elections on the aggregate level in four types of Jewish urban communities, classified according to size (cities or towns) and date of establishment as Jewish communities (old or new) — with the year 1948 (marking the establishment of the State of Israel) as the dividing line. Cities are urban communities with appropriate municipal status which generally have populattions of 20,000 or more. Towns are smaller and are governed by "local councils." We will employ the term "towns" throughout, although official statistical terminology refers to such communities as "urban settlements."

Of far greater significance for election geography is the division of Israel's urban communities into old and new, which incorporates a clear distinction in terms of the socio-economic characteristics of the resident population. The population of the old Jewish urban regions is largely characterized by higher socio-economic status and Ashkenazic (i.e. European or American) ethno-cultural origin. Many such communities are located in central Israel, in or near the metropolitan regions of Tel Aviv and Haifa. A number of them developed from *moshavot* — rural settlements which underwent varying degrees of urbanization.

During the 1950s, many immigrant housing developments were constructed on the outskirts of the old urban communities. At present, most are populated by people of Sephardic (i.e. Middle Eastern and North African) origin, of lower socio-economic status than their counterparts in the inner urban neighborhoods. Such population concentrations may also be found in old neighborhoods of the three large cities: Jerusalem, Tel Aviv (including Jaffa) and Haifa. Old urban communities are of a heterogeneous nature in terms of population composition and socio-economic status.

In general, the new urban communities — established or settled by Jews since 1948 — are populated primarily by Sephardim, who constituted the majority of the immigrant population during the 1950s, when most of these areas were established or settled. Moreover, internal migration processes have stripped these communities of many of their upwardly-mobile residents. Thus, by comparing old and new cities and towns on the aggregate level, we may find differences in electoral behavior between the two major components of Jewish society: the social and economic core of the country, with its heterogeneous population, versus the periphery composed of new towns, where ethnicity and socio-economic status assume a distinct character.

Table 1 summarizes measures of electoral data for the two major lists during the period between the 1965 and 1981 elections. In general, a rise in Likud support and a concomitant decline for the Alignment was common to all four types of Jewish urban communities. However, the most significant change occurred in the new cities and towns, wherein Alignment votes decreased by 50% between 1965 and 1981, while the percentage of Likud votes more than doubled. The electoral swing in the old urban communities was not so extreme: the two political blocs achieved virtually equal support in the 1981 elections.

The Relative Representation Quotient (RRQ) recorded in Table 1 facilitates examination of electoral change by type of urban community, comparing the proportion of votes given to a particular list in a specific type of community and in the country as a whole. A rating of more than 1.0 means that community support of the list in question exceeded its proportion of the overall vote.

Table 1 clearly shows that since the 1965 elections, the new cities and towns have gradually become centers of Likud over-representation. In 1981, the proportion of Likud votes in new urban communities was one-third larger than that of the country as a whole. At the same time, the Alignment has

Table 1: **Alignment and Likud Votes by Type of Jewish Urban Community, 1965—1981**

	% of Votes			RRQ*		
	1965	1973	1981	1965**	1977	1981
Type of Community and List						
Old Cities:						
Alignment	50.0	39.7	36.8	0.97	1.00	1.01
Likud	26.5	34.8	39.7	1.24	1.15	1.07
Old Towns:						
Alignment	57.9	43.8	39.9	1.13	1.08	1.09
Likud	19.2	31.5	38.5	0.90	1.04	1.04
New Cities:						
Alignment	54.2	41.4	29.5	1.05	1.04	0.81
Likud	22.2	32.0	49.0	1.04	1.06	1.32
New Towns:						
Alignment	53.8	38.1	26.1	1.05	0.96	0.72
Likud	19.8	32.1	49.1	0.93	1.06	1.33
Entire Country:						
Alignment	51.2	39.6	36.6	—	—	—
Likud	21.3	30.2	37.1	—	—	—

RRQ (Relative Representation Quotient) = % of vote in community / % of total vote.

**Alignment = ILP + Mapam + Rafi; Likud = Gahal.*

Source: Central Bureau of Statistics, 1970 and 1981.

experienced a severe drop in representation in the same communities, far exceeding its decline in national representation. This drop has been greatest in the new towns, which are characterized by a high proportion of Sephardic population, low socio-economic status and severe economic problems due to their small size and dependency upon too few industrial plants and economic sectors.

Although the proportion of Alignment votes declined in the old urban communities betwee 1965 and 1981, relative Alignment representation remained virtually unchanged, with the RRQ approaching 1.0. The heterogeneous nature of their population — particularly the middle-to-upper class Ashkenazic component — was undoubtedly responsible for this situation. This trend was of particular significance in the old towns: in the 1965 elections, Alignment component parties together received 57.0% of the votes, the highest representation among the four types of urban communities. Their support declined to only 39.9% in 1981, although still registering an RRQ of 1.09, higher than the 1.0 recorded for old cities. In this context, it is interesting to note that in the 1977 elections, the old towns served as important bases for the Democratic Movement for Change (DMC), a one-election party that attained support primarily among middle-class Ashkenazim.

From a geographical point of view, a fundamental change has been taking place in the electoral competition between the Alignment and the Likud. In 1965, the Alignment parties amassed about half the votes in all types of Jewish urban communities. Labor, although not yet finally consolidated as a unified electoral list, was the dominant political component all over urban Israel. In 1965, the Labor Party still maintained the role of a country-wide dominant party (Shapira 1980). Gahal, the predecessor of the Likud, was then a small political bloc whose proportion of votes in the four types of urban communities varied between only 1/5 in the new cities up to 1/4 in the old ones, primarily due to its electoral strength in Tel Aviv and Jerusalem. in short, there was very little geographical differentiation in the representation of each of the two competing political camps in 1965. By 1981, this geographical uniformity gave way to differentiation, wherein the Likud shifted its major weight from the old to the new cities and towns. Labor, which up to 1965 was able to win over the recently-formed social periphery of Jewish society, has since lost its electoral dominance. Consequently, by 1981, a clear-cut, country-wide division emerged between the old and new urban communities: the old ones were split electorally between the Likud and the Alignment while the new ones swung towards the Likud.

The emerging geographical division between old and new communities, which has affected electoral competition between the two major political blocs since 1977, has also characterized the remainder of the political spectrum of the Jewish population in the 1981 campaign. Tami, for example, broke away from the National Religious Party (NRP) on ethnic grounds in 1981. The NRP relied primarily upon its religious Ashkenazic supporters in the old urban communities, while Tami drew its strength from Sephardic voters (of North African — particularly Moroccan — origin) in the new cities and towns, as indicated in Table 2. Tami attained a level of over-representation in the new urban communities (as indicated by the RRQ) twice as high as that of the Likud. As such, it emerged as even more a party of the periphery than the Likud and was the latter's chief competitor for the votes of this population sector.

Table 2: RRQ* by Party and Type of Urban Community — 1981

		Type of Urban Community			
Party	% of National Vote	Old Cities	Old Towns	New Cities	New Towns
Alignment	36.6	1.01	1.09	0.81	0.71
Likud	37.1	1.07	1.04	1.04	1.33
CRM	1.4	1.29	1.36	0.57	0.50
Shinui	1.5	1.00	1.20	0.46	0.46
Independent Liberals	0.6	1.00	0.83	0.66	0.50
Telem	1.6	1.06	1.13	0.75	0.88
Techiya	2.3	1.09	1.16	0.65	0.83
NRP	4.9	0.98	1.12	0.57	0.92
Tami	2.3	0.70	0.78	2.61	2.26
Agudat Israel	3.7	1.27	0.65	0.73	1.35
Poalei Agudat Israel	0.9	1.00	0.66	0.88	1.88

Source: Central Bureau of Statistics, 1981.
*See Table 1.

In the 1981 elections, the old urban communities served as major electoral bases not only for the Alignment but also for most of the small parties, especially those which derived their electoral support from Ashkenazic middle-to-upper class groups. These small parties are situated in various locations along the political spectrum, from Shinui on the "dovish" side to Techiya at the far "hawkish" extreme, even beyond the Herut component of the Likud. All these parties were over-represented in the old urban communities, especially the old towns, with their high proportion of middle-to-upper class Ashkenazim (see Table 2). It appears that this type of population gave rise to small parties of particular ideological or political inclination. At the same time, residents of the new urban communities, characterized by a different ethnic and socio-economic composition, showed very little interest in the small parties, as indicated by the very low RRQs in Table 2.

Among the small parties, only the orthodox ones (Agudat Israel and Poalei Agudat Israel) were able to achieve any noteworthy representation in the new towns, in addition to the major support from the large concentrations of orthodox population in Jerusalem and Bnei Brak, which are categorized as old cities. Recently, orthodox groups have made an effort to increase their hold in some new towns, especially through promotion of orthodox neighborhoods and institutions. Nevertheless, the case of the orthodox parties is rather an exception to the general dichotomous pattern recently emerging in the geography of elections in the urban Jewish population. The new cities and towns have developed a political composition which is substantially different from that of the old ones. This clearly indicates a substantial change in the voting behavior of the lower-class Sephardic population in recent years — a topic which will be considered towards the end of this chapter. Prior to this, however, we proceed to investigate the geography of election results on the intra-urban level.

The 1981 Competition within the Large Cities

Israel's cities and towns, like many other urban regions, are characterized by social differentiation (Gradus, 1971; Hershkowitz 1979; Shahar *et al.* 1978 and Shinan 1975). The social map of the old cities and towns includes ethnically homogeneous as well as heterogeneous residential areas.

Those with large Sephardic majorities are generally of lower socio-economic status than areas with a majority of Ashkenazim. The relationship between ethnicity and voting began to emerge in data on statistical quarters as early as the 1969 elections (Lissak 1969). This chapter will further explore this possible relationship, investigating voting data of the 1981 elections and utilizing statistical subquarters which represent the ethnic and socio-economic quarters. Data on the ehtnic composition of these subquarters are based upon the percentage of foreign-born by continent of birth (a surrogate for ethnicity in much of Israel's social research) in 1977. These statistics, the most recent data available, approximate description of the gross ethnic composition of the population. There are certain inherent drawbacks to utilizing these statistics, such as their date, for example. Nevertheless, the four-year difference between them and available voting data does not constitute a serious shortcoming in light of the low rate of residential mobility. A far more serious drawback is the partial nature of the data:

(Fig. 1)

11. Givat Hamivtar, Ramot Eshkol, Maalot Dafna, Sanhedria Hamurhevet
12. Mea Shearim, Beit Israel, Bucharim, Sanhedria, Mahanaim
13. Morasha, Mamilla (foot of Agron Street)
14. Downtown
15. Rehavia, Kiryat Shmuel
16. Mahane Yehuda, Nahlaot, Zichronot, Shaarei Hesed
17. Geula, Kerem Avraham, Mekor Baruch, Zichron Moshe
21. Romema, Romema Murhevet, Mei Naftoah, Givat Shaul
22. Kiryat Hauniversita, Neve Shaanan, Kiryat Hamemshala
23. Kiryat Moshe, Beit Hakerem, Bayit Vegan, Ramat Sharett, Ramat Danya
31. Kiryat Hayovel, Ein Kerem, Hadassah
32. Kiryat Menahem, Ir Ganim, Manahat
41. New Gonen (Katamonim)
42. Givat Mordechai, Rassco
51. Old Gonen (Katamon), German Colony (Emek Refaim Street), Greek Colony
52. Komemiut (Talbieh), King David Hotel
53. Yemin Moshe, Givat Hanania, Abu Tor, Geulim, Talpiot, Mekor Haim, Beit Zefafa
71. Atarot Airport, Beit Hanina, Neve Yaakov, Shuafat and Refugee Camp, Ramot
73. Mt. Scopus, Augusta Victoria, Givat Shapira (French Hill)
74. Jebel Makbar, Government House, Sur Baher, Gilo, Beit Zefafa (south), Shuafat

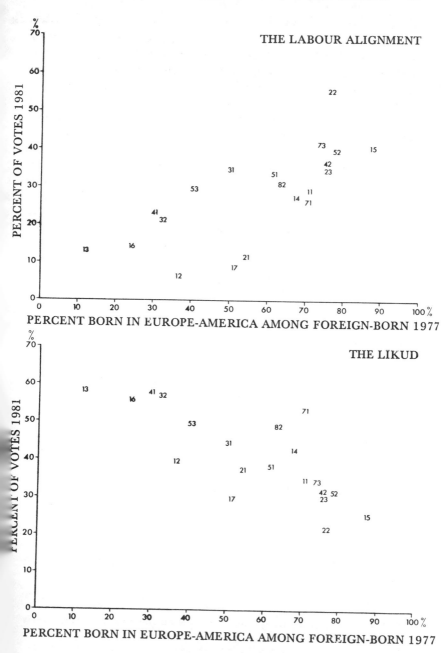

FIG. 1. JERUSALEM

the Israel-born population — whose ethnic make-up in certain residential areas is of a slightly different nature from that of the foreign-born — is unaccounted for. In general, however, there is a systematic bias in the difference, as the proportion of Sephardim among the Israel-born is larger than among the foreign-born, due to differential birth rates between them. Another factor allowing for leniency in use of data on the foreign-born is the fact that many of the Israel-born were still under voting age in 1981.

Figures 1—3 plot the proportion of 1981 votes for the Alignment and the Likud in the three large cities, by sub-

---

(Fig. 2)

11. Tochnit Lamed
12. Ramat Aviv, Sheikh Munis, Kiryat Hauniversita, Afeka, Neve Avivim, Avivim
22. Yad Hamaavir, Ramat Hahayal, Tel Baruch
31. Northwest: Tel Aviv Port, Nordau Avenue
32. Arlosoroff Street (west of Ibn Gvirol Street)
33. West of Dizengoff Circle: Mahlul Quarter
34. East of Dizengoff Circle: Malchei Israel Square, Habima Area, Nordiya Quarter
41. Northeast: Bavli, Givat Amal, Yehuda Hamaccabi Street
42. Kikar Hamedina area
43. Ichilov Hospital area, Neve David, Beeri Street
51. Northern downtown region: 29 November Square, Rashi Street, Trumpeldor Street
52. Kerem Hatemanim, Carmel Market
53. Southwest: Menashiya, Neve Shalom, Neve Zedek
54. Magen David Square, Kalisher Street, Eliot Street
55. Hamoshavot Square, southern Rothschild Boulevard
61. Hakirya, Wholesale Market
62. Harakevet Quarter, Montefiore Quarter
71. Florentine Avenue, Old Maccabi area, Bloomfield Stadium area
72. Old Jaffa (West): Ajami, Givat Haaliya
73. Central Jaffa: Jerusalem Avenue
74. Nuzha, Sakhnat Darwish, Abu Kebir
81. South: Central Bus Station area, Neve Shaanan, Wolfson Street area
82. Shapira Quarter, Givat Herzl, Kiryat Hamelacha
83. Kiryat Shalom
91. Nahalat Itzhak, Ramat Israel, Bitzaron
92. Yad Eliyahu, Ramat Hatayasim, Neve Zahal, Shikun Amami, Givat Shimshon, Caucasian Quarter
93. Hatikva Quarter, Ezra Quarter, New Maccabi
94. Kfar Shalem

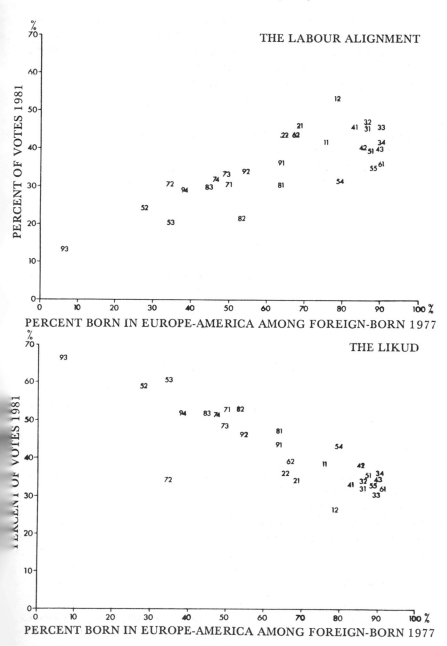

FIG. 2. TEL-AVIV — YAFO

quarter, against the percentage of residents of foreign origin born in Europe and the Americas in 1977. In all three cities, subquarters with higher proportions of Asian and African-born residents, generally of lower socio-economic status, vote percentages were higher for the Likud and lower for the Alignment. The population of such subquarters is very similar to that of the new cities and towns; their respective voting patterns did not differ substantially in 1981. Generally, these subquarters are divided into three principal types: pre-1948 old Jewish neighborhoods of Sephardic ethnic composition, old neighborhoods initially inhabited by Arabs and populated by Jews after 1948 and immigrant housing developments built in the 1950s and 1960s. Settlement and social processes in all such subquarters led to their eventual evolution as concentrations of a lower socio-economic status Sephardic population.

The current rise in electoral support for the Likud in concentrations of lower-status Sephardic population has become a familiar process. Contrary to the widespread image of dichotomous ethnic voting, however, there has been no significant converse increase in electoral support for the Alignment in subquarters of middle-to-upper class Ashkenazic majorities, as shown in Figures 1—3. Rather, the pattern in Ashkenazic majority subquarters could be described as electorally split with a clear advantage for the Alignment. In such subquarters the Alignment received 35% — 40%. In many of them, the

---

(Fig. 3)

11. New Kiryat Haim (west), Kiryat Shmuel
12. Old Kiryat Haim (east)
13. Industrial Zone, Shemen coast
21. Old City, Wadi Salib
22. Lower City, Railroad Station, Haifa Port
23. Wadi Nisanis, German Colony
31. Kiryat Eliyahu, Kiryat Eliezer, Bat Galim
32. Ein Hayam, Mahane David, Shaar Ha'aliya
41. Ahuza
42. Western and Central Carmel, Carmeliya, Romema
43. French Carmel, Ramat Shaul, Kiryat Sprinzak
51. Upper Hadar: Kisch Avenue, Golomb Street, Ramat Hadar, Abas Street
52. Central Hadar: Hehalutz Street, Herzl Street
61. Tel Amal, Neve Shaanan, Yizraeliya
62. Ziv Quarter, Ramot Remez, Kiryat Hatechnion, Kiryat Hauniversita

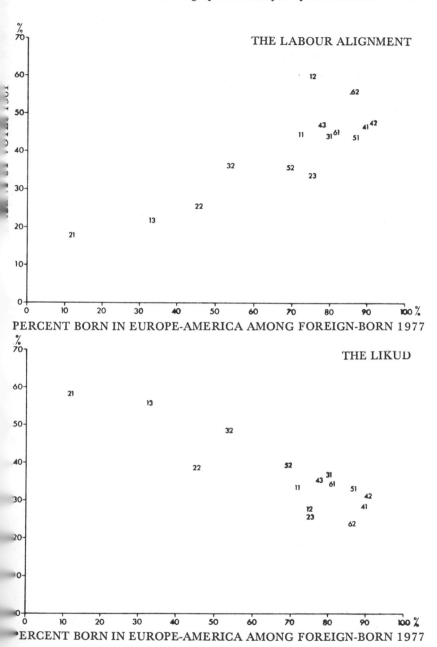

THE LABOUR ALIGNMENT

PERCENT BORN IN EUROPE-AMERICA AMONG FOREIGN-BORN 1977

THE LIKUD

PERCENT BORN IN EUROPE-AMERICA AMONG FOREIGN-BORN 1977

FIG. 3 HAIFA

difference between the Alignment and the Likud did not exceed 10%. This split implies that the electoral behavior of the population in question is not necessarily ethnically motivated or class-bound, despite the relative homogeneity in this respect. The phenomenon may indeed be rooted in differences in political tradition: Alignment electoral strength stems largely from persons who — despite their upward social mobility — remained loyal to the political ideals and interests traditionally embodied in Labor's social-democratic image. Conversely, the Likud draws its electoral support from people who follow one of the two political traditions which joined together to form this political bloc: on the one hand, the class-boind political tradition of the Liberal Party and on the other that of Herut, which emphasizes national rather than social and economic issues. These two Likud political traditions, together with those of Labor, characterized the Ashkenazic population even during the 1920s and 1930s, when political differentiation followed status or class lines. In recent decades, much of the Ashkenazic population has been incorporated into the upper half of the social ladder; nevertheless, despite this upward social mobility, political divisions are preserved.

During the 1950s, Sephardic immigrants were drawn into the long-standing European-rooted political conflicts of the Ashkenazic population. During the first two decades of the new State of Israel, the Labor camp managed to mobilize the electoral support of the newly-arrived Sephardic population, especially in the new towns and immigrant housing developments (Gonen & Hasson 1981). However, since the 1960s, a rising proportion of the Sephardic population has lent its electoral support to the Herut party. The formation of Gahal in 1965 and subsequently the Likud in 1973 created a coalition not only within the Ashkenazic population residing in the inner urban middle-class neighborhoods but also between this population and the largely Sephardic one inhabiting the urban or national periphery. On the municipal election level, this has meant that after many local elections in old urban communities had been won by Labor in the 1950s, with the electoral support of the population residing in immigrant housing developments, the Likud was able to recapture many of these municipalities with the support of this same Sephardic population, which eventually joined with part of the residents of the largely Ashkenazic neighborhoods in the heart of the old urban communities (*ibid.*). A similar trend took place in some of the new cities and towns even without the support of a large Liberal constituency, virtually non-existent in such communities.

A few of the subquarters in Figures 1—3 fail to conform fully to the relationship between ethnicity and voting for the Likud and the Alignment and consequently merit some explanation. One such pattern relates to subquarters with a high proportion of Ashkenazim in which the vote was not split but rather clearly favors the Alignment. These include large Histadrut (Labor Federation) housing developments established between the 1930s and 1950s; the ethnic composition of their population has remained stable and the Labor voting tradition therein precludes any substantial inroads of support for the Likud.

Another type of non-conforming subquarters was evident in Jerusalem, in inner urban neighborhoods with an overwhelming majority of religious Ashkenazim. In such cases, the population barely voted for the Alignment at all, instead offering large electoral support to the orthodox parties, primarily Agudat Israel. Even the Likud received fewer votes in these subquarters than could be predicted according to their ethnic composition.

Haifa and Tel Aviv displayed a third exception: subquarters with only limited support for the Likud and a "more than anticipated" vote for the Alignment, despite their high proportion of Sephardim. Such areas included a substantial number of Arab residents, whose votes are reflected in electoral data even though they do not figure in calculations of the Jewish population's ethnic composition. Arab voters hardly supported the Likud in 1981, but were somewhat more generous towards the Alignment.

The 1965—1981 Competition in the Large Cities

We now proceed to a geographical examination of the electoral competition between the Alignment and the Likud in the three large cities between 1965 and 1981. The main electoral process in this period — the rise of the Likud and the decline of the Alignment — did not occur in an identical manner in all subquarters. We may distinguish among three types of subquarters, according to the nature of electoral change taking place within them between 1965 and 1981.

In one rather rare type of subquarter (e.g. A1, A2 and A3 in Figure 4), the Likud has led the Alignment in percentage of votes since 1965, with the electoral gap widening substantially in each election year. This type includes old inner urban neighborhoods, inhabited by an overwhelming Sephardic majority and characterized by lower socio-economic status. Most were established as Sephardic population clusters from the outset, although others have become so following Arab exodus and Jewish resettlement in 1948.

The second type of subquarter (D1, D2 and D3, in Figure 4) represents the other extreme: i.e. those inhabited by a majority of Ashkenazim of middle-to-upper socio-economic status throughout the period 1965—1981. The Alignment did lose some of its electoral strength to the Likud in these subquarters; nevertheless, it remained in the lead throughout, except for the 1977 elections, in which the DMC took a substantial bite out of Alignment support, particularly

Figure 4: Percentage of Valid Votes for the Likud and the Alignment in Large Cities, by Selected Subquarters, 1965 — 1981

JERUSALEM	TEL AVIV—YAFO	HAIFA
A1: Mahane Yehuda Nahlaot	A2: Hatikva, Ezra	A3: Old City Wadi Salib
B1: Gonen	B2: Yad Eliyahu Hatayasim	B3: Mahane David Shaar Haaliya
C1: Downtown: Jaffa Road — Ben Yehuda St.	C2: 29 November Square area	C3: Central Hadar: Hehalutz St. — Herzl St.
D1: Rehavia — Kiryat Shmuel	D2: Arlosoroff St. (West)	D3: Ahuza

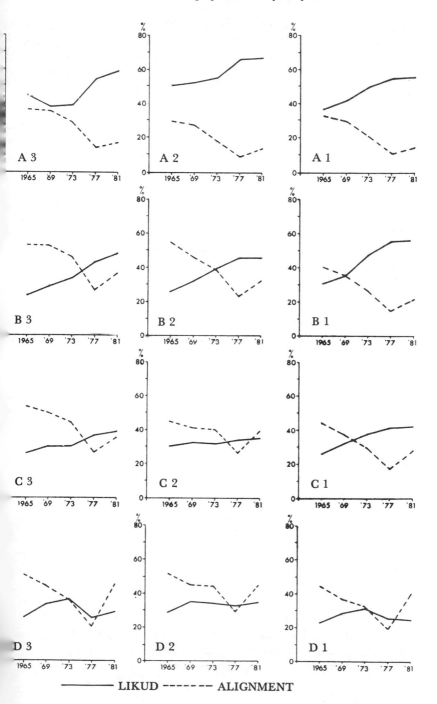

LIKUD ------ ALIGNMENT

in this type of subquarter. In the 1981 elections, the Alignment regained its 1977 loss to the DMC when the latter disappeared from the political map. However, the situation of electoral split with an advantage for the Alignment, which commenced during the 1970s, has not changed as a result of Labor's 1981 comeback.

Between the two aforementioned subquarter types — one evolving as a stronghold for the Likud and the other maintaining a weakening allegiance to the Alignment — lies the third, in which a substantial swing took place: the Alignment lost its leading position to the Likud during the period under observation. There are many such subquarters in all three cities; we may safely suggest that it is primarily this type of subquarters which was responsible for the general rise in Likud electoral strength and the concomitant weakening of the Alignment, and therefore is worthy of a detailed analysis.

Subquarters of Electoral Swing

Foremost among the subquarters of electoral transition are the immigrant housing estates constructed during the 1950s and early 1960s to house the huge influx of immigration which characterized the first years of the state (e.g. B1, B2 and B3). After their construction, many of estates underwent demographic processes, including migration, which led to increased ethnic homogeneity (Cohen 1966). Consequently, the proportion of Sephardic population therein often reached a level of 75% — 90%. In the 1965 election, about half the votes in these housing estates went to the Alignment. By 1973 or 1977, however, the Likud had secured the lead in these estates, as it had in many other Sephardic population clusters.

Similar immigrant housing estates — with parallel demographic processes and ethnic compositions — may be found in medium-sized old cities. Differential outward migration left an overwhelming Sephardic majority in these estates (Gonen & Hasson 1974). By the end of the 1970s, areas such as Pardes Katz in Bnei Brak, Amishav in Petah Tikva and Dora in Netanya had shifted from Alignment to Likud support.

Certain public housing estates constructed prior to or soon

after 1948 were not designed to house recent immigrants, but rather to serve the housing needs of a veteran population capable of helping to finance their construction. The Histadrut and other organizations, generally those with obvious political affiliations, were involved in developing such housing projects for their members and followers (Gonen 1975). Similar projects were constructed by government organizations in the 1950s for low-to-middle income households whose small capital and steady employment enabled them to afford housing more spacious than standard immigrant accommodations. At the time, this meant that non-immigrant housing estates were largely inhabited by Ashkenazim. Moreover, most were built by the Histadrut and were established from the start as centers of electoral support for the Labor camp. Such support was continuously accorded to the Alignment from these estates so long as no major demographic changes took place. In certain cases, however, locational circumstances — such as proximity to lower-status residential areas — led to an exodus of the original residents, followed by an influx of new ones from neighboring areas, i.e. immigrant housing estates or old inner urban ethnic neighborhoods, thereby changing the population's ethnic composition. It appears that the newly arrived Sephardic residents brought with them political traditions which had recently become consolidated in their former places of residence, thus increasing the proportion of Likud votes in their new neighborhoods. This electoral behavior continued even though the change in residence was often accompanied by upward social mobility. The result has been a rising percentage of votes for the Likud.

Social changes — with electoral ramifications — took place in old residential areas located in the heart of the large cities (such as C1, C2 and C3); penetration of commercial services and small industries ultimately led to deterioration in the quality of life, fostering an exodus of the upwardly mobile population. As a result, Ashkenazic residents left for new neighborhoods and lower-middle class Sephardic residents moved in, leading to electoral transition.

Electoral behavior was identical in residential areas of other old urban communities which underwent similar social processes. In middle-to-upper class areas with an Ashkenazic majority, the Alignment continued to lead the Likud, although it did suffer some decline in share of the electorate. In immigrant housing estates and inner urban commercialized areas, a transition took place from the Alignment to the Likud as the leading political bloc. Other types of residential areas prevalent in the three large cities are virtually non-existent in the remaining old cities and towns.

A twofold overall pattern thus emerges in the electoral geography of the large cities. Although there is some correlation between ethnicity and voting in lower-status residential areas with large Sephardic populations, there is an electoral split in the middle-to-upper class areas with an Ashkenazic majority; hence it is impossible to find a straightforward correlation. We may therefore suggest that ethnicity is a major electoral factor in lower-status Sephardic population clusters. In areas with middle-to-upper class Ashkenazic majorities, tradition and change in political ideology are more likely to be associated with electoral behavior.

Spatial Diffusion of the Swing to the Likud

From a social-geographic standpoint, the most important factor in the rise of Likud electoral strength since 1965 has been the shift in its direction among Sephardic population clusters, especially those characterized by lower socioeconomic status. A process of spatial diffusion becomes evident when this electoral swing is examined on both the intra and inter-urban level. This diffusional process is displayed in Table 3, which lists neighborhoods and towns of overwhelmingly Sephardic majority, according to the election year in which Likud votes exceeded those accorded to the Alignment.

The first nucleus of Likud support in Sephardic population clusters emerged in the old inner urban neighborhoods of the three large cities, where the Likud had led Labor since the 1965 elections. In some of these areas, sympathy for the Irgun paramilitary organization and the Revisionist movement, the ideological forerunners of the Herut Party, had existed as early as the 1940s during conflicts with the British Mandatory authorities.

From the old, inner city neighborhoods, support for the

Table 5. Urban Cluster by Geographical Type and by Year the Likud Surpassed Labor in Votes

Type of Cluster	1965	1969	1973	1977	1981
Old inner-urban in large cities	Musrara (Jerusalem) Nahlaot (Jerusalem) Kerem Hateimanim (Tel Aviv-Yafo) Hatikva (Tel Aviv-Yafo) Kefar Shalom (Tel Aviv-Yafo) Neve Zedek (Tel Aviv-Yafo) Wadi Salib (Haifa)	—		—	—
Immigrant Housing Estates in Old Cities		Romema (Jerusalem) Gonen (Katamonim) (Jerusalem)	Kiryat Hayovel (Jerusalem) Ir Ganim (Jerusalem) Pardes Katz (Bnei Brak) Amidar (Bat Yam) Ramat-Yam (Bat Yat) Tel Giborim (Holon) Amishav (Petah Tiqva) Hamizrah (Rishon Leziyon)	Tel Kabir (Tel Aviv-Yafo) Mahane David (Haifa) Yad Hatish'a (Herzliya) Jessie Cohen (Holon) Ramat Herzl (Netanya) Dora (Netanya)	—
Immigrant Towns (Near Old Cities)	—	Or Yehuda (Tel Aviv-Yafo) Bet Dagan (Tel Aviv-Yafo) Mevasseret (Jerusalem) Kiryat Eqron (Rehovot) Rosh Ha'ayin (Petah-Tiqva)	Or Akiva (Hadera) Tirat Hacarmel (Haifa) Kiryat Ata (Haifa)	Yahud (Tel Aviv-Yafo) Lod (Tel Aviv-Yafo) Ramla (Tel Aviv-Yafo) Kiryat Yam (Haifa)	—
Development Towns	—	Netivot	Hatzor Yavne	Eilat Ofakim Ashdod Be'er Sheva Bet She'an Bet Shemesh Dimona Yokneam Yeruham Migdal Ha'emek Mitzpe Ramon Kiryat Gat Kiryat Malachi Kiryat Shmona Sderot Shlomi	

Likud spread first to immigrant housing developments on the
outskirts of the old cities. This process began as early as 1969,
but reached a peak in most such developments in the 1973
elections.

The 1969 elections also marked the beginning of Likud
preference in new immigrant towns which sprang up near
the centrally-located old cities. In order to distinguish these
towns from the new urban communities in Israel's periphery,
the former are called "immigrant towns" and the latter
"development towns," following familiar Israeli terminology.
In the 1969 elections, the Likud vote surpassed that of the
Alignment in the immigrant towns of Or Yehuda and Beit
Dagan (near Tel Aviv), Mevasseret Zion (near Jerusalem),
Kiryat Ekron (near Rehovot) and Rosh Haayin (near Petah
Tikva). In 1973, these immigrant towns were joined by Tirat
Hacarmel and Kiryat Ata (near Haifa) and Or Akiva (near
Hadera).

The last wave of diffusion occurred in 1977 in the development towns, which were the most peripheral type of Sephardic
population clusters. In a few development towns (Hatzor,
Netivot and Yavne), the relative significance of the religious
vote facilitates the Likud's surpassing the Alignment at
the polls as early as 1969 or 1973. In most others, however,
the Alignment still led the Likud in those election years.
Only as late as 1977, the year the Likud won the national
elections, did the development towns swing over to the Likud.
By the 1977 elections, therefore, the spatial diffusion of the
Likud vote was completed. Three development towns did
not even join this swing in the 1981 elections, namely Upper
Nazareth, Carmiel and Arad, whose late date of establishment
and demographically planned process of initial settlement
singled them out as communities with a substantial proportion of middle-class Ashkenazim.

Explaining the Diffusion — An Hypothesis

The spread of Likud electoral support — from the ethnic
inner urban neighborhoods of the three large cities, through
immigrant housing developments on the outskirts of old
cities and nearby immigrant towns, to development towns in

peripheral areas — is easily traceable through available election statistics. Nevertheless, it is difficult to find an explanation for the process which may be substantiated with evidence. In this respect, we suggest a hypothesis based upon the overall geographical structure of Israeli society.

The rise in Likud electoral support is generally attributed to certain overall changes in the social and economic structure of the country. So long as there was direct personal dependence upon Labor-run governmental and adminsitrative organizations with regard to matters of employment, housing and social services, Labor was able to secure widespread support within all strata of the Jewish electorate and particularly the lower strata, in which much of the Sephardic population was concentrated. However, with the application of increased rationality and universalism in the operation of many governmental and administrative organizations engaged in the allocation of resources, this personal material dependence upon Labor has diminished gradually. Moreover, general economic development in Israel has led to upward socioeconomic mobility among many residents of housing estates new cities and towns, thereby further weakening such dependence. Consequently, the lower-status Sephardic population felt free to express its political views — i.e. anti-Alignment and pro-Likud — at the polls.

Several alternative or complementary suggestions have been offered with regard to the roots of this latent political tendency. One is based upon class grievance, wherein the Alignment is considered as representative of the upper and middle classes, whose interests are promoted by Labor through its means of government. A second widely-suggested theory is ethnically-based, perceiving of the Labor establishment as serving the needs of the Ashkenazic population. According to this view, the vote for the Likud was mainly an ethnic protest against Labor. It was also often mentioned that the Sephardic political culture is more inclined towards strong and charismatic leadership, provided by the image of Menachem Begin, leader of the Likud, once David Ben-Gurion, Labor's long-standing leader, left the political scene and eventually passed away. Another significant factor is the religious issue: the Sephardic population is said to be more religiously inclined and consequently attracted by the many religious overtures and gestures accompanying the political posturing of Herut, the major component of the Likud. Last but not least is the hawkish attitude that was attributed to the Sephardic population in the sphere of the Arab-Israel confrontation, one which conforms more to the position of the Likud than that of the Alignment (Shamir & Arian 1982). Without examining the validity and relative weight of each factor, we may state that several such factors could indeed potentially tip the electoral balance in favor of the Likud among the Sephardic population. Furthermore, the weakening of material dependence upon the governmental-administrative system, long headed by Labor, apparently made this change possible.

In the context of this analysis, we seek to determine how to associate the pattern of spatial diffusion of the shift from the Alignment to the Likud and the general weakening of material dependence upon the former Labor-headed govern-mental-administrative system. The answer lies in the geo-graphical location of the various types of Sephardic clusters in the urban-economic system of the country. The first to enter the diffusional process were the old inner urban neigh-borhoods of the three large cities. In these neighborhoods, opportunities for employment and housing were only minimally controlled by the governmental-adminstrative system headed by Labor. The private sector, operating intensively in the commercial and industrial centers of the large cities, had been providing a wealth of employment opportunities since the early 1960s. Almost all local housing was — and still is — private, while nearly all public housing was concentrated on the urban periphery. Moreover, in the large cities, organizations affiliated with the Likud parties were long engaged in provision of non-governmental social services, foremost among which were health services, which competed with the nationwide system developed and managed by the Labor-dominated Histadrut.

The immigrant housing estates on the outskirts of the old cities and nearby immigrant towns joined in the second phase of diffusion of the Likud's electoral rise. These Sephardic population clusters, in geographic proximity to the economic systems of the old cities, were able to utilize the wide variety of employment opportunities provided by the private commercial and industrial sectors, especially in metropolitan regions, as well as by Likud-headed municipalities in some of the old cities. Nevertheless, they were more dependent upon government housing services than were residents of the inner urban neighborhoods. However, most of the housing in these immigrant developments and towns had already been built by the mid-1960s. Thus a sizeable share of housing transactions gradually began taking place between individual sellers and buyers, a tendency which in turn weakened dependence upon the public sector for housing.

Peripheral development towns were the last to join the spread of the Likud vote, as their dependence upon government and Histadrut-controlled employment opportunities was far greater than in other clusters of lower-status Sephardic population. The private sector hardly moved into the development towns during their early decades of formation. A few large public sector employers characterized the labor market in these towns, as contrasted with the heterogeneity which prevailed in central Israel. Certain development towns were virtually one or two company towns in this respect. Social services were also monopolized by the government or the Histadrut, as was housing. Nevertheless, factors contributing to weakening of material dependence were operative here as well, albeit at a later date, which may be explained in terms of "political economy." The nature and pace of change was influenced by the peripheral location of the development towns and the role the government played during their early stages. By the 1970s, employment had diversified and the housing reserve was sufficient to sustain private transactions. Income rose, as did levels of professional skill and education. Moreover, by the late 1970s, the tendency of a Sephardic swing towards the Likud was already in evidence; hence it was inevitable that development towns would join this trend as well.

The diffusion of the Likud vote was conditioned not only by the geography of political economy among the various components of the urban system but was also propelled by the momentum already achieved in other peer clusters. These cultural facets of electoral diffusion have yet to be explored, as does the entire process as a whole. All we can suggest at this point is that the diffusion of Likud support

though the urban Sephardic clusters is related to the geography of government and Histadrut control of the urban
economy and to the geographical spread of economic development from the core to the periphery. Further investigation of
this phenomenon demands in-depth studies of the details of
the electoral swing's spatial diffusion and the various factors
and agents which delayed or hastened the process.

Conclusion

A geographical examination of the electoral competition
between the Alignment and the Likud, currently the two
major political blocs in Israeli elections, reveals several
geographical changes and processes which shed light upon
the nature of this competition in Jewish urban communities.

One such change is increased differentiation in the geography of this electoral competition. In the 1965 elections,
there was marked geographical uniformity in the electoral
strength of each of the two political blocs: the Alignment had
about half the votes and the Likud approximately a quarter.
in each type of urban community. By the late 1970s, the
Likud attained the upper hand in clusters of Sephardic population. This change was expressed by a widening difference in
electoral behavior in centrally-located old cities and towns
and new ones on the periphery with large Sephardic majorities.
In the old urban communities with a sizeable Ashkenazic
component, the two political blocs reached a state of equilibrium in terms of electoral strength. In the new cities and
towns, the Likud replaced the Alignment as the dominant
political bloc.

Within the large cities, a similar geographic pattern has
emerged since the 1965 election. At the beginning of this
period, there was very little geographical differentiation
among residential areas. In most of them, the Labor parties
were by far the dominant force. Since then, however, residential areas of lower-status Sephardic population have swung
over to the Likud. At the same time, Labor lost some of its
electoral strength to the Likud in middle-to-upper class
residential areas with Ashkenazic majorities. Consequently,
a state of electoral split, with an advantage for the Alignment,

developed in these areas in the 1981 elections. This trend indicates that on the whole, there is no sharp ethnic dichotomy. While ethnicity does appear to influence the electoral behavior of Sephardic residential areas, those with Ashkenazic majorities exhibit an electoral split which should be related to a growing political or ideological differentiation within the Ashkenazic population.

The spatial diffusion of growing electoral support for the Likud — at the expense of the Alignment — in Sephardic population clusters, as revealed in the geographical examination of 1965—1981 election data, appears to be associated with the geography of economic development, upward socio-economic mobility and weakening of material dependence upon the governmental-administrative system formerly headed by Labor. This association between electoral spatial patterns and spatial manifestations of basic processes underlying the fabric of Israeli society indicates that the gradual electoral swing taking place in the competition between the Alignment and the Likud is not only a change in political opinions but is also embedded in structural, social and economic changes. Geographical analysis may thus contribute towards our understanding of this process.

BIBLIOGRAPHY

Alker, H.R.
  1969   "A Typology of Ecological Fallacies." in: Dogan,
            M. and Rokkan, S.(eds.), *Quantitative Ecological
            Analysis in the Social Sciences.* Cambridge
            (Massachusetts): MIT Press, pp. 69-86.
Butler, D.E. and Stokes, D.E.
  1969   *Political Change in Britain: Forces Shaping the
            Electoral Choice.* London: Macmillan.
Central Bureau of Statistics.
  1970   "Results of Elections to the Seventh Knesset
            and Local Authorities, October 28, 1969."
            Special Series no. 309, Jerusalem (Hebrew).

  1981a   "Population Survey: June 30, 1977." Special
            Series no. 673, Jerusalem (Hebrew).

1981b   "Results of Elections to the Tenth Knesset, June 30, 1981." Special Series no. 680, Jerusalem (Hebrew).

Cohen, E.
1966   "Problems of Development Towns and Urban Housing Developments." *Riv'on Lekalkala* (Economic Quarterly) 13, 49-50, pp. 113-117 (Hebrew).

Cox, K.R.
1971   "The Spatial Components of Urban Voting Response Surfaces." *Economic Geography* 47, pp. 27-35.

Garrahan, P.
1977   "Housing, the Class Milieu and Middle-Class Conservatism." *British Journal of Political Science* 7, pp. 125-126.

Gonen, A.
1975   "Locational and Ecological Aspects of Urban Public Sector Housing: The Israeli Case." in: Gappert, G. and Rose, H.M. *The Social Economy of Cities* (Urban Affairs Annual Reviews, Vol. 9). Beverly Hills and London: Sage, pp. 275-295.

—— and Hasson, S.
1974   "Ethnic Differences in Change of Residence: Immigrant Housing Projects on the Outskirts of Medium-Sized Cities in Israel." *Megamot* 20, 3, pp. 310-315 (Hebrew).

1981   "Public Housing as a Spatial-Political Measure in Israeli Cities." *Medina, Mimshal Vihasim Ben-leumiyyim* (State, Government and International Relations) 18, pp. 27-37. (Hebrew).

Gradus, Y.
1971   "The Spatial Ecology of Metropolitan Haifa, Israel: A Factorial Approach." Ph.D. Dissertation, the University of Pittsburgh.

Hershkowitz, S.
1979   "The Spatial Structure of the Population of the Tel Aviv Metropolitan Area: 1961-1972." Ph.D. Dissertation, The Hebrew University of Jerusalem (Hebrew).

Johnston, R.J.
1982   "Short-Run Electoral Change in England: Estimates of it Spatial Variation." *Political Geography Quarterly* 1,7, pp. 41-55.

Lissak, M.
1969   *Social Mobility in Israel.* Jerusalem: Israel Universities Press.

Robinson, W.S.
1950   "Ecological Correlation and the Behavior of Individuals. *American Sociological Review* 15, pp. 351-357.

Rokkan, S.
1970   *Citizens, Elections, Parties.* New York: McKay.

Shahar, A., Hershkowitz, S. and Stier, M.
1978   "Social Areas in the Tel Aviv Metropolitan Region in the 1960s." *Mehkarim Bageographia shel Eretz Israel* (Studies in the Geography of Israel) 10, pp. 1-30 (Hebrew).

Shamir, M. and Arian, A.
1982   "The Ethnic Vote in Israel's 1981 Elections." *Medina, Mimshal Vihasim Benleumiyyim* (State, Governemtn and International Relations) 19-20, pp. 88-105 (Hebrew).

Shapira, J.
1980   "The End of a Dominant Party System." in Arian, A. (ed.), *The Elections in Israel, 1977.* Jerusalem: Academic Press, pp. 23-38.

Shinan, L.
1975   "The Social Ecology of Jerusalem, 1961." M.A. Thesis, the Technion — Israel Institute of Technology, Haifa (Hebrew).

Taylor, P.J. and Johnston, R.J.
1979   *Geography of Elections.* Harmondsworth (Middlesex), England: Penguin.

4

THE ETHNIC FACTOR IN ELECTIONS

Yochanan Peres* and Sara Shemer**

Historical Background

Although Israel's population tripled in size between 1948 and 1960, its political map did not change significantly (Smith 1972). The customary explanation for this surprising stability in the face of a demographic "revolution" is that new immigrants, a decisive majority of whom were of Asian-African (also called Sephardic or Oriental) origin, were distributed among the various political blocs† in approximately the same proportions as veteran Israelis. This equal distribution resulted partly from the sectoral structure which the state inherited from the *Yishuv* (pre-1948 organized Jewish community) (Eisenstadt 1967, pp. 332—367). The sectors struggled for political power while controlling important services required by both immigrants and veteran settlers, i.e. housing, employment, education and health. A series of written and unwritten agreements led to division of resources among the sectors in accordance with size. These resources included the new manpower joining the system, i.e. students, youth and new immigrants. In sum, the ethnic factor led to no far-reaching political changes during the first decade of Israel's independence.

Associate Professor of Sociology, Tel Aviv University
**Director: "Modi'in Ezrachi" Institute of Social Research, Tel Aviv.

†*"Political blocs" are not precisely equivalent to Knesset election lists: rather, the party map may be divided into three blocs: socialist, right-wing (or center) and religious. The changes which took place in each bloc which may be attributed to the influence of migration: in the socialist bloc, Mapai increased its strength, whereas the more left-wing Mapam became weaker. On the right, the Liberals lost support and Herut gained, while among the religious parties, the NRP grew stronger at the expense of Agudat Israel.*

By the mid-1960s, sociologists and political observers began to suspect a challenge to this social-political equilibrium. Resources were transferred from the sectors (and especially the most developed among them, the socialist bloc) to the state; immigrants of the 1950s — and especially their children — were no longer completely dependent upon services provided by public bureaucracies. At the same time, the number and geographic mobility of the voting public increased, processes which hampered even a semblance of control over the voting practices of individuals, families and communities. Conditions were thus created for appreciable alteration in voting behavior, particularly among Sephardim.

Association Between Ethnicity and Voting Patterns

Asher Arian, in surveys undertaken prior to and immediately after the 1969 election (Arian 1972), was the first to reveal that this potential mobility had become a fact. Three demographic variables were found to influence voting patterns: ethnic background, age and number of years in Israel. Likud voters are characteristically of Oriental origin and young, while Alignment voters are Ashkenazic and older and have been in Israel for a relatively long time. Arian, guided by the "dominant party" conception, interpreted these findings as leading to preservation of the existing political constellation. Young voters will eventually grow older and adapt their voting patterns to the "demands" of maturity. The narrowing of inter-ethnic gaps in the areas of employment, education and lifestyle will exert an influence in the same direction. Following the 1973 elections, Peres, Ya'ar and Shafat (1975) undertook further research which corroborated and even reinforced Arian's findings. Their results, however, were given a different interpretation: groups whose proportion in the overall population was *on the rise* (i.e. Oriental and Israel-born youth) tended to vote for the Likud, while members of the shrinking demographic groups (the elderly, Ashkenazim, the foreign-born) were more loyal to the Alignment. In other words, long-range trends, based upon demographic developments, tend to favor the Likud over the Alignment.

"Explaining Away" the Ethnic Factor

The notion that ethnicity plays a key role in shaping political realities has encountered much criticism. Some observers do not accept ethnic affiliation alone as a determinant of political positions; hence they seek other factors behind it. These critical approaches may be divided into two categories, those emphasizing class and culture, respectively. According to the former view, a group which superficially appears to be ethnic is actually a social stratum. Shlomo Swirsky (1981, p. 356) has expressed this approach most eloquently:

> ". . . The Israeli bourgeois is Ashkenazic . . . because most of the processes and symbols of bourgeois control of economics, politics, education and communications are familiar to him from birth, from his home and his neighbor - hood . . . because he is used to finding Ashkenazim in positions parallel to his own and Orientals in lower positions . . . because he considers it his mission to transmit the values of goal-oriented, competitive ethics to the Orientals in the army, at school and at the factory . . . The Jewish worker is an Oriental . . . because his social situation is universally described as the product of Oriental characteristics: large families, poor education . . . because he expects to find Orientals in positions parallel to his own and Ashkenazim above him . . . "

The cultural approach, recently expressed succinctly in an article by Harvey Goldberg, tends to analyze the behavior of the respective ethnic groups in terms of unique history and culture. Groups are defined according to shared cultural histories, whose boundaries only partially overlap those of the countries of origin (Goldberg, to be published in *Megamot*].

Issues Investigated

The above-mentioned developments and their sociological analysis raise certain empirical problems which we attempt to discuss using data accumulated during the 1981 election campaign:

1. Has ethnic polarization increased over the four years
    between the 1977 and 1981 election campaigns?
2. How does the demographic factor (i.e. the relative size
    of various ethnic groups) influence change in the balance
    of electoral power?
3. Are the political behavior patterns of various components
    of the Sephardic community similar, or do they differ,
    as does cultural history?
4. Are most differences in electoral behavior of ethnic
    groups based upon class or value divergence — thus dis-
    appearing upon control of such background factors as
    education, income and political attitudes?

Procedure

(1) *Population and Sample:* The findings presented herein
are based upon a series of surveys undertaken just prior to
the Tenth Knesset (June 1981) elections and one undertaken
during the Ninth Knesset campaign (May 1977). All data
were collected by the Research Institute of *Modi'in Ezrachi,*
Ltd. Sample sizes were approximately 1,200 subjects and
were designed to represent the adult Jewish population of
Israel (with the exception of residents of kibbutzim, who
constitute 3% of the overall population). An "area sampling"
procedure was adopted: The country was divided according
to geographical region (North, Central and South) and type
of settlement (large cities, small towns, development towns,
rural settlements). Cities and other settlements in the sample
were divided into statistical subregions; two streets were
selected in each, at which houses, flats and interviewees from
among the adults in each household were sampled at random.
Once the surveys were completed, their representativeness
was determined through comparing the distributions of
demographic background variables with those of the overall
population, as published in the most recent edition of the
Statistical Abstract of Israel (1981, pp. 77—80). The following
table indicates the degree of similarity between the demographic profiles of our sample and of the overall population
of Israel. Note that the differences do not exceed ±2%.

Table 1: Comparison of Background Variables — Sample and Overall Population of Israel (%)

Variable:	1 Sample (N=1207)	2 Overall Population (Jewish)	3 Difference (1 − 2)
Sex:			
Male	50.9	48.9	2.0
Female	49.1	51.0	−2.0
Age Group:			
12−30	25.7	25.3	0.4
31−40	21.5	22.1	−0.6
Origin:			
Asia/Africa	41.7	43.0	−1.3
Europe/America	49.8	52.0	−2.2
Israel (father also Israel-born)	7.0	5.0	2.0

Source: Statistical Abstract of Israel 1981.

(2) *Research Methods:* The survey involved distribution of questionnaires which primarily comprised closed questions covering a variety of topics of public interest. This article analyzes only a small fraction of the data, those which deal with voting tendencies, demographic background and a projected definition of hawkishness/dovishness.

Processing of the data necessitated a measure of association among nominal variables (e.g. origin and ovting pattern), for which Cramer's V was applied. Cramer's V is a derivation of the well-known and widely-accepted χ^2 test. The details and rationale of this coefficient may be found in Blalock 1960, p. 230.

Similarly, a measure of ethnic homogeneity was sought. Assuming that the population of Israel may be divided into two large ethnic groups (at least for purposes of this index), we applied the following simple formula for assessing ethnic homogeneity (of a political party):

$$\frac{J-I}{J+I}$$

where J denotes the larger ethnic component of the party and I the smaller.

Findings

1. *Changes in Ethnic Polarization Between the 1977 and 1981 Elections*

A quantitative measure of polarization is required to compare ethnic polarization at two specified time periods. One approach is to consider the link between origin and electoral behavior as such a measure. As we are considering two nominal scales (ethnic groups and political parties), we have selected Cramer's V (see above) as an index of the extent of this association (V ranges between 0 — association — and 1).

Table 2 displays the voting patterns of five main ethnic groups in 1977 and 1981. For sake of clarity, only the two large parties were considered, which together account for 60%–70% of the voting public. The coefficient V was calculated for each period. The association between origin and voting patterns clearly increased from 0.25 in 1977 to 0.46 in 1981.

Another, more detailed approach to the same problem is to compare the extent to which the various ethnic groups are homogeneous in terms of political affiliation. We apply a simple homogeneity index for the two parties under consideration: the difference between the number of voters for the large party and the small one divided by the sum of the two figures:

$$H^* = \frac{J+I}{J-I}$$

where J indicates the number of voters for the large party and I the number of voters for the smaller one. This homogeneity coefficient, too, clearly ranges from 0 (equal distribu-

Table 2: Likud and Alignment Voters by Origin and Election Campaign: V Coefficient and Indices of Homogeneity

	SEPHARDIM			ASHKENAZIM			ISRAEL-BORN (Self & Parents)	ENTIRE SAMPLE	V (P)
	Foreign-born	Israel-born	Total	Foreign-born	Israel-born	Total			
1977									
Likud	42	56	46	21	29	23	47	34	0.25
Alignment	24	19	23	30	18	27	22	25	(0.001)
N	(362)	(131)	(493)	(475)	(191)	(666)	(74)	(1,233)	
Homogeneity Index	0.27	0.49	0.33	0.18	1.23	0.08	0.36	0.15	
1981									
Likud	44	58	49	19	21	20	28	34	0.46
Alignment	19	13	17	52	39	48	34	33	(0.001)
N	(343)	(206)	(549)	(381)	(196)	(577)	(83)	(1,207)	
Homogeneity Index	0.40	0.63	0.48	0.46	0.30	0.41	0.09	0.01	

tion of voters between the two parties) to 1 (full homogeneity).

Note that all ethnic groups (with the exception of the second-generation Israel-born) have become more politically homogeneous, thus disproving the popular misconception that only Sephardim vote in an "ethnic" manner. The H coefficients reveal that Ashkenazim — at least the first generation thereof — are no less electorally homogeneous than their Oriental counterparts.

We may also comprehend the concept of "ethnic polarization" in terms of the ethnic homogeneity of the political parties. To what extent have the two major parties become more ethnically homogeneous? (see Table 3).

The first two columns of Table 3 indicate the distribution of ethnic groups (Asian/African immigrants and their children vs. European immigrants and their children) in each of the two major parties just before the 1977 elections, while the next two provide parallel data concerning the 1981 elections. A brief glance at these distributions indicates that the two parties have indeed become more ethnically homogeneous. Indices of homogeneity which appear in the following two columns point to the same phenomenon.

2. Comparison of the Electoral Behavior of Asian and African Immigrants

To what extent may we justify the widespread tendency among Israeli social scientists to combine immigrants from the various Asian and African countries into a single category and those from Europe into a parallel one? In the present work, validity of the classification is examined solely for the analysis of electoral behavior. In an effective categorization, differences between the categories are expected to exceed those existing within each. Our sample is not sufficiently large to be divided into countries of origin; nevertheless, we may distinguish Asian immigrants from African ones, as well as the first (foreign-born) generation from the second (Israel-born) within each. We thus isolated seven sub-samples, whose voting pattern distributions are shown in Table 4.

Table 3: Principal Ethnic Group Representation (%) Among Likud and Alignment Voters (1981) — Indices of Homogeneity*

	1977		1981		Homogeneity 1977	Index 1981	Number of Voters 1977	1981
	Sephardim	Ashkenazim	Sephardim	Ashkenazim				
Likud	60	40	70	30	0.20	0.40	(373)	(381)
Alignment	39	61	25	75	0.22	0.50	(293)	(369)
N	(345)	(420)	(360)	(390)				

Homogeneity index = Ma-Mi/Ma+Mi, where Ma = Majority and Mi = Minority.

Table 4: Voting for Various Parties, by Ethnic Group (%) – 1981

Birthplace Self Parents	Asia Asia	Africa Africa	Europe Europe	Israel Israel	Israel Asia	Israel Africa	Israel Europe	Entire Sample	N
Party									
Likud	47	42	19	28	58	59	21	34	410
Alignment	29	16	52	34	13	14	39	33	400
NRP	8	7	6	–	2	5	7	6	69
Others	6	27	19	31	14	13	25	20	238
Did not vote	9	8	4	7	13	9	8	7	92
TOTAL %	99	100	100	100	100	100	100	100	–
N	(160)	(183)	(381)	(83)	(120)	(86)	(196)	(1,209)	(1,209)

Table 4 shows that as far as the two large parties are concerned, differences between Asian and African immigrants
are minor in comparison with the wide gap between these
two groups and voters of European origin. This is especially
evident with regard to the second generation, among whom
differences between Asian and African origin are virtually
negligible. Regarding the first generation, we note the prominent difference in support of other parties (27% of African
immigrants versus 6% of Asians). A more detailed investigation indicated that the phenomenon was due to support of
North African immigrants for the new Tami list, which
"stole" voters of this ethnic group from both the Likud and
the Alignment. Nevertheless, this interesting phenomenon,
the continuity of which is so far undeterminable, does not
disprove — even for the first generation — the convenient
and widely-accepted division of Israel's population into
groups of Asian/African versus European origin.

3. *The (Isolated) Long-Range Influence of the Domographic Factor*

Now that we have demonstrated the existence of ethnic
polarization in elections, we proceed to inquire how this
polarization, should it persist, will influence the balance of
political power in the future. This question became especially relevant after the 1981 elections, whose results constituted
a kind of "draw" between the two major parties. Assuming
that the distribution of voters among the various parties
within each ethnic group will remain stable, while the size of
the respective groups will change in accordance with current
and projected rates of natural increase, we may calculate the
influence of the demographic factor when *isolated* from
others. The results are presented in Table 5.

Table 5: Projected Electoral Support for the Likud and the Alignment (%), Based Upon Fixed Voting Patterns (1981) and Variable Population Makeup

A) Birthplace:

Self	Asia/Africa	Israel	Europe	Israel	Israel	Entire Sample	N
Parents	Asia/Africa	Asia/Africa	Europe	Europe	Israel		
Likud	44	58	19	21	28	34	(1,207)
Alignment	19	13	52	39	34	33	(1,207)

B) Projected Population Makeup: **C) Projected Results:**

	Asia/Africa Asia/Africa	Israel Asia/Africa	Europe Europe	Israel Europe	Israel Israel	Likud	Alignment
1980	31	14	35	15	5	33	33
1985	28	19	30	16	6	34	32
1990	25	24	25	18	8	36	31
1995	21	28	20	19	12	37	30

Source: Central Bureau of Statistics, Special Publication no. 568.

The upper two rows of Table 5 again display voting patterns (for the two major parties) among the five principal ethnic groups. The first five columns of rows 5—6 indicate the proportions of these groups within the overall population, according to a Central Bureau of Statistics projection for 1980—1995. Multiplying the voting rates for the Likud and the Alignment by the appropriate weights (i.e. the size of the relevant groups in the year considered), we derive the projection indicated in the two final columns of those rows.

This projection commences with a state of equal distribution (1980), predicts a constant rise for the Likud and a concomitant decrease for the Alignment up to a gap of 7% (37% vs. 30%, respectively) in 1995.

We again stress that the validity of this projection is limited by rather strong assumption — namely that the rate of support for the major parties remains constant within each ethnic group. There is no certainty that this condition (and hence the projection based thereupon) will indeed be fulfilled. The statistics in Table 5 are more abstract in nature: the Likud is apparently "swimming with the current;" the projected demographic change works in the Likud's favor at a rate of approximately 2% per election campaign. A similar phenomenon in the opposite direction implies that the Alignment is "swimming upstream."

4. *The Influence of Origin Upon Voting Directions with Control of Education, Income and Political Attitudes*

We proceed to investigate the association between origin and voting patterns with respect to level of education. If it is true that social stratum or class actually underlie the ethnic factor, we would expect that controlling key socio-economic parameters would eliminate or at least considerably reduce the corrleation between origin and voting pattern.

Table 6 is essentially a combination of three joint distributions: origin X voting for three educational levels — elementary, secondary and higher education:

Table 6: Percentage of Likud and Alignment Voters by Ethnic Origin and Educational Level (1981)

Education	SEPHARDIM			ASHKENAZIM			Entire	V
	Foreign-born	Israel-born	Total	Foreign-born	Israel-born	Total	Sample	(P)
Elementary								
Likud	56	62	57	14	22	21	45	
Alignment	18	14	17	57	62	61	32	0.52
N	(97)	(29)	(126)	(55)	(7)	(62)	(188)	(0.001)
Secondary								
Likud	57	72	64	22	40	28	51	
Alignment	25	11	18	64	45	58	36	0.49
N	(123)	(121)	(244)	(143)	(62)	(205)	(449)	(0.001)
Higher								
Likud	39	47	41	29	20	25	29	
Alignment	39	47	41	63	58	61	56	0.19
N	(39)	(17)	(56)	(91)	(69)	(160)	(216)	(0.001)

As we recall (from Table 2), the coefficient V between origin and voting was 0.46 for the entire sample. Will the indices of association between origin and voting be much lower if we calculate them for each educational level separately? From Table 6, it emerges that a substantial drop in the association between origin and voting was noted only in the category of "higher education," while for the two lower educational levels (elementary and secondary), which together comprise some 75% of the sample, the association even increased somewhat.

Table 7 displays the results of a similar procedure, this time with respect to three levels of income (low, moderate and high). Here, the V coefficients were somewhat lower than for the entire sample (0.32 rather than 0.46). Nevertheless, they still indicate a rather strong association. Hence education and income level account for only a very small part of the association between origin and voting.

Other research has indicated that Oriental voters tend to express more aggressive ("hawkish") views in foreign policy (Peres 1977, pp. 92—97). This tendency may underlie their support for the more hawkish Likud and that of Ashkenazim for the more moderate Alignment. We measured the correspondence among "hawkishness," ethnic origin and voting patterns, assessing the first parameter in terms of attitudes towards settlements in Judea, Samaria and Gaza. This topic, we believe, combines several elements which are generally linked with the concept of "hawkishness": claims of ownership of territory, stalwartness in the face of international pressure, a firm stand regarding the Arabs, etc. The relevant question was: "Do you support or oppose additional settlements in Judea, Samaria and the Gaza Strip?" Responses were classified into the following categories: (1) Support; (2) Support under certain conditions (that it does not harm the peace process, that it not constitute too heavy a financial burden, etc.); (3) Oppose. Unqualified supporters were defined as "hawks," conditional supporters (for whatever reason) as "centrist" and the opponents as "doves." We are aware that the middle category comprises a wide variety of views, but it is nonetheless sufficiently differentiated from the two extreme categories.

Table 7: Percentage of Likud and Alignment Voters by Ethnic Origin and Income Level (1981)

| Income | SEPHARDIM | | ASHKENAZIM | | Entire | V |
	Foreign-born	Israel-born	Foreign-born	Israel-born	Sample	(P)
Low						
Likud	71	74	31	42	56	
Alignment	29	26	69	58	44	0.37
N	(97)	(46)	(78)	(24)	(245)	(0.001)
Moderate						
Likud	66	82	57	30	56	
Alignment	34	18	43	70	44	0.32
N	(76)	(28)	(53)	(33)	(190)	(0.001)
High						
Likud	63	57	34	23	39	
Alignment	36	43	66	76	61	0.32
N	(41)	(42)	(91)	(78)	(252)	(0.001)

Table 8: Percentage and V Coefficients of Likud and Alignment Voters by Ethnic Origin and "Hawkishness"

	Hawks	Centrists	Doves	Entire Sample	V (P)
Sephardim					
Likud	79	54	52	70	
Alignment	21	45	48	30	
					0.32
N	(232)	(68)	(52)	(352)	(0.001)
Asheknazim					
Likud	58	26	7	32	
Alignment	42	74	93	68	
					0.46
N	(157)	(104)	(134)	(395)	(0.001)
V	0.23	0.29	0.51	0.37	
(P)	(0.001)	(0.001)	(0.001)	(0.001)	

Table 8 may be considered as a combination of five partial tables. The three columns (hawks, centrists, doves) are essentially the joint distributions of origin and voting (for the two major parties only), with stand on foreign policy and security (hawkishness) as the fixed variable. The V coefficients in the last row (each of which sums up the data of one column) indicate that ethnic polarization among the hawks and the centrists is considerably lower (in comparison to the overall population), although certain obvious differences remain (for example: 79% of the Oriental hawks vote Likud as compared with 58% among the Ashkenazim). In contrast, among the doves, ethnic polarization has increased beyond the levels prevailing in the population of Israel as a whole. Virtually no Ashkenazim with dovish outlooks supported Likud (7%!), as compared with more than half of the doves of Oriental origin.

The upper and lower sections of the table examine the association between hawkishness and voting when origin is controlled, with the relevant V coefficients appearing in the extreme left column. A comparison of the various V coefficients leads to several conclusions:

1)   In the final analysis, the impact of the ethnic factor on electoral behavior is no less important than that of hawkish/dovish views.

2)   Hawkishness/dovishness constitutes a more important factor in voting patterns among Ashkenazim than among Sephardim (0.46 and 0.32, respectively).

3)   Ethnic origin is a more important factor for determining voting among doves than among hawks.

Conclusion

The conclusion which follows consistently from all data presented herein is that ethnic origin or affiliation is an important factor affecting the political behavior of the Jewish population of Israel in the early 1980s. We have shown that the overlap between origin and voting has increased since the last elections, that the gap between Ashkenazim and Sephardim is indeed larger than that between Oriental Jews of Asian and of African origin. Hence the frequently-criticized generalization which divides the Jewish population of Israel into two major ethnic groups is valid at least insofar as prediction of electoral behavior is concerned. We then proceeded to estimate the long-term influence of changes in the demographic-ethnic makeup of the population upon the balance of parliamentary power, discovering that this factor alone — assuming that all other conditions remain constant — would increase the gap between the two major parties (in the Likud's favor) at a rate of some 2% in each election campaign. Finally, we attempted to interpret the ethnic gap in voting patterns as a direct result of stratificational differences among the groups. When key stratificational characteristics — such as education and income — were held constant, the association between origin and voting remained clearly intact nonetheless.

Many observers find it difficult to accept this finding intellectually: it does not appear likely that ethnic origin would exert a direct influence upon political behavior. Shamir and Arian, for example, write that "explaining voters' behavior on the basis of ethnic origin alone implies accepting the existence of inherent differences among the groups, differences which are somehow expressed in voting patterns. We cannot accept this claim from either a methodological or theoretical point of view" (Shamir & Arian 1982, p. 93).

The operative conclusion of this approach is that the researcher dare not rest until he finds intervening or mediating variables which enable discovery of the "true factors" underlying origin. We will take our chances and reject this conception on the basis of logic, as well as experience. In principle, note that it is impossible to disprove the claim that an as-yet un-identified intervening variable may transform an empirical correlation into a spurious one; an empirical correlation which remains valid after 100 attempts to fix various background variables may theoretically disappear on the 101st trial. Hence when one claims that the correlation between origin and electoral behavior may disappear when we find and control the "correct" intervening variable, he has not related specifical-ly to the topic at hand . . . Research experience indicates that once you have controlled a group of basic background variables without an empirical correlation disappearing (or weakening considerably), it is highly unlikely that this will occur as a result of controlling further variables.*

We do not claim that ethnic origin "itself" affects political behavior; we, too, realize the need for finding explanatory or linking factors between ethnic origin and voting. However, the factors suggested herein affect such a vast majority of Oriental Jews (at least those who immigrated during the 1950s) that there is no possibility whatsoever of separating them from ethnic background through statistical manipulation. These factors (described briefly below) constitute an in-separable part of the very essence of the Sephardic Jewish population in Israel.

a. *History of Subjugation to Arabs/Moslems:* Israelis of Asian/African backgrounds are also referred to as "immigrants from Islamic countries." Throughout the ages, nearly all Oriental Jews have suffered to some extent from deprivation

*Shamir and Arian, whose analysis includes such factors as crowded housing con-ditions, a feeling that the party represents the ethnic group, the importance of the leader, traditionalism and hawkishness — in addition to income and education — do not ultimately succeed in "explaining the decisive majority of the inter-ethnic differences in voting" (ibid., pp. 98—110).

or humiliation by their neighbors. Tensions between Moslems and Jews intensified virtually everywhere upon the outbreak of national awakening in the "Third World" in general and upon the establishment of the State of Israel in particular (Peres 1977, pp. 51, 54, 94).

b. *Dissociation from Israel Arabs:* Israeli Arabs not only "remind" immigrants from Islamic countries of the nations to whom they had been subject in the past but also represent backwardness and crudeness. An even more serious factor is the ambiguity concerning Arab loyalty to the State of Israel. Hospitality and repulsion regarding Israeli Arabs therefore fulfilled several functions for Asian/African immigrants: "settling the accounts" of the past, keeping themselves far from the bottom of the socio-economic scale and finally constituting an unambiguous expression of their decision to belong to and identify with the rest of the Jewish people. The Likud was perceived as more steadfast and decisive in its attitude towards Arabs both in and out of Israel's boundaries and therefore expressed the tendencies and sensitivities outlined above better than did the Alignment.

c. *Emancipation from the Establishment (of the 1950s):* We emphasized the rather effective control which the parties exerted over their voters during the 1950s through provision of essential services. This control gradually eroded during the 1960s and set the stage for *possible* political mobility. The fact that many strata of Sephardim utilized this opportunity to abandon the largest and best-developed political sector, which ruled Israel during its first 30 years, is explained in part by the aforementioned factors a) and b). In addition, we should consider the mental process which accompanied these objective developments. The era of absorption was characterized by passivity on the part of the "absorbed.' They were flown in from abroad, housed, educated and healed. Government representatives, veteran Europeans, planned and administered their lives. Even if all this took place without distortions, deprivation or any signs of domination whatsoever, after a generation and a half it would have aroused a desire to replace the benevolent establishment with another one towards which Oriental Jews could feel less awesome respect and more of a sense of partnership. Thus, the previous establishment, controlled by the Labor Party (later, the Alignment), had to pay for its *achievements* in immigrant absorption no less than for its mistakes during its 30 years of dominance.

d. *Ethnic Consciousness — A Self-Reinforcing Process:* As the aforementioned factors generated a visible political trend, this trend itself became a factor as well. In this context, we note the existence of ethnic political leaders who built their careers around an ethnically-defined constituency (for a theoretical analysis of this phenomenon, see Smooha 1980). Nevertheless, it would be erroneous to view the personal ambitions of politicians as the sole or even major cause of increased ethnic tension in the political arena.

e. *Organizational Factors:* Political struggles are often complementary to economic ones. Each individual may choose to face the challenges of the economy using his own powers or those of relatively small common interest groups. Powerful forces reduced the effectiveness of too large economic unions:

(a) The more an organization expands, the smaller the basis for common interests and the greater the need for compromise; (b) the more an organization expands, the more difficult it is to obtain economic benefit without collapse of the entire economy. When an ethnic group finds itself in an inferior economic position and simultaneously grows from minority to majority, there is an increased temptation to transfer the arena of struggle from economics to politics. Forces which deter large-scale organization are operative in politics as well, but are counterbalanced through considering the common basis (in this case, ethnic consciousness) as more important than the specific interests of individuals and subgroups. In other words, now that sectors have been weakened and the demographic balance has changed, the political struggle has become more expedient than the economic one from the Oriental population's point of view.

Finally, we should consider the dynamics of organization within conflict. We have seen that ethnic voting is not the lot of Sephardim alone: in 1977, the Ashkenazim were less homogeneous in their voting patterns than were the Sephardim, while in 1981 the first generation of European immigrants were no less homogeneous than their Asian/African counter-parts (the gap between the respective second generations remained, however). Ethnic political organization on one side thus impels parallel organization on the other. The more the conflict intensifies, the greater the pressure exerted upon those who vote "contrary to expectations" regarding their respective ethnic groups. Voting which deviates from ethnic patterns is made more difficult, especially for those who live in an environment populated by a decisive majority of their own ethnicity.

Applying a broad perspective, one may interpret the afore-mentioned process as an instance of the domination of collective (or majority) consciousness over individual con-sciousness. In other words, even if a particular Sephardic Jew or his family did *not* suffer oppression or humiliation in an Islamic land and did not undergo absorption pangs during the 1950s, he would be likely nonetheless to consider himself as if he *did* undergo these experiences. Similarly, European immigrants and their children who did not take part in the pioneer elite of the early Jewish community in Palestine and the beginning of the State of Israel are able to identify with the work of this elite and share psychologically in its responsi-bility. Thus, group histories become "personalized" and un-suspecting people find themselves "involved" in an ethnic conflict.

The findings and analysis presented herein lead towards two potent and mutually reinforcing processes. Overlap between the ethnic and political conflict is increasing on the home front, while with regard to foreign policy, there is a growing tendency towards uncompromising attitudes and the use of force to maintain them. Are these tendencies praiseworthy or regrettable? This issue is clearly beyond the scope of the present article.

BIBLIOGRAPHY

Arian, A.
1972　　"Electoral Choice in a Dominant Party System."
in: Arian, A. (ed.), *The Elections in Israel.*
Jerusalem: Academic Press.
Blalock, H.M.
1962　*Social Statistics.* New York: McGraw-Hill.
Central Bureau of Statistics.
1981　*Statistical Abstract of Israel* — 1980. Jerusalem.
Eisenstadt, S.N.
1967　*Israeli Society.* London: Weidenfeld & Nicholson.
Goldberg, H.
in press　"Historical and Cultural Trends in Ethnic
Research in Israel." *Megamot* (Hebrew).
Peres, Y.
1977　*Ethnic Relations in Israel.* Tel Aviv: Sifriat
Poalim (Hebrew).
——— , Yuchtman-Ya'ar, E. & Shafat, R.
1975　"Predicting and Explaining Voter's Behavior in
Israel " in: Arian, A. (ed.) *The Elections in Israel,
1973.* Jerusalem: Academic Press.
Shamir, M. & Arian, A.
1982　"The Ethnic Vote in Israel's 1981 Elections."
Medina Mimshal Vihasim Benleumiyyim (State,
Government and International Relations) **19-20,**
pp. 88-105 (Hebrew).
Smith, H.
1972　"Analysis of Voting." in: Arian 1969.
Smooha, S.
1977　"A Theoretical Framework for Research on
Ethnic Leadership." *Rivon Lemehkar Hevrati*
(Social Research Quarterly) **9-12,** pp. 1-26
(Hebrew).
Swirsky, S.
1981　*Neither Weak Nor Weakened.* Haifa: Research
and Critical Monographs (Hebrew).

5

POLARIZATION AND VOLATILITY AMONG VOTERS*

Avraham Diskin

1. Introduction

The election campaign for the Tenth Knesset was apparently differentiated from all previous campaigns by two distinct features: *polarization* among voters and politicians and extreme *volatility* in flow of votes among the contending lists. As we will clarify below, the exact meaning of these two concepts depends upon the phenomena researched. We will indeed attempt to prove that polarization and volatility on one particular plane do not resemble those of others.

Polarization between political camps was indicated by a long series of phenomena. For the first time since the State of Israel was established, all but one of the lists ultimately represented in the Knesset declared their affiliation with one of the two large political camps: the National Religious Party (NRP), Agudat Israel and Tami announced their intentions to join a Likud coalition after the elections, while the Movement for Change (Shinui) and the Citizens' Rights Movement (CRM) avowed that they would join with the Alignment, if such a coalition were possible.

The Techiya Party presented itself as the opposition to the right of the Likud, while Hadash placed itself to the left of the Alignment, leaving no doubt as to its affiliation. Telem, led by Moshe Dayan, was the only list to withhold its post-election intentions. Cooperation between the two major lists — the Likud and the Alignment — in forming the future coalition appeared to be in no way feasible. The entire election campaign was characterized by exchanges of mutual attacks

*Data for this article were accumulated in a cooperative research effort with Prof. E. Gutmann and Dr. D. Caspi, funded primarily by the Adenauer Stiftung (Germany).

and accusations between the leaders of these two lists. The tensions that arose between them simply intensified and worsened during the final days of the campaign. Perhaps it is somewhat symbolic that the comedians the two lists had hired — Sefi Rivlin for the Likud and Dudu Topaz for the Alignment — expressed regrets after the elections concerning exclamations to which they had been driven.

The tension between the right and left camps — and especially between the two major lists — reached a climax during the last two weeks of the campaign in a long series of manifestations of physical violence, including fist fights, incessant heckling and disturbances at rallies and even arson at a party branch office. But as early as March, before the elections to the Histadrut, the inter-party struggle had already adopted an extremely violent verbal character. In Kiryat Shmona, for example, the Likud circulated proclamations inciting the public against the kibbutz-dwelling "Ashkenazic Commissars" of the Alignment. In Tel Aviv, on the other hand, leaflets were distributed which included jokes (actually personal insults) directed against Moroccan-born David Levi, one of the prominent Likud leaders. The most popular bumper stickers read either "Anything but Likud" or "Only Likud."

Polarization of the major lists was blatantly ethnic. We will not consider this issue at length, but it suffices to say that according to all available data, the Likud received more than 70% of the votes of (Israel-born) Sephardim. This contrasts with the majority supporting the Alignment from the same population in 1969. Among young people from families of North African origin, Likud support approached 90% The Alignment, which had always been strikingly pluralistic was supported this time primarily by Ashkenazim. More than half of the Ashkenazim born in Europe and North America voted for the Alignment, as opposed to less than a quarter who supported Likud this time. (This ratio has not changed significantly over the years; however, it appeared striking in light of the Alignment's loss of Sephardic votes and the gain of an overwhelming number of Ashkenazim who voted DMC in 1977.)

An additional characteristic of polarization in the 1981 elections became evident from the election results: the two major lists received almost the same number of votes (an advantage of only 0.5% for the Likud). For the first time since the establishment of the state, the two lists together won more than 70% of all valid votes cast; the smaller lists were overrun by the two leading blocs. Three parties which had been represented in every previous Knesset — Poalei Agudat Israel, The Independent Liberals and the Arab lists — now disappeared from the scene. The NRP — which more than once had been the third-largest party — attained only half of its traditional strength. Several theories (Downs 1957; Wright 1971) claim that when a multy-party system changes into a two-party system, differences of opinion between the two major lists are blunted and parties tend towards the center of the political spectrum. Signs of this phenomenon are apparent in Israel as well (for example, foreign policy and security issues during the Likud's first four years in office); however, considering the atmosphere which prevailed during the election campaign, it appears that the close race and electoral successes of the Likud and the Alignment emphasized the very differences which distinguish between them.

Alongside the polarizaiton which apparently prevailed between the two political camps emerges a peculiar and seemingly contrasting phenomenon — mobility of votes between camps (floating votes), including vote flow from one election campaign to the next, as well as between lists during the campaign. Until the 1970s, it was commonly believed that the Israeli voter was extremely stable: despite the tremendous growth in number of eligible voters (from 0.51 million in 1949 to 1.75 million in 1969), election results were largely consistent. For example, all the parties which formed the Alignment in 1965 collectively won from 65 seats (1949) to 56 seats (1969). Interestingly, now that the magnitude of the electorate has stabilized (2.04 million in 1973 and 2.49 million in 1981), a major change has taken place in the strength of this camp, which won only 32 seats in elections to the Ninth Knesset. Even if we add to the Alignment total all votes for lists which preferred an Alignment-led (or Mapai-ed) government over Likud (or Herut) rule, the floating vote remains prominent nonetheless. In the 1981 elections, the road-based camp (i.e. the Alignment and the Communists, Arab lists and centrist parties such as the Progressives or

Shinui) won 55 seats, as compared with some 70—80 in elections between 1949 and 1969.

Still more extreme volatility was apparently in evidence during the six months preceding the elections. In late December 1980 and early January 1981 — upon announcement of the decision to hold early elections — all public opinion polls predicted that for every Likud voter there were three Alignment supporters. Hence many projected that the Alignment would win an absolute majority of the votes. As election day approached, however, most polls forecasted a struggle over a one-seat plurality between the two major lists — a prediction which indeed came true.

The floating vote phenomenon may well contrast with the polarization effect: if there is indeed such a large gap between camps on the *voter* level, it is not likely that supporters of one camp would move so freely to the other side of the fence (in such a short period of time and in so demonstrative a manner); only when two main contenders are extremely close in ideology is it reasonable that the visible supporters of one party would become enthusiastic proponents of the other.

Is there indeed polarization? Is there really a floating vote? How did these two conspicuous phenomena come about? We will attempt to prove that polarization between the supporters of the two major lists — at least on the ideological plane — was not at all determinate. Secondly, we will demonstrate that *volatility* between the two major lists was relatively low despite the considerable extent of the *net floating vote*. The Israeli political system has entered a stage in which explicit and extreme phenomena of polarization are likely despite the fact that the *ideological distance* between voters of the two camps is not inordinate. Under such conditions, a major change in the strength of lists is likely even if most voters stick to their traditional preferences.

2. Measuring Polarization

The following formula may be used as a measure of polarization between supporters of the two major lists (A and B) at time t on a given issue j consisting of k ordered categories (assuming that the intervals between them are equal):

or, in abbreviated form,

$$
P_{jt} = \left| \frac{\sum\limits_{i=1}^{k} (i-1) f_{Ajti}}{(K-1) \sum\limits_{i=1}^{k} f_{Ajti}} - \frac{\sum\limits_{i=1}^{k} (i-1) f_{Bjti}}{(K-1) \sum\limits_{i-1}^{k} f_{Bjti}} \right|
$$

indicate the frequency of belonging to category i on issue j at time t among supporters of lists A and B, respectively. It is clear that $0 \leqslant P_{jt} \leqslant 1$; the index will attain its maximum value (1.0) when *all* supporters of list A belong to one extreme category (1) and *all* supporters of list B belong to the opposite one (k). Conversely, it drops to a minimum (0) when $M_{jtA} = M_{jtB}$ — that is, when the mean ratings of supporters of lists A and B are equal.

3. *Ideological Polarization Between Supporters of the Likud and the Alignment*

Polarization between Likud and Alignment supporters may be investigated through a long series of ideological questions. One common method of categorizing these questions utilizes the three central ideological issues which have divided Israeli parties since the establishment of the state: religion and state; security and foreign policy; social and economic policy (see, for example, Horowitz and Lissak 1972). Furthermore, the most interesting times to consider are (a) mid-May 1977 (elections to the Ninth Knesset; (b) early January 1981 (when the date of elections to the Tenth Knesset was advanced and when a great Alignment advantage was predicted); (c) mid-June 1981 (just before Tenth Knesset elections, when the Likud was perceived as possessing some advantage).

We begin by examining polarization in terms of voters' self perceived overall placement within the three ideological dimensions. Respondents were asked to rank themselves on a seven-degree scale, wherein a score of one indicated that one defined himself as "extremely anti-religious" on questions of religion and state, as an "extreme dove" on matters of security and foreign policy or as an "extreme leftist" on social and economic issues. The other extreme, 7, corresponded to "extremely religious," "extreme hawk" and "extreme rightist," respectively. Table 1 indicates the polarization between Alignment and Likud supporters upon the three aforementioned occasions:

Table 1: Index of Polarization Between Alignment and Likud Supporters (P_{jt}) — by Time and Ideological Dimension

Ideological Dimension	5/77*	1/81	6/81
Religious/Anti-religious	.07	.09	.12
Hawk/Dove	.10	.10	.13
Right/Left	.09	.13	.17

Placement for 1977 was determined according to respondents' declarations in a survey conducted in January 1981.

The dominant phenomenon apparent in Table 1 is the striking lack of polarization between supporters of the two major lists at each of the three times. We also note that the most frequent answer for each of the three times periods with respect to each of the three ideological dimensions — for both Likud and Alignment voters — was the fourth category, i.e. the center of the ideological spectrum. Despite this, it appears that parallel to the increase of external effects of polarization at the end of the election campaign, in June 1981, polarization itself increased on ideological issues in comparison to the two previous dates. This phenomenon arouses some surprise in light of the fact that there was no extreme change in the percentage of Alignment supporters in June 1981, while the proportion of potential Likud voters increased significantly (especially among the "undecided" of previous surveys) and included a population group much broader than the "hard core" who supported the Likud even at its ebb in January 1981 (i.e. staunch right-wing former Herut supporters). This point will be considered in greater detail below.

Another phenomenon linked to placement of voters for the two lists (see below) is that polarization is apparently lowest for the religion-and-state dimension and most extreme regarding social and economic policies. (A slight deviation from this phenomenon is the index of low polarization on the right-left continuum among 1977 voters, which may be explained by the success of the DMC — the "Ashkenazic" party of the time.)

It is also interesting to ascertain the mean placement of voters(M_{jtA} and M_{jtB}) in the three ideological dimensions. Table 2 displays this placement, as well as that which voters ascribed to the lists they supported in January 1981. A rating of 1.00 in Table 2 implies (following Downs 1957) "extreme conservatism" (with the mean rating on all scales), while a rating of 0 means "extreme liberalism" (1.00 is the mean rating on all scales).

Table 2: **Independent Placement of Supporters of the Two Major Lists and Placement Attributed to the Lists in the Three Ideological Dimensions (Mjt Index) — January 1981**

| | PLACEMENT | | | | | |
| | Self-Determined | | | Attributed to List Supported | | |
Ideological Dimensions	Polarization	Likud	Alignment	Polarization	Likud	Alignment
Religious/Anti-religious	.09	.50	.41	.13	.55	.42
Hawk/Dove	.10	.59	.49	.14	.62	.48
Right/Left	.13	.72	.59	.18	.75	.57
Mean	.10	.60	.50	.15	.64	.49

Three phenomena are evident in Table 2:

a) *voters* for both lists consider both *themselves* and the *lists* as more conservative on the socio-economic continuum and as more liberal on the religious one;

b) polarization in placement of lists is greater (in all dimensions) than that which respondents indicated for themselves;

c) the lists (especially Likud) are perceived as more "extremist" than their supporters.

None of these phenomena are unique to Israel and the reasons for them are discussed at length in the literature (for example, see Inglehart & Klingman 1976). However, one consistent phenomenon which is peculiar to the Israeli system is the perception of the Likud as more conservative according to both self and list placement in all ideological dimensions. Even this finding is no great innovation and has already been noted in various contexts (see Arian 1980; Diskin & Felsenthal 1981). Nevertheless, in light of voters' self-placement and that which they ascribed to the lists they proceeded to support, the distance between the Likud and the Alignment hardly points to extreme polarization. The extent of polarization, moreover, is less than is usual for major parties in other regimes (see Laponce 1970; Converse 1966; Inglehart & Klingman 1976; Inglehart 1977).

Placement of the lists and their supporters over the three ideological dimensions discussed is a rather abstract notion. Hence the phenomenon was also investigated through a series of specific questions with operational significance. The results of this test, shown in Table 3, were obtained by presenting respondents with a fixed statement to which they expressed their agreement or disagreement on a scale of 1 to 6 (1 = agree strongly; 2 = agree; 3 = tend to agree; 4 = tend to disagree; 5 = disagree; 6 = strongly disagree).

Concretization of the ideological questions clearly increased polarization between supporters of the two lists, a conclusion also evident from comparison of the questions presented in Table 3. At first glance, it appears that significant polarization is indicated in June, more so than in January. However, the questions asked in June maintained a more concrete character, which apparently contributed to this difference. Statement 9, for example, was presented several days after the bombing of the Iraqi atomic plant. Statement 10, on the other hand, is of a strictly abstract nature.

The major conclusion derived from Table 3 is that polarization on concrete questions is far from extreme, although it does not disappear completely. Note that the split among supporters of both lists generally tended to be normal (or asymmetric with an obvious center). In other words, the

Table 3: **Index of Polarization Between Supporters of the Likud and the Alignment (P_{jt}) on Selected Issues**

Statement (Abridged Version)	1/81	6/81
Religion and State:		
1. It is desirable that religious institutions and considerations be involved in political issues	.12	—
2. Equal legal status should be granted to the various trends of Judaism	—	.20
3. Civil marriage should be instituted in Israel	—	.23
4. The government should decrease allocations to religious institutions	.23	—
Security and Foreign Affairs:		
5. The government should encourage Arab emigration from Israel	.10	—
6. Government support of Arab clubs should be discontinued	.14	—
7. The government should increase its involvement in Lebanon	—	.21
8. A compromise should be reached concerning Judea, Samaria and the Gaza Strip.	—	.23
9. Israel should concede on the issue of these territories if her security is guaranteed by nuclear armaments	—	.33
Social and Economic Issues:		
10. The government should be involved in directing industry and commerce	.08	—
11. The government should abstain from granting subsidies for food products	.22	—
12. Control of the *Kupat Holim* Health Fund should be transferred from the Histadrut to the government	—	.29

majority of respondents tended towards middle-of-the-road answers (wherein standard deviations were similar for both parties). A blatant deviation from this pattern occurred regarding questions of religious matters: although respondents tended to categorize themselves as center-oriented on this issue as well, as manifested in a general manner (see Table 2), they evidently do have definite opinions on the concrete issues. This phenomenon, singular to one ideological dimension only, is illustrated in Table 4.

Table 4: Inter-Party Polarization on the Statement: "Civil Marriage Should be Instituted in the State of Israel"

	strongly agree					strongly disagree	
	1	2	3	4	5	6	Total
Party supported							
Likud	18.9	14.9	10.6	6.4	16.2	33.0	100%
Alignment	37.3	25.8	9.4	6.6	7.4	13.5	100%

The "U distribution" displayed in Table 4 indicates that for several issues (such as the example provided), internal polarization within each party is greater than the mutual polarization of Likud and Alignment supporters (prominent in the Table). In other words, with regard to several concrete issues of clear ideological significance, the position of respondents supporting the respective parties is far from indicative of absolute polarization between them; hence their positions — even if rather extreme — are adequate as predictors of voting intentions. Moreover, even questions indicating clear polarization between Likud and Alignment supporters (see also Table 6, below) found party adherents who took a stand opposite from that of the majority of their colleagues.

4. Polarization on the Issue of Government Performance

It appears that the government totally altered its performance during the six-month period between the decision to advance elections and the elections themselves. During 1980, the government's public image had deteriorated progressively, apparently the result of a chain of events indicating inadequate performance in almost all major areas of activity. In the economic sphere, inflation was most prominent, climaxing in an annual rise of 133% in the cost-of-living index, rendering Israel the country with the world's highest inflation rate for

that year. Several economic indicators of positive developments were overshadowed by this rate of inflation. In the
area of foreign policy, the public responded to such negative
incidents as postponement of autonomy talks with Egypt
and tensions with countries not directly involved in the Israel-
Arab conflict — expressed symbolically by the departure
from Jerusalem of all embassies that had been located there
upon ratification of the Basic Law determining the status of
unified Jerusalem as the capital of Israel. With regard to
security, the most striking issue was agitation in Judea and
Samaria: first, the soldier Yehoshua Saloma and then another
six Jews were murdered in Hebron, following which the
mayors of Hebron and Halhul and the *Kadi* of Hebron were
deported. Still later, there were attempts upon the lives of
the mayors of Nablus and Ramallah. None of these events
were likely to be perceived by the public as evidence of
government control. The government itself suffered from
bitter differences of opinion among its members — a phenomenon which included unpleasant exchanges, frequently leaked to the press. Another effect of these differences was the
resignation of Defense Minister Ezer Weizman (who was also
suspended from the Herut movement) and Justice Minister
Shmuel Tamir. In early January 1981, the Finance Minister,
Yigal Hurwitz, resigned as well; it was the dissociation of
his party, Rafi, from the Likud which actually led to the
decision for early elections. In late 1980, an ethical shadow
was also cast upon the coalition when police commenced an
investigation of the Minister of Religious Affairs, Aharon
Abuhatzeira, ultimately deciding to bring him to trial. At
the end of December, when Police Inspector-General Herzl
Shafir was relieved of his position, suspicions were publicized
concerning offences within the Ministry of the Interior,
headed by Dr. Yosef Burg — leader of the party to which the
Minister of Religious Affairs belonged. This combination of
events placed the government in a humiliating position in
terms of its public image, as illustrated in Table 5, below.

In Table 5, a rating of 1.00 implies absolute satisfaction
with government performance, while 0 means utter dissatisfaction. The results show a considerably low rating for the
government, even from Likud supporters; only in the area of
security was the government accorded a relatively high score.

Table 5: Measure of Satisfaction with Government Performance in Selected Areas (M_{jt} Index) and Polarization Between Likud and Alignment Supporters on the Issue of Government Performance (P_{jt} Index) — January 1981

	Likud Supporters	Alignment Supporters	Polarization
Overall performance	.43	.17	.26
Economic affairs	.31	.13	.18
Religious issues	.52	.38	.14
Foreign Policy	.53	.37	.16
Security	.75	.65	.10

Note that every Israeli government has received a high rating on this issue, at least since the Six-Day War (according to statistics compiled by the Israel Institute for Applied Social Research — 1967—1980). Nevertheless, the ratings shown in Table 5 relating to security are generally lower than those accorded to the previous government. On the other hand, low ratings in economic performance need not necessarily be attributed solely to the drastic rise in the cost-of-living index for 1980 nor the national budget crisis which led to the Finance Minister's resignation (and indirectly to the decision to hold early elections). A propos the outstandingly low performance generally accorded the government on economic affairs, particularly among Alignment supporters, we emphasize that *all* previous governments were rated lowest for their performance in this area.

Table 5 does not indicate unusual polarization between voters for the two major lists in their perception of the government's performance, except, perhaps, for the issue of "general performance." On the other hand, extreme polarization was revealed in response to the statement which implied that the Begin government performed "worse than the Rabin government." When the two governments were compared, Likud supporters awarded their own list a rating of 0.73, while Alignment supporters in January 1981 rated the Begin government only 0.19. Recalling that Rabin was not overly popular even within his own party at the time, the high polarization index (0.54) on this question is even more outstanding.

(About a month before the survey, Shimon Peres defeated Itzhak Rabin in the Labor Party Conference race for the position of party candidate for Prime Minister, with Rabin receiving less than 30% of the vote). Nevertheless, we note that in comparisons between the Begin and Rabin governments on the four aforementioned specific issues, inter-list polarization narrowed almost to a minimum (0.08, 0.14, 0.19 and 0.15, respectively). Specification of the respective Prime Ministers' names in the question on general performance led to considerable polarization. We will consider the significance of this phenomenon below.

It appears that the government's performance underwent a change during the six months preceding the elections. The new Finance Minister, Yoram Aridor, took a number of steps which were defined by the Alignment as "election economics" — confirming the popularity of these steps among the public. In the areas of security and foreign affairs, a number of dramatic events took place druing the month preceding the elections (and prior to the survey, the results of which are presented below): two Syrian helicopters were shot down over Lebanon, leading to deployment of Syrian anti-aircraft missiles; a summit meeting between Prime Minister Begin and the late President Sadat of Egypt; unprecedented attacks by the Prime Minister upon several European heads of state and especially the bombing of the Iraqi nuclear reactor. During those six months, no crises rocked the government and internal differences were reduced to a minimum. About a month before the elections, the Minister of Religious Affairs was acquitted of criminal charges, although the judges did condemn his behavior. All these events (most of which lent themselves to public debate) may explain the increase in government performance ratings recorded by Likud supporters in June and for the stability (and even occasional decline) in such ratings by Alignment supporters. Thus, relatively high indices of polarization were noted in June on the question of government performance (see Table 6).

Note that in contrast to the tendency towards intensified polarization as a result of ideological concretization, the reverse generally occurs regarding the question of performance. Polarization on specific policy areas progressively decreased both in January and in June, as it did in cases of direct comparison between the Rabin and Begin governments in specific areas. Moreover, even lower indices were found when the question of performance was further concretized. Thus, for example, in the field of security, polarization regarding the question of satisfaction with the government's handling of the crisis in Lebanon was 0.25 (as compared with 0.28 on overall security performance and 0.43 on general government performance). This was also true for the economic field when polarization was noted for government performance on the labor relations issue (strikes and the like). Here the polarization index reached 0.25, as compared with 0.35 for economic performance as a whole. Only in isolated cases were there deviations from this phenomenon, as in the case of agreement with government activities regarding settlements in Judea and Samaria (polarization index of 0.38).

Table 6: Measure of Satisfaction with Government Performance in Selected Areas (M_{jt} Indices) and Polarization Between Likud and Alignment Supporters on the Issue of Government Performance (P_{jt} Index) — June 1981

	Likud Supporters	Alignment Supporters	Polarization
Overall performance	.65	.22	.43
Economic affairs	.50	.15	.35
Religious issues	.65	.43	.22
Foreign Policy	.70	.32	.38
Security	.81	.53	.28

The conflicting effects of concretization in the ideological sphere and on questions of performance demand an explanation, to be provided below. Prior to this, however, we consider the question of the floating vote: Between January and June 1981, various differences were noted in the characteristics of supporters of the two major lists; our comparison of polarization during these two months — regarding both ideological issues and performance — would not be complete without a description of various developments among the respective populations.

5. Floating Vote from One Election Campaign to the Next

Our general impression of the floating vote phenomenon is derived firstly and foremostly from the considerably large scope of the net floating vote in the last three election campaigns. One popular example of this phenomenon is the fact that the Alignment list won 51 seats in the Knesset in 1973, only 32 seats in 1977 and increased its representation to 47 seats in 1981. Another representative phenomenon concerns the DMC in 1977: this new list — which obviously had no seats in the previous Knesset — won 15 seats during that year, although its successor, Shinui, obtained only two seats in the Tenth Knesset. Note that the connection between these two phenomena is not entirely justifiable: the overwhelming majority of DMC votes in 1977 did not come only from 1973 Alignment supporters, but also from those of the Likud, the small center lists and new voters (Diskin & Wolffsohn 1978; Arian 1980).

The net floating vote (from period s to t) is often calculated according to the following formula:

$$N_{s,t} = \frac{1}{2} \Sigma \, |P_{is} - P_{it}|$$

P_{is} and P_{it} represent the proportion of votes that list I received in the two time periods, with k lists competing. Indices of this type have been used extensively in both general and Israel-specific literature (for example, see Dodd 1976; Caspi 1972). Figure 1 presents the development of the Ns,t index since the elections to the Second Knesset. Other indices frequently used to indicate the evident volatility of the Israeli voter are displayed in the same figure.

General trends illustrated in Figure 1 indicated steady increments in the net floating vote, a gradual increase in strength among parties comprising the Likud and consistent decline among those making up the Alignment, as well as a consistent increase in the power of the two major lists combined. These phenomena are particularly striking in the later election campaigns and are especially impressive in light of the stability in number of lists attaining representation in the Knesset and the number of eligible voters in the later period. All these factors constitute a comprehensive indication of the

Figure 1: Common Indices for Depicting Acceleration
of Volatility in Israel

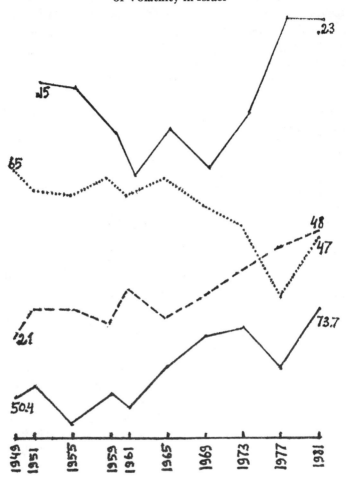

Key:

———— — Ns,t index

•••••• — number of mandates received by parties comprising the Alignment

– – – – – — number of mandates received by partis comprising the Likud

———— — Percentage of votes received by the two major lists.

true scope of voter volatility. Thus, for example, a large
floating vote is likely between the lists without having an
impact upon the Ns,t index. In fact, votes drifting from one
list to another ought to counterbalance one another. On the

other hand, the Ns,t index may indicate a larger flow of votes than that which resulted from frequent changes in electorate structure and the loss of "counterbalancing drifts," as described above. A different aspect of the volatility phenomenon is therefore presented in Table 7.

Table 7: Minimum Estimate* of Vote Stability (%) — by Party and Year

% of voters among list's supporters	1965	1969	1973	1977	
% of voters continuing to support same list	1969	1973	1977	1981	Mean
Likud	64	79	79	80	76
Alignment	80	65	45	75	66
Religious Lists	88	80	73	52	73
Mean	77	75	66	69	72

*Voters who refused to declare their vote for the later year were considered as unstable even if they actually did vote for the same list.

Source: The table is based upon statistics supplied by the Israel Institute for Applied Social Research and upon data accumulated by the author on various occasions.

Table 7 creates an impression which differs considerably from the general ones summarized in Figure 1. The overwhelming majority of voters in Israel clearly do not change their votes from one election campaign to the next, even when the respective lists are struck hard — as were the Alignment in 1977 and the religious lists in 1981. Even under these catastrophic electoral conditions, about half of the old supporters of the losing list clung to their earlier vote. The findings illustrated in Table 7 summarize the results of parallel analyses of shorter time periods (Caspi 1972; Arian 1975 and 1980). In any event, the Israeli voter, according to this index, is much more stable than those of other Western democracies (compare, for example, the findings of Butler & Stokes 1969, Rose 1974). The high mean of the Likud in Table 7 and the increase in percentage of stability of this list in the five election campaigns is correlated with the increase in electoral strength of this list. However, this graded increase in stability raises a question regarding the measure of party loyalty beyond that of two consecutive election campaigns and a consequent question regarding its extent (i.e., the measure of proximity to the "hard core" list supporters).

The issue of long-term party loyalty was examined in two ways: firstly, veteran voters who participated in at least three Knesset elections were asked if they always voted for the same list, including municipal elections. Secondly, we asked respondents questioned in January and June 1981 to indicate when they first participated in Knesset elections, how they voted at that time, in 1973, in 1977 and how they intend to vote in the coming elections. We then determined how many were consistent in their declarations. The findings based on the direct question of party loyalty and an investigation of voting intentions for the different elections indicate that about half of the veteran voters did not change their vote at any time. "Consistent voters" obviously included those who had voted in any earlier election for one of the components of the large blocs and continued to support this bloc since its establishment. No striking differences were found in this respect between the Likud and the Alignment. Furthermore, the loyalty index of 50% is higher than parallel figures calculated for other Western democracies. In the United States, for example, party loyalty ranges from about 30% to 40% for the Democratic and Republican Parties, respectively (for example, see Campbell, Converse, Miller & Stokes 1960). The term "volatility" was only recently applied in the United States, when party loyalty indices fell below these figures. In this context, we note that the claim that party loyalty was even greater in Israel until the 1960s does not conform to reality. Available data from these periods attest to a significant flow of votes between camps (Diskin 1976). Furthermore, in 1969 the percentage of Gahal voters who considered the Alignment as their second choice — and likewise the percentage of Alignment voters whose second choice was Gahal — ranged from 40% to 60%! (*ibid.*, p. 99). These findings thus indicated the advent of the 1977 upheaval. By 1981, the trend decreased considerably: in January, only 18.5% of Alignment supporters considered the Likud as their second choice, as compared with a mere 8.4% of Likud supporters who indicated likewise regarding the Alignment at that time. By mid-June, these differences had narrowed somewhat, reaching 14.4% and 5.8%, respectively. In this respect, there is no doubt whatsoever that Alignment supporters were considerably polarized from Likud supporters. Readiness for transition from support of one list to the other decreased greatly, while the potential for transition of votes from the Alignment to the Likud was greater than the potential flow in the opposite direction.

All the data apparently contradict the election results and their expression in development of the Ns,t index over the past three elections. This contradiction, however, is in accord with the unidirectional flow of votes between lists. Under such conditions, even a meager transition has a decisive impact upon the potential composition of the Knesset. Thus, for example, a unidirectional transition of approximately 7% from one major list to the other creates a difference of approximately 18 seats (nine for one list and nine for the other) in the election results. In both the 1977 and 1981 campaigns, vote flow tended to be unidirectional. In 1977, for example, the Alignment lost approximately 15% of the total vote from the lower socio-economic strata. These votes were for the most part transferred directly to the Likud, without any significant flow in the opposite direction. During the same year, the Alignment lost a similar percentage of votes to the DMC among the higher social classes, without gaining any substantial compensation in the reverse direction, even if we consider other small center lists, such as the Independent Liberals and the CRM. (The Likud lost votes among the upper social classes to all three of the aforementioned lists.) These phenomena, which are expressed in a general sense in survey data and accumulated results, have already been discussed at length in several analyses of election results to the Ninth Knesset (for example, see Arian 1980; Diskin 1980; Diskin & Wolffsohn 1978).

Four surveys undertaken during the last two weeks of the campaign (one by the Israel Institute for Applied Social Research, two by *Dahaf* and one by the Jerusalem local newspaper *Kol Ha'ir*) indicate that in the 1981 election campaign as well, vote flow tended to be unidirectional, as shown in Table 8.

In 1981, there was clearly a two-way flow of votes, albeit infinitesimal in scope, between the two lists. According to data accumulated by the Israel Institute for Applied Social Research relating to mid-June 1981, approximately 6% of 1981's Likud supporters voted for the Alignment in 1977 and vice versa. Other surveys indicate an even smaller vote drift between the two major lists. Most votes floated in one direction — from the small lists to the major ones. About 5% of 1981 Likud voters had supported the NRP in 1977, as compared with none in the opposite direction. About 17% of the Alignment supporters supported the DMC in 1977

Table 8: Estimates of 1981 Vote Flow According to Various Surveys*

Vote in 1977	Likud	Alignment	NRP/AI/-PAI	Tami	Techiya	CRM	Shinui	Hadash	Telem	TOTAL
Likud	88	5	0	1	4	0	1	0	1	100%
Alignment	9	86	0	0	0	2	2	0	1	100%
NRP/Agudat Israel Poalei Agudat Israel	21	1	56	14	8	0	0	0	0	100%
DMC	14	65	0	1	1	4	11	0	4	100%

Includes only respondents who declared their 1981 voting intentions

Source: see text.

(according to data supplied by the Israel Institute for Applied Social Research); a similar percentage of Shinui supporters came from among 1977 Alignment voters, although this is no evidence of a two-way flow in light of the enormous difference in the dimensions of the two lists. (In fact, the number of DMC supporters who transferred to the Alignment is at least 15 times greater than the number of Alignment voters who subsequently supported Shinui.) Obviously, the votes received by the new lists — Techiya, Tami and Telem — also attest to a dominant trend of floating votes in one direction only. One may thus explain the differences in representation of the different lists in consecutive elections: notwithstanding the Israeli voter's high degree of party loyalty, the considerable net floating vote in the last election campaign was the result of a continuing trend towards unidirectional vote flow. Nevertheless, the vast difference in strength among the two major lists — as manifested in the last six months of the campaign — demands further explanation.

6. Vote Drift During the 1981 Election Campaign

The best method of following vote drift during an election campaign is the panel technique. Unfortunately, we possess no such data. However, similar conclusions may be derived from samples taken at different times in the course of the campaign:

a) The perceived vote flow in January 1981 tended to be much greater than the flow reflected in actual election results. A large proportion of 1977 Likud voters decided to support the Alignment in early 1981 but later regretted their decision and ultimately did vote for the Likud after all.

b) A strong tendency among voters not to commit themselves was dominant in January 1981. In the surveys, most claimed that they were "still undecided," a minority declared that they had no intention of voting and an even smaller minority refused to answer the question. The majority of these voters eventually did support the Likud. The January 1981 situation is described in Table 9.

Table 9: Voting Intentions of Regular Likud, Alignment and DMC Voters in January 1981

	1981 Voting Intentions						
	Align-ment	Likud	Other List	Won't Vote	Un-decided	No Reply	Total
Vote in 1977							
Likud	31.2	22.5	5.6	5.5	31.5	3.7	100%
Alignment	83.0	1.6	2.9	0.8	10.1	1.6	100%
DMC	47.1	2.3	1.6	3.4	35.6	0.0	90%

Additional data at our disposal support the above conclusions. It appears (according to other surveys) that approximately 10–15% of a large group of Alignment supporters indicated the Likud as their second choice in January 1981. As noted above, the number of Alignment voters who saw the Likud as a viable alternative decreased to 6% by mid-June. As the number of Alignment supporters decreased in June in comparison to January, there is apparently no escaping the conclusion that some January Alignment supporters indeed "crossed lines" towards their second choice. In other words, had elections been held in January, it is likely that conclusions regarding vote flow from one campaign to the next would have been somewhat different.

However, the essence of the Likud's recovery came from the "undecided" of January 1981. There is no doubt that these voters — according to past record — were closer to the Likud than to the Alignment, a phenomenon already recognizable in January. Table 9 indicates the overwhelming contribution of Likud supporters in 1977 to the undecided population, as opposed to the limited contributions of the Alignment and even the DMC. Moreover, beyond the percentages indicated in Table 9, we recall that the Likud-supporting population in 1977 was initially much larger than the Alignment-supporting population; furthermore, the DMC's impact in this respect is clearly marginal.

It is therefore interesting to note that in January, the undecided were somewhat closer to the position of Alignment voters on all issues relating to government performance. This relative proximity (Z_i), may be measured according to the following formula:

$$Z_i = \frac{|M_{jtc} - M_{jti}|}{P_{jt}}$$

M_{jtc} represents the "mean rating" of the undecided on a given question, M_{jtc} the parallel rating of Alignment and Likud voters, respectively and P_{jt} the polarization index between Alignment and Likud voters for the same question. A rating of 0, according to the Z_i index, implies maximum proximity of the hesitant to party i. In this case, the index of proximity to the second party (j), Z_j, is equal to 1.0. Table 10 displays the results of our calculations.

The determining factor for the undecided voter was ultimately previous party affiliation, rather than his January position regarding government performance, although this, too, led to hesitation at the beginning of the campaign.

Table 10: Relative Proximity of Undecided Voters to the Positions of Alignment and Likud Supporters on Questions of Government Performance (Zi Indices)

Issue	Proximity to Supporters of	
	the Alignment	the Likud
General government performance	.43	.57
Performance of the Begin government as compared with that of the Rabin government	.44	.56

7. Conclusions

We commenced this article with the question of how polarization between voters for the two major lists could occur simultaneously with voter volatility within the two large camps. After all, exaggerated willingness to change party affiliation does not conform to the perception of polarized competing parties. This apparent contradiction is shown to be non-existent. We noted that supporters of the Likud and the Alignment are not as polarized in their positions as one might surmise according to the character of the Tenth Knesset campaign. On the other hand, we realized that party loyalty among supporters of the two lists is quite high (unless we consider as disloyal those who hesitated and entertained thoughts of "crossing lines" to the other camp but supported their old choice in the end).

However, the discovery of these results was accompanied by the emergence of two additional problems: (a) It became apparent that polarization between Likud and Alignment voters was higher for most questions in June — when the campaign ended — than in January, when it commenced. In January, supporters of the various lists (and especially the Likud) were characterized as "diehards" with fixed party affiliations; hence it was reasonable to assume that polarization would decrease concomitantly with the undecided voters' joining Likud (and to a lesser extent, Alignment) supporters; (b) Polarization on all questions of general government performance was generally greater than on basic ideological issues. Nevertheless, when the questions on these two issues were concretized, polarization decreased for questions of government performance and increased regarding ideological issues.

The explanation of these phenomena is inherent in an additional apparent contradiction: party loyalty intrinsic to vote (i.e., the scope of limited volatility from one campaign to the next) as opposed to volatility and hesitation among a significant number of voters in the course of the campaign.

One of the basic norms characterizing the Israeli voter — as well as his counterparts in other Western democracies — is undoubtedly attachment to the center of the political map. Hence the most frequent response to the self-placement question according to various ideological scales corresponds to the center of these scales. This is also the reason that party supporters tend to place their parties in a more extreme position than they place themselves. On the other hand, Israeli voter loyalty is necessarily accompanied by certain ideological affinities, although these are exposed only when ideological issues are concretized. In other words, as long as the voter is not pressed by a practical question deriving from an ideological perception, he will lean towards a center position — the "correct" one. Concretization of ideological questions blocks this escape route which allows for simultaneous adoption of apparent ideological moderation and party extremism (expressed as exaggerated loyalty). The relatively high polarization on general questions dealing with government performance is the result of similar factors. Most voters undoubtedly perceived the government either as parallel to their own party or as its major rival. It is therefore only natural that broad party loyalty would increase concomitantly with polarization on the question of performance. This is also the reason for intensification of polarization when an explicit comparison was made between the Rabin government — the last Alignment government — and that of the Likud led by Menachem Begin. At the same time, there was considerably wide consensus with respect to government performance (or lack of it on concrete questions which do not lead to a clear ideological or party dispute: hence the decrease in polarization upon the concretization of questions on government performance. This phenomenon was especially evident in January, when the general opinion was that the government was doomed to failure, expressed even in the words of the Prime Minister regarding "short circuits" in government activities.

Polarization on the question of performance increased upon implementation of government activities considered to be matters of public debate (and not necessarily negative) during the election campaign. A number of them bore "concrete ideological" features which intensified polarization.

Polarization was at its lowest in January, as the inter-party struggle was yet to erupt. However, the major reason for increased polarization in June is a result of controversial government policies. Government activities generally strengthened old party loyalties. The undecided — a large portion of whom were Likud voters in 1977 — considered the government's performance during the campaign as justification for "reconciliation." Those who supported the Likud even in its "worst" moments certainly found its later activities to constitute good reason to vote as they had intended from the start, a phenomenon which found expression in the improved ratings they accorded to government performance. "Die-hard" Alignment loyalists (as distinguished from 1977 Likud voters who considered voting for the Alignment in January 1981 but later changed their minds) also identified the government with the Likud; for this very reason, they did not credit the Likud with their later activities and continued to condemn its performance. All in all, government performance during 1980 served to undermine party loyalty at the outset of the election campaign. However, during the first six months of 1981, it did not induce any vote movement between the two major lists; rather, the opposite phenomenon was engendered, i.e. overall reinforcement of old party loyalties. Thus, nearly all 1977 Likud voters returned to support the party, thereby insuring its victory. The same holds true for a portion of the Alignment voters, who had deviated from their usual vote in the elections to the Ninth Knesset.

BIBLIOGRAPHY

Arian, A.
   1975   "Where the 1973 Elections Critical? in: Arian A. (ed.) *The Elections in Israel — 1973.* Jerusalem: Academic Press.

   1980   "The Israeli Electorate." in: Arian A. (ed.) *The Elections in Israel — 1977.* Jeurslam: Academic Press.
Butler, D.E. and Stokes, D.
   1969   *Political Change in Britain.* London: Macmillan.
Campbell, A. Converse, P., Miller, W. and Stokes, D.
   1960   *The American Voter.* New York: Wiley.
Caspi, D.   "Floating Vote and Floating Voters in Israeli Elec-
   1972   tions." *Medina U'mimshal* 3, pp. 81-97. (Hebrew).

Converse, P.
   1966   "The Problem of Party Distances in Models of Voting Changes." in: Jennings, K. and Zeigler, H. (eds.) *The Electoral Process.* Englewood Cliffs (New Jersey): Prentice-Hall, pp. 175-207.
Diskin, A.
   1976   "The Competitive   Multi-Party System of Israel." Ph.D. Dissertation, Jerusalem, the Hebrew University (Hebrew).

   1980   "The 1977 Inter-party Distances: A Three-Level Analysis." in: Arian 1980.
      and Felsenthal, D.
   1981   "Do They Lie?" *International Political Science Journal* 2, 4, pp. 407-422.
      and Wolffsohn, M.
   1978   "Das Ende des Dominanspartei-Systems: Israels Wahlen vom 17 Mai 1977". *Politische Viertel-jahresschrift* 18, 5, pp. 773-843.

Dodd, L.C.
1976   *Coalitions in Parliamentary Government.* Princeton (New Jersey): Princeton University Press.
Downs, A.
1957   *An Economic Theory of Democracy.* New York: Harper and Row.
Horowitz, D. and Lissak, M.
1972   "From 'Yishuv' to State." Jerusalem, The Hebrew University, Department of Sociology. (Hebrew).
Inglehart, R.
1977   "Political Dissatisfaction and Mass Support for Social Change in Advanced Industrial Society." *Comparative Political Science* 10, 3, pp. 455-472.
    and Klingman, H.D.
1976   "Party Idnetification, Ideological Preference and the Left-Right Dimension, Among Western Mass-Public." in: Greve, I. and Farlie, D., *Party Identification and Beyond.* New York: Wiley.
Israel Institute for Applied Social Research Survey (Hebrew).
1967-1980
Laponce, J.A.
1970   "A Note on the Use of the Left-Right Dimension." *Comparative Political Studies,* 2, 4, pp. 481-502.
Rose, R.
1974   *Electoral Behavior.* New York and London: The Free Press and Collier Macmillan.
Wright, W.E.
1971   "Comparative Party Models: Rational-Efficient and Party-Democracy." in Wright, W.E. (ed.), *A Comparative Study of Party Organization.* Columbus (Ohio): C.E. Merrill.

6

THE NRP IN TRANSITION — BEHIND THE PARTY'S ELECTORAL DECLINE

Menahem Friedman *

Introduction

Since the establishment of the State of Israel (1948), the National Religious Party (founded by the Mizrachi and Hapoel Hamizrachi movements[1] has been characterized by relatively stable electoral support. In the Ninth Knesset elections (1977), voters "punished" not only the Alignment but also its traditional coalition partner — the Independent Liberals (Progressives.[2] However, despite the fact that the NRP had been part of virtually all Labor (Mapai) governments — and despite the party's "historic alliance" with Mapai in the Zionist Executive and "National Institutions," extending back to the 1930s — the NRP not only retained but actually increased its support in those elections.[3] In light of this impressive achievement, NRP circles expressed the view that party appeal had extended beyond its traditional stronghold — the national-religious public — reaching other sectors of the population who maintained positive attitudes towards the Jewish religion and traditions. Thus, the NRP might become a centrist party.

Following the elections, a new pattern of relations developed between the NRP and the Likud, unlike those which traditionally prevail between a small party and its dominant coalition partner. The NRP no longer considered its role to be protection of its own vital interests and those of its members from the major party (as it did in Mapai/Alignment governments), but rather as a partnership between two movements which have identical social goals and joint political ob-

*Senior Lecturer in Sociology, Bar-Ilan University

jectives. This new relationship is reflected in the heretofore unparalleled proportion and significance of key ministries accorded to NRP members within the Likud-led cabinet.

This background underscores the significance of the NRP's electoral decline in Tenth Knesset elections (1981), after four years of coalition partnership with the Likud, a phenomenon which apparently resulted from severe internal crisis. A study of recent internal party affairs has revealed struggles for factional domination within the NRP and serious tension within the party leadership, as in the Young Guard's bid for control of the *Lamifne* faction and the all-out battles waged with *Likud Utemura*. There are even some signs of an ideological crisis, in light of growing religious extremism among certain population sectors and the "Greater Israel" issue (see below). We thus note that the NRP's decline indeed appears to be rooted in internal crisis. Yet there is still room for further speculation, as party history includes a series of similar crises which had never before affected NRP voting adversely. Until the Tenth Knesset elections, in fact, the party was characterized by virtually unconditional voter support. Hence we proceed to investigate the changes in voting patterns among traditional NRP supporters, analyzing the major processes they have undergone against the background of more extensive changes which took place within the party itself since the 1950s.

Analyses of the historic basis for social change may tend to adopt a positivistic approach; i.e. they may posit that the changes under consideration were the positive result of past processes. Hence we hasten to clarify our claim that the decline of the NRP is connected with processes of social change in religious society which have been taking place since the 1950s, as these processes are ultimately of dialectic character. In the final analysis, historical realities are ultimately determined by a combination of social circumstances which pertain to the development of Israeli society as a whole.

The "Camp Party" as a Factor Promoting Stability

The issue of NRP electoral stability — up to the last elections — has been considered in a most productive and intensive analytical study (Don-Yehiya 1980). Don-Yehiya perceives of the NRP as a party with "essential stability" expressed on both the organizational and ideological planes. Don-Yehiya utilizes two concepts to explain the phenomenon: "camp party" and "institutionalized factionalism." The former term refers to "a party which represents a particular subculture within the population, distinguished by its values and life-styles and maintaining a comprehensive system of institutions and organizations reciprocally connected with the party" (*ibid.*, p. 26). The NRP, therefore, is a "camp party," as it represents a population with a specific religious lifestyle and culture, preserved and transmitted through a particularistic educational system whose protection, welfare and development are perceived as a primary obligation by the political leadership. In addition to these educational institutions, the party also maintains affinity for a wide variety of financial and mutual aid institutions which reciprocally link the party and its members. This definition of a "camp party" suits most political parties in Israel, primarily labor parties. Nevertheless, Don-Yehiya justifiably contends that since the 1950s, the affinity between such parties and discernibly consolidated social groups within the population has been weakening steadily. All religious parties may essentially by considered as "camp parties"; according to Don-Yehiya, this fact at least partially explains the obligation of the "camp" to support its representative party at election time.

The concept of "institutionalized factionalism" explains the organizational stability of the party despite the variety of opinions and interests therein. This stability is fostered through "official recognition by party institutions and regulations of the status of factions as an integral part of the party system" (*ibid.*, p. 27). "Institutionalized factionalism" is thus institutionalization of the concept of "parties" within a single party. Don-Yehiya explains the phenomenon by way of a paradox: even though party factions generally threaten organizational stability, in the religious parties, which are "camp parties," institutionalized factionalism is functional for this purpose. Such parties are characterized by social pluralism, which demands official expression within the various factions. Furthermore, institutionalized factionalism allows for expression of characteristic internal party tensions while maintaining an external appearance of solidarity.

These concepts undoubtedly enable evaluation of several internal processes within the NRP. It is doubtful, however, whether they suffice for explaining the key phenomenon of long-term organizational and electoral stability. Moreover, if these concepts are indeed capable of explaining electoral stability and the obligation of the NRP-voting public (the "camp") towards the party, the question of why this obligation was not preserved in the Tenth Knesset elections acquires increased relevance. Furthermore, a group maintaining a particular subculture — with discernible values and lifestyles and a comprehensive system of institutions and organizations — need not express itself on the political level within the framework of a camp party. Rather, it may defend itself and demand fulfillment of its unique needs within a party pressure group or through competition among various parties for its electoral potential. On the other hand, it would not be difficult to demonstrate that institutionalized factionalism may, under certain conditions, constitute the basis for splitting a party. We apparently do not yet possess a satisfactory explanation of why the religious parties — and particularly the NRP — were formed and consolidated as camp parties and under what conditions institutionalized factionalism is indeed functional for party solidarity.

Complete and detailed answers to these questions undoubtedly demand coverage of an area extending far beyond the scope of this article. We will perforce limit ourselves to key issues which account for past stability and attempt to explain the drop in NRP support in the last elections.[4]

Erosion in Religious Life

Erosion in religious lifestyle is a phenomenon largely responsible for molding religious society in Israel and its relations with secular populations. The image of Jewish society has been constantly changing since the late eighteenth century. The disintegration of traditional Jewish society and processes of secularization have taken their toll and have created a new social reality: adherence to *Halacha* (Jewish religious law) according to its orthodox interpretation has become the lot of the minority, while the majority has somehow abandoned the religious-traditional Jewish lifestyle.[5] This dynamic process of alienation from tradition takes place against the background of dramatic social changes in both overall and Jewish society. Permeation of modernity expressed itself in revolutionary technological changes which fundamentally changed lifestyles and challenged the validity of tradition. Among European Jews, the political and social changes which came in the wake of technological advancement led to steadily-worsening social, economic and political crises.

By the end of the nineteenth century, all of these factors led to phenomena of uprooting and migration from rural to urban areas, from villages to the large cities, from Eastern Europe, which was still largely traditional, to Palestine, Western Europe and the United States. The process of abandoning tradition has led to a severe *Kulturkampf* between the guardians of tradition and the revolutionary social movements which seek to change the character of Jewish society and the role of the Jew in history. The result was that this *Kulturkampf* penetrated the family unit and set children against their parents.[6] The rapid changes and their unambiguous character with regard to affinity for tradition challenged the security of the traditional world and created a feeling of anxiety or even perhaps of extended trauma.

Anxiety — one might even say paranoia — over the actions and intentions of the militant secular movements, over the secular-modern culture and those who represent it, is apparently the dominant phenomenon which determined the relationship of orthodox religious society in all its variations towards secular Jewish society. Vestiges of this approach persist to this very day. As shown below, there was no uniform orthodox religious reaction to the challenge of modern culture. However, irrespective of attitudes towards modern culture *per se,* anxiety over the secular social environment, over the deeds and misdeeds of the secular socio-political movements, was largely shared by all shades of orthodoxy. The historic experience in Palestine only strengthened these feelings, as in the battle over educational institutions in immigrant camps during the first years of statehood.[7] For the orthodox, this incident was a warning sign of what could happen to the entire religious educational system if they do not maintain the political power demanded *a priori* for protecting values, norms and vital needs. It thus follows that public support of religious parties in Israel stems primarily from feelings of anxiety over the "secular environment" and the need to "protect" the traditional individual and public and provide them with their essential needs, especially in the area of education. We may indeed concur with Don-Yehiya's definition of religious parties as "camp parties"; however, party loyalty is not only a result of obligation to shared culture and lifestyles; rather, it results also from consciousness of a threat to the very existence of the "camp" by hostile factors which control society's chief financial and social resources.

Even when the "Yishuv" (Jewish community in Palestine) political institutions were first established (1917—1936), there was conflict between the religious and the secular Zionist political establishments (the Chief Rabbinate and the National Council and Zionist Executive, respectively), wherein the former felt anxious and threatened by the intentions of the latter. The Chief Rabbinate, which considered itself as representing religion and tradition, perceived a direct confrontation with a political system which it did not trust but upon which it was almost entirely dependent financially. From this point of view, intensification of the power and influence of Mizrachi/Hapoel Hamizrachi apparently helped restore balance and mutual trust between the religious and political establishments, a fact which ultimately enabled the autonomous *Yishuv* institutions to develop to their fullest extent (Friedman 1978, pp. 116, 385—388).

The link between the religious party and its "camp" thus also derives from the "threat" to the latter's vital interests, a dynamic variable which may define the intensity of affinity between "camp" and "camp party."

As the Zionist enterprise developed, the pioneering left was considered as representative of a militant anti-religious outlook, proposing alternative values for the newly-forming Jewish society in which there was no room for traditional Sabbath and Festival observance, dietary laws or even religious marriage and divorce.[8] The rise of Mapai to power within the *Yishuv* (1931) thus intensified the threat to the religious camp. The "historic alliance" between Mapai and Mizrachi/-Hapoel Hamizrachi, forged when the former was the dominant party in the *Yishuv* and Zionist movement (1931—1935), thus appears to be more of an act of defense — guaranteeing, through political partnership, that the basic needs and rights of the religious sector would be provided by the senior partner in government — than an ideological and methodological association (Bat-Yehuda 1979).[9] Despite this alliance, relations between Mapai and the two components of the Mizrachi movement were fraught with conflict over attacks upon religion and tradition — intentional and otherwise — on the part of various factors within the labor camp *ibid.,* pp. 429, 433, 444—448), which invariably reawakened feelings of hostility and mistrust. This led to a rather paradoxical situation: those very suspicions over the left's intentions towards religion and its institutions actually bolstered the historic alliance, as the religious camp realized that its dissolution was liable to cause them irreparable harm.

This is only one component of the complex relationship between the Mizrachi — and especially Hapoel Hamizrachi — movements and Mapai and the Labor Party. However, it is this particular aspect which acquired increasing significance as the parties became more estranged from their social and ideological roots and began turning into centrist movements — slightly to the left of center.

In summary: the consistent loyalty of the NRP voting public to its party was indeed based upon the existence of a subculture with discernible values and lifestyles. However, the need to express this culture on the political plane — as a party traditionally participating in government and struggling for allocation of power and financial resources in society — is connected with the feeling of anxiety over the continued existence of this very subculture in the face of dominant social forces. This anxiety was corroborated in the long historical experience of alienation from religion and tradition and of conflicts — chiefly with the socialist left — over preservation of religious and traditional values in the *Yishuv* and during the first years of Israel's independence. It thus stands to reason that when confidence in the existence and continuity of religion and its institutions is reinforced and when anxiety over the "threat from without" decreases, party affinity and electoral support is likely to diminish as well.

The Generation Gap Within the NRP

The NRP has recently been characterized by generational conflict, expressed in the Young Guard's ambitions of attaining a dominant position within the party and accompanied by a religious-cultural change of delegitimization of the culture and political methods of the older generation. There are various manifestations of this change, including retreat from the principles of the *Torah Vaavoda* (Torah and Labor) movement and what has been termed "religious extremism." The topic merits extensive and intensive research far beyond the scope of this study, which will consider only those aspects which pertain directly to the issue at hand.

1. The dialectic character of relations between Mapai/Labor and the NRP (Mizrachi/Hapoel Hamizrachi) within the framework of the historic alliance necessarily bred tension within the latter. As the arrangement was a system of relations between unequal powers, it was only natural that compromise would be demanded, including turning a blind eye to various "sins of commission and omission" which the religious population perceived as injurious to Jewish tradition. Partnership in government demanded a practical policy and constant differentiation between the real and the ideal. This brought groups which felt more obligated by religious values, such as young people, into conflict with the senior partner, which is perceived as "dealing" in values and religious affairs. The greater one's self-confidence over facing the secular environment, the greater the basis for delegitimization of the veteran leadership and its historical path. On the other hand, once the State of Israel was established, Mapai was challenged as the representative of Labor movement values. Furthermore, once these values ceased to be of significance for most of the population, young NRP members — who did not experience the veteran's struggle for securing their special religious rights within the developing Israeli society — felt that another basis had been eliminated for justification of the NRP's historic path.

2. As indicated above, estrangement from religion and tradition has apparently been the main problem facing the orthodox religious establishment in recent generations. This

problem is seen to exist on two planes: *public* — i.e. religious society's obligation to impart its lifestyles to the coming generations and *individual* — i.e. parents' natural desire for their children to remain loyal to all that they cherish and hold sacred. Within the framework of religious Zionism (the Mizrachi movement), this problem was reflected on still another plane, the *national* plane, i.e. the religious-Zionist movement's obligation not only to impart religious and traditional values to the coming generations but also to participate actively in the construction of a modern Jewish society in Israel — hence the obligation to prepare the next generation for fulfillment of all roles within this society.

The Mizrachi movement consequently assumed responsibility for development and establishment of a multi-faceted educational system, including kindergartens, elementary schools, secondary schools and teachers' seminaries. The movement sought to redesign the traditional educational system to prepare the new generation in Israel to take part in modern society while maintaining loyalty to the orthodox lifestyle. Essentially, this system closely resembled the general educational system; even the curricula were similar, with the exception of religious studies.

Jewish studies were indeed accorded more time and significance in Mizrachi schools, but this in no way upset the balance among the various subjects. On the other hand, the absence of *yeshivot* (Talmudic academies) in this educational system was most prominent. During the *Yishuv* period, there were several attempts — most of which ended in failure — at establishing yeshivot in the spirit of the Mizrachi movement. It was only towards the end of this period that foundations were laid for a yeshiva high school (Midrashiyat Noam — 1944). At the time, however, it was considered only a marginal phenomenon.[10]

Mizrachi schools indeed strove for full integration in the renewing Jewish society in the Land of Israel, with affinity for both modern and special Jewish culture. However, it was particularly in the area of education that the Mizrachi movement — as a religious movement in which parents who sought to educate their children towards loyalty to religion and its values — had to face a most frustrating situation: a developing secular Jewish culture whose symbols, heroes and ceremonies attracted and unified Israel's youth and which Mizrachi educators could not combat successfully. No precise statistics are available concerning this phenomenon. However, members of the generation in question have declared that only a minority of Mizrachi school graduates remained loyal to religious principles (Bar-Lev 1977, pp. 83–87).

The "failure" of the Mizrachi school system served as yet another basis for delegitimization of the parents' generation, the founding fathers. The schools were perceived as shallow in terms of Jewish content and the parents' homes were unable to serve as models for full Jewish lives (a detailed explanation follows below).

3. Up to now, the term "erosion" was understood as overall abandonment of an orthodox religious lifestyle, wherein the individual considers himself to be "non-religious" and is defined as such by his environment. However, the concept of religiousness may also be defined as a continuum, such that any systematic and public diversion from *Halacha* and tradition would express erosion. It would be most productive to investigate the religious culture which developed in Israel among the population which identifies with the Mizrachi movement. Such research is currently only in its initial stages; nevertheless, we may claim that within this population sector — especially among members of Hapoel Hamizrachi kibbutzim — diversion from accepted traditions has been legitimized to some extent. Negation of Diaspora Jewish lifestyles not only led to changes in traditional clothing and appearances, but also to adoption of the Hebrew language in its Sephardic pronounciation for prayers, liturgy and religious studies. This enabled intermingling among immigrants from various countries and traditions into an overall religious community with a "neutral" religious culture. The rejection of key components of Diaspora religious culture could be accomplished only within the framework of a "holy war" (Fishman 1979, p. 21) against the Diaspora and all it represents. The religious culture represented by Hapoel Hamizrachi members on kibbutzim, moshavim and even in cities was generally less demanding and less restrictive — and therefore less "pious" (Bar-Lev, in press). There are numerous examples: relations between the sexes, institutionalization of the custom that married women need not cover their heads, less obligatory

attitudes towards public prayer, afternoon and evening services, ritual hand-washing, grace after meals, etc. In a general sense, we may define this phenemenon as "diminished piety," more lenient towards deviation from *Halacha* than the traditional approach.

As ideological justification could be found for the change in pronunciation of the prayers and in the language of religious study — which apparently were not legitimized by any senior rabbinic authority[11] — it is characteristic that the innovators did not require any Halachic opinions regarding the change. The strength of their Zionist experience and rejection of the Diaspora as a central component of their *Weltanschauung* were sufficient reasons for institutionalizing this decisive religious change. However, no such formal justification could be found for other deviations from religion and tradition. The institutionalization of such phenomena may be explained in light of the following factors:

a)   The experience of renewal and change resulting from a radical change in lifestyle was in constant conflict with traditional Judaism.

b)   Abandonment of religion and tradition, erosion and adoption of the values of democratic society, including the right to privacy. This atmosphere precluded meticulous social supervision of the deeds and misdeeds of every individual. Hence no obligatory organizational or individual conclusions could be derived.

c)   Individual and collective desire for minimizing external conflicts with the dominant culture, on the one hand and stressing the difference between the new religious culture and the traditional one, which was "Diaspora-like," non-pioneering and anti-Zionist, on the other hand. This implies that the modern religious society forming in Palestine was indeed united in its obligation to *Halacha,* although relative tolerance was displayed towards varying shades of diversion therefrom.

Such innovations and changes could not be instituted without arousing reaction. From the very outset, they exposed religious Zionism to criticism and delegitimization on the part of Agudat Israel. With the change in historical circumstances (which we will consider briefly below), they served as an additional basis for delegitimization of the parents' generation, wherein children contrasted their parents' lifestyles with the tenets of religious law.

In summary: Changes in conditions and circumstances exposed the founding fathers of religious Zionism in Israel to criticism from their children regarding three central issues:

a)   Over-subservience to the secular ruling party and political lobbying;
b)   Failure to halt erosion; lack of success in education;
c)   "Diminished piety."

The Educational Crisis in the Religious Camp

The rise of the Young Guard faction within the NRP occurred against a background of comprehensive economic, religious and social changes which reshaped the image and character of modern religious society in Israel. The clearest expression of these changes focused primarily upon education, rather than politics: institutionalization of the yeshiva high school (and later the *Ulpana* for girls) as a dominant pattern of secondary education since the latter half of the 1950s (Bar-Lev, in press (b)). The yeshiva high school essentially supplanted the religious high school — a change whose comprehensive social significance cannot be exaggerated. This is a topic which demands a far more extensive and intensive study than can be provided here. Hence we relate to only a few of the most significant aspects of the phenomenon.

There are four principal reasons for the institutionalization of the yeshiva high school:

a)   *The Holocaust Crisis:* The tragic and brutal disappearance of traditional Judaism in Eastern Europe and the destruction of centers of Jewish learning in Poland and Lithuania aroused guilt feelings among Jewish communities in Israel, particularly among movements for which "revolt" against the Diaspora was a central ideological component. As a result, there developed an increasing tendency to consider the once-derided traditional pre-war past in a positive, romantic light. Furthermore, religious Jews maintained the additional incentive of reestablishing the destroyed world of learning. Many of the founding fathers — who had "rebelled" but remained loyal to *Halacha* — sustained even stronger guilty consciences. The renewed post-Holocaust legitimization of the yeshiva was thus an expression of parents' desire to reconstruct, through their children, a bridge to a past world which no longer exists.

b) *The "Failure" of the Religious High School:* The fact that the "erosion" of the second generation in Zionist religious society was not arrested during the entire Yishuv period pointed an accusing finger at the Mizrachi educational system — and particularly its high schools — as primarily responsible for the situation. It was claimed that teachers had little religious faith and that religious studies (Talmud) were not sufficiently covered in the curriculum (see opinion of R. Maimon (Fishman) in Bat-Yehuda 1979, pp. 482—483). However, it was not only the high school which was perceived as "guilty." The parents' generation effectively felt that it too had failed to transmit its religious heritage to the children. Moreover, the renewed legitimization of traditional Judaism necessarily implied at least partial delegitimization of the new religious culture which formed during the Yishuv period ("diminished piety"). This situation prepared parents for adoption of a new educational pattern, wherein responsibility for molding the children's Jewishness is transferred to other factors serving *in loco parentis* within the younger generation's primary agent of socialization. This is one of the main reasons that yeshiva high schools are generally boarding schools.

c) *"Creeping Secularism":* Another factor which encouraged the rapid development of yeshiva high schools is the institutionalization of Western, urban secular norms in Israel. The 1950s also marked a period of crisis for militant secularist culture, that self-assured culture which constituted an alternative and a most outspoken critic of the old world in which tradition and religion played a major role. In its place, however, emerged a "creeping secularism" — i.e. day-to-day life which included substantial contravention of religious conceptions and *Halacha* without any premeditated or demonstrative (i.e. spiteful) intention to harm religion or its adherents. One key component of this secular culture is sexual permissiveness, as expressed in women's clothing, advertising, theater, cinema,[12] television and literature, in the press, in parlor conversations, etc. In many respects, this situation "frightens" the religious person more than militant secularism. The latter is better-defined and even more "legitimate," despite its rejection of religion, as it suggests an alternative of social and national values. "Creeping secularism," on the other hand, is "frightening" because it somehow characterizes a situation of anomie, attacking modern man on all fronts and invading his home and bedroom. Furthermore, it offers no alternative of social and national values, considering daily life and pleasure within Western consumer culture to be a legitimate objective. The religious Jew feels that he has no choice other than to remove his children from their home, where they are exposed to the attractions of creeping secularism, and place them in a closed educational system which covers all hours of the day.

d) *The Establishment of the State of Israel and the Rise in Standard of Living:* The steadily-rising standard of living in Israeli society aids parents in bearing at least part of the heavy financial burden of boarding school costs and maintenance. Other financial factors include:

1. Western Diaspora Jews, whose financial status and sensitivity to the well-being of Israeli society has become a key factor in maintaining cultural and educational institutions in Israel.

2. These schools (like other educational and cultural institutions) also benefit from the support of various governmental agencies, including the Ministry of Education and other national and public factors (the Ministry of Religious Affairs, the Jewish Agency, etc.)

Yeshiva high schools rapidly became the preferred path for religious youth with affinity for the NRP. From these schools there developed a new generation ("the knitted skullcap generation") whose values and lifestyles indeed maintained continuity with their parents' culture. Even more prominent, however, was their revolt and criticism of the founding fathers regarding the issues indicated above. The development of yeshiva high schools signified halt to erosion. For the first time since the secularization process began, there were signs of generational continuity within the religious population, as feelings of self-confidence permeated its ranks. Regardless of whether this development is to be credited entirely to the yeshiva high schools or to other social-communal factors, the former are considered as primarily responsible for this historic change and are among its principal beneficiaries.

These comprehensive schools led to the development of a new religious culture, accompanied by inculcation of new political national conceptions. This was a comfortable framework for molding a new generation: the pattern of studies demanded constant confrontation between accepted lifestyles and the ideal presented in *Halachic* literature. The modern religious home necessarily emerged from this confrontation at a disadvantage. The political traditions of national-religious society were similarly put to the test. Thus, in parallel to the attenuation of ideological and militant secularism arose a new, self-assured religiousness which demanded the right to mold the image of the Jewish people not only in the narrow religious sphere but also in terms of its social-national character. This situation was accorded prominent expression after the Six-Day War (1967) and especially following the 1973 Yom Kippur War.

The development of yeshiva high schools was not initiated by the NRP political leadership. Rather, this solution to the severe problems facing national-religious society was provided through its youth movement (Bnei Akiva). Although the first yeshiva high schools did not officially belong to this movement, there is no doubt that Bnei Akiva helped transform them into select institutions for modern religious youth. To a certain extent, the atmosphere prevailing at these schools continues the romanticism of the youth movement. Most are connected with the "Bnei Akiva Yeshivot Center," although their financial dependence upon the NRP political establishment is marginal.

The young modern religious Jew, especially if of Ashkenazic origin, is thus educated today from kindergarten until his induction into the Army — and in certain cases even during military service (in the *Nahal* corps or *Yeshivot Hesder*) — within a special religious framework. At adolescence, he finds himself in a closed and comprehensive society together with his friends, most of whom are old youth movement acquaintances. Thus not only is his social and religious image formed, but also informal social frameworks which retain their validity for years afterward. Moreover, the school provides him with tools for playing an active role in the economic and professional components of modern society. From the 1960s on, we find young religious people attending institutions of higher learning and from there to continuing on to assume key positions in government, the economy and the free professions, thereby according them financial security. As participation in national institutions becomes more and more institutionalized, they feel increasingly more confident of their own capabilities, on the one hand and their non-dependence upon any party apparatus on the other.

In parallel to the development of yeshiva high schools, there emerged a process of "ghettoization" — i.e. an increasing tendency among the religious population to live in special residential areas. This phenomenon, too, is a result of "creeping secularism" and a rise in standard of living. "Creeping secularism" created a situation which makes it difficult for religious people to maintain primary friendship relations with non-religious persons as a result of the "secularization" of leisure-time activities and entertainment. In the past, acceptable entertainment and leisure-time patterns (social evenings, excursions and the like) were perceived as "neutral," at least by the modern religious Jew. Today, however, it is impossible for a religious family to spend time with non-religious persons, owing to potential violation of Sabbath or dietary laws, for example. This obligates the religious person to seek social outlets among people who resemble him. The new "ghetto" is thus not of a defensive character and does not express anxiety or inferiority. Rather, it fulfills a social need among people whose social and financial security in Israeli society generally does not require bolstering. These changes had an even more far-reaching social consequence: in contrast to the humdrum attitude induced by a decrease in ideological-Zionist tension — even within bodies which once stood for pioneering and self-sacrifice for Zionist objectives — there is a prominent display of national affinity, readiness for sacrifice and obligation towards Zionist ideology on the part of national religious youth. Such attitudes were easily expressed on an organizational plane, thanks to the social relationships consolidated through special youth movement education, yeshiva high schools, *Nahal* units, *Yeshivot Hesder* and the "ghetto."

In summary, the social changes which befell the national-religious "camp" — the rise of the yeshiva high school, halting of erosion towards the secular camp and processes of "ghetto-ization" — necessarily influenced religious and social patterns and increased self-confidence among modern religious individuals and the religious public as a whole within Israeli society. This implies a challenge to one of the fundamental components of the heretofore uncontested obligation to vote for the NRP. Once again, the "camp" has no essential need for the services and protection of the "camp party. "

The NRP Young Guard — Revolt and Continuity

The rise of the Young Guard within the NRP and the system of relations between them and the traditional party leadership constitutes yet another manifestation of the afore-mentioned processes. The changes which took place in NRP political platforms over the past few years accurately reflect the social changes which affected national religious society, represented on the political plane by the NRP Young Guard (see parallel discussion in Deshen 1978, pp. 115—158).

Historically, the leadership of the NRP Young Guard faction developed from the Young Guard organization, initially established not as a special ideological movement but rather as a means of providing leisure-time activity for young religious people who — upon returning home to the city following *Nahal* service — found themselves alienated from secular entertainment and activities. The organization ceased functioning within a few years; in the meantime, however, Young Guard leaders began to present themselves as an alternative to the veteran NRP leadership, acquiring incentive from young people's overall discomfort with the veteran leadership (see above discussion). The relatively facile and swift rise of the NRP Young Guard to the front lines of party leadership may thus be partially explained by feelings of failure among parents and their desire for their children's success.

From the very outset, the NRP Young Guard constituted an opposition to the traditional party leadership. Their criticism focused upon two key issues: (a) The system of internal party relations, based upon "institutionalized factionalism" and (b) the tactics and strategy of the party in all that pertains to partnership with Mapai (and subsequently the Alignment).

Don-Yehiya describes institutionalized factionalism as a mechanism which enables expression of internal differences of opinion while maintaining external party unity. Clearly, this mechanism is functional primarily within a "camp party" — i.e., one which senses that the "threat from without" is so great that sacrifices must be made to preserve unity, at least superficially, thus allowing for internal differences only. Furthermore, there is a virtual consensus among all factions regarding political issues on an overall, national scale, so that differences are considered "insignificant" in light of the impending "threat" to religion and religious society. However, "institutionalized factionalism" has other functions: it allows the veteran establishment to retain its status when threatened by a new factor and serves as a power base for party politicians, who attain their objectives through internal arrangements among the factions. According to our investigation, institutionalized factionalism indeed enabled the veteran factions to delay the rise of the Young Guard and to block several of their demands for long-term personnel changes. For example, consider the Young Guard's demand for a "beautiful NRP," the thrust of which was directed against Itzhak Raphael, then head of the *Likud Utemura* faction. Regardless of whether the accusations leveled against Raphael were true or false, it is important to note that the young NRP members presented themselves as standard-bearers of righteousness, as opposed to the "corrupt wheeler-dealers." Furthermore, we note that Raphael's status remained strong so long as his faction supported him. The Young Guard did not succeed in eliminating factional rule and itself became a faction among others.

Consequently, they did not have the means to oust Raphael except through his faction ("Oslo," in party jargon). However, it was this very act which intensified tensions within the party and created the backdrop for the crisis among young people in the second-large faction, *Lamifne*. Since institutionalized factionalism was not eliminated, the condition for normal party functioning was the relative security of faction leaders regarding "outside interfention" by other factions. The success of the Young Guard's initiative in causing a "court revolution" with the *Likud Utemura* faction necessarily fostered reform among *Lamifne* leaders anxious over challenge to their own status.

In the area of external relations, the NRP Young Guard played a decisive role in the party's rightward swing. This approach paralleled second generation discomfort over partnership with the Alignment and the ILP. By "rightward swing," we refer primarily to opposing territorial compromise and supporting the demands of Gush Emunim settlers. A far-reaching change occurred in the NRP's involvement in national political activity. Identification with Gush Emunim's principles led to overlap between the most important global overall national political question and the religious demands by which the NRP considers itself bound. This introduced some ferment with which institutionalized factionalism could not contend, as noted below. However, this approach did not lead to partership with the Likud until the latter became the largest party and was to form the government coalition (the "upheaval" of 1977).

It is against this background that we investigate the difference between the NRP's achievements in the 1977 (Ninth Knesset) and 1981 (Tenth Knesset) elections. In the former, the results — 12 mandates — were most impressive, while in the latter, the NRP sustained a mighty blow as their representation was cut in half. The reasons for these vastly different results may be explained in terms of the processes which have been described extensively above.

The processes which challenged the role of the NRP as a religious "camp party" were in effect during the Ninth Knesset elections as well. Nevertheless, the NRP was not hurt in those elections because it appeared highly probable that the Alignment would again form the government and that the NRP — not the Likud — would continue to be the main partner in   the coalition. Consequently, the NRP would assume the same obligation it had fulfilled in previous governments: prevention of relinquishing territory, primarily in Judea and Samaria. Greater Israel supporters among the NRP voters considered a vote for the Likud to be wasted, whereas the NRP represented the primary factor capable of preventing the Labor-headed government from relinquishing territory. A different situation confronted voters in 1981: prior to the elections, NRP leaders had already committed their party to joining a Likud coalition. On the other hand, the Alignment posed a threat to continued Likud rule. As a result, many of those religious voters who felt no obligation to the NRP, their "camp party" (see above), instead came to the aid of the Likud.

The NRP, Gush Emunim and the Techiya Movement

Perhaps the best proof of the theory presented above is the history of relations between the NRP and Gush Emunim and the establishment of the Techiya Party as a joint religious-secular movement. As indicated earlier, the political path of Young Guard is characterized by revolt and continuity. Gush Emunim, which became consolidated chiefly after the Yom Kippur War, is considered a more authentic expression of national religious youth, the yeshiva high schools, *Ulpanot* and *Yeshivot Hesder*. There is surely a need for an intensive and fundamental study of Gush Emunim as a religious, social and political phenomenon[13]. We do not propose to fill this gap herein, but rather to raise several ideas which pertain to the subject at hand.

Gush Emunim is based upon those very social frameworks which were consolidated in the yeshiva high schools, *Nahal* or *Yeshivot Hesder*. It subsumes continuation of the youth revolt, ideological commitment, youth movement romanticism and a desire to depart the "secular city" and live together in a small community. But Gush Emunim is more than this. It is a political-religious movement with a leadership which has unified and led the masses. Relations between the NRP Young Guard and Gush Emunim are complex in nature: initially, the former considered themselves as the political patrons of the latter. This necessarily led to tension between them, as the NRP's central role in government demanded that it maintain political realism and condemn violations of the law, whereas Gush Emunim is a religious movement, functioning by the power of faith and internal fortitude, which is not always prepared to consider "day-to-day" national regulations. On the other hand, Gush Emunim does not want to be identified with the NRP because it prefers recruiting a varied political lobby comprising representatives of different parties who recognize it as a pioneering, idealistic movement, prepaired to sacrifice itself for national objectives. However, it would have been naive to posit that Gush Emunim would not ultimately assume some form of political, parliamentary expression. The Likud's victory and partnership with the NRP demanded such expression, as it was then that differences emerged between the ideological-religious-messianic obligation to Greater Israel and ideological commitment tempered by practical considerations. Had the NRP been in opposition to Likud government, it could then have served as a tool for Gush Emunim's criticism of the government's reneging on commitments to Greater Israel. Gush Emunim's political activity thus laid the foundations for limiting its obligations to the NRP. Furthermore, operating within the NRP as an independent faction or together with the Young Guard was irrelevant for another reason: Gush Emunim focused upon an issue which was by nature religious but also politically significant from an overall, national point of view. Institutionalized factionalism, as indicated above, could not cope with issues in this dimension.

The establishment of the Techiya Party by a number of Gush Emunim members and secular extremists from the "Land of Israel" movement expresses a change which took place among at least part of the NRP voters regarding their obligation to vote for a religious party. Techiya had but one political demand — the imposition of Israeli sovereignty over Judea, Samaria and Gaza. This does not mean that Gush Emunim members in Techiya reject or belittle the vital importance of those social-religious needs which the NRP, as a "camp party," is supposed to guarantee. On the contrary, a significant portion of those who identify with Gush Emunim are among the prominent representatives of the renewed "meticulous piety" trend ("extremism") in the NRP camp. Rather, such people do not anticipate any danger to these social-religious needs; they consider them to be ensured or assume that they are capable of defending their rights without the aid of the party. Once again, there is no need for a "camp party" because the basic and vital needs of the "camp" are guaranteed, in one way or another, by other factors.

Religion and Ethnicity — Tami and the NRP

The resignation of Aharon Abuhatzeira from the NRP and the establishment of Tami just prior to the elections was one of the major factors leading to the drop in NRP electoral support. A brief glance at the election returns from a number of development towns in southern Israel reveals that the NRP was essentially "deserted" for Tami by entire party branches. However, it appears that not all Tami supporters formerly voted for the NRP; rather, Tami clearly attracted votes from the Likud and the Alignment as well.

Note that Tami is an ethnic party, primarily based upon religious and traditional observance, which has succeeded where others have failed. Paradoxically, religion and tradition were key factors in Jewish national unity throughout the period of Exile. This may be explained through a relatively simple sociological analysis: it was the geographic dispersion of the Jews that fostered development of local traditions expressed in daily life, in synagogue and in Jewish law. So long as there was dispersion, the unifying aspects of Judaism were emphasized over the differentiating factors (Katz 1979, p. 155). However, once groups of Jews with different traditions converge upon one place, it becomes clear that particularistic traditions make it difficult even for them to pray together; hence separate congregations are established.[14]. In the old Yishuv, these differences acquired powerful historical significance not only with respect to relations between Sephardim and Ashkenazim but also those among adherents of the various Ashkenazic traditions. These differences were so influential that it was impossible to organize a unified Jewish community in Jerusalem, for example. Research on

Agudat Israel's settlement attempts (*Mahane Israel* — 1924) reveals that one of the difficulties in consolidating the settlers' society was rooted in the fact that they belonged to groups with different traditions (*Hassidim, Mitnagdim,* German Jews and *Yerushalmim*), which made intermingling difficult. On the other hand, abandoning the tradition of the country of origin, adoption of Sephardic pronunciation and instituting uniform versions of prayer and liturgy enabled the consolidation of Hapoel Hamizrachi training and settlement groups into a unified religious-social community.

The NRP, as a religious subculture, contributed decisively to the absorption of Sephardic (Asian and African) Jewish immigrants who maintained loyalty to *Halacha* (Deshen 1978, pp. 164–165). This culture included elements which the Sephardim could adopt without difficulty or loss of identity (such as the use of Sephardic pronunciation in prayer and religious study), as well as those which bridged the gap between religion/tradition and modern culture.[15]

However, none of this sufficed to create a uniform religious culture. No one synagogue was established which could express the existence of a single religious community. In order to implement this dramatic change, both sides had to continue the "holy revolt," but were unwilling to do so. The Sephardic Jews did not come to Israel through negating tradition; rather, the opposite was true. In the painful process of absorption, they were forced to give up an important part of their former lifestyles, such that the traditions of prayer and liturgy remain the major focus of their past and self-identity. For veteran Ashkenazim, as indicated above, the era of revolt has already passed and a new affinity for *Halacha* and Ashkenazic tradition ("meticulous piety") is developing. Furthermore, the social-demographic processes ("ghettoization") analyzed above have imposed additional difficulties on intermingling of ethnic groups and traditions. The processes of "ghettoization" are connected with the rise in standard of living and economic status, which itself creates a tendency towards isolation — even on an ethnic-religious basis. This situation also influences the ability to maintain reasonable integration in state religious schools.[16]

Latent ehtnic schism has apparently existed for some time within the NRP. The reasons behind its outbreak in the 1981 elections are certainly linked with various incidents within the party and Israeli society which created the appropriate atmosphere. The rise of the maturing young leadership and the fact that the synagogue, which is ethnic in nature, is the primary organizational base of the religious parties enabled Tami to commence operation successfully even without an independent organizational infrastructure.

In summary, we may obviously inquire whether Tami will become a permanent fixture in Israeli politics. The above analysis hints at an affirmative answer. However, it is difficult to predict at this stage, primarily because of the personal difficulties nad problems which face several key figures in the movement. Nevertheless, it is unlikely that we will witness a return to the NRP. It is more reasonable to assume that if Tami's infrastructure disintegrates, the majority of its supporters will prefer the Likud, which already has a strong nucleus of traditional Oriental Jews.

Conclusions

The reasons for the drop in NRP support in the 1981 elections to the Tenth Knesset were shown to be linked with significant changes taking place in the status of the national-religious "camp." A challenge was posed to the camp's traditional commitment to support the religious party. The religious voter's feeling of dependence upon the party because of the "threat" from the secular government to essential religious services and needs apparently diminished considerably. The social-economic and religious revolutions undergone by the NRP's younger generation led to delegitimization of their parents' ways and strengthened confidence in their ability to confront the various expressions of secularism and emerge "victorious" without needing the party and its institutions.

Nevertheless, it would not be correct to state that this weakening commitment *necessarily* led to the drop in the NRP support. The NRP could have obtained many votes because of its political stand on the issue of Greater Israel, as it apparently did in the 1977 elections. Rather, reduced support of the NRP resulted from the rise of the Likud to power. The two parties were rivals for voter potential, with the Likud

making inroads among some of the traditional NRP supporters. The Likud's attraction to such voters is reinforced by
their confidence in Menachem Begin as a traditional Jew. The
tendency of Sephardic voters towards the Likud is likely to
foster further abandonment of the NRP; moreover, Tami
voters formerly associated with the NRP are not likely to
return. The Likud's rise to power and partnership with the
NRP necessarily intensified differences between these parties
and extreme supporters of the Greater Israel concept within
Gush Emunim, forming the basis for the establishment of
Techiya.

In light of the above, it appears that an NRP comeback
will be possible only if there is a drastic change in the political
situation — one which is currently considered to be highly
unlikely — and Likud support drops to a level so low that it
cannot possibly form and head a coalition government.

NOTES

1. Merged in 1956.
2. This party obtained 1.2% of the vote (20,384 votes) in the 1977
   elections, as compared with 3.6% (56,560 votes) in 1973.
3. Its strength increased from 8.3% (130,349 votes) in 1973 to
   9.2% (160,787 votes) in 1977.
4. From 9.2% (160,787 votes) in 1977 to 4.92% (95,232 votes) in
   1981.
5. This was expressed in the concepts of "old" and "new" generations in eastern Europe, wherein the former described traditional
   Judaism and the latter those who had abandoned traditional life.
   See also Note 7, below, as well as Friedman 1974, p. 457, n. 7.
6. For example, consider the following representative quotation
   from *Hahavatzelet* (May 5, 1909): ". . . The anxious Jew . . . is
   struck a twofold blow: not only is he not given his rightful place
   among his people but he also suffers by seeing that his children
   do not follow the true path . . . He sees the new generation
   digging a grave for all of Judaism, for which he has sacrificed his
   very soul . . . Alas! How sad is this tragedy . . . He cannot defend
   his children and family. He has no weapons, he has no protection.
   What can he do? He can only weep bitterly . . . "
7. 1949–1950. See Friedman 1982, pp. 11–12.
8. The problem of observing Jewish holidays (including Passover
   and the Day of Atonement) and other traditional customs, particularly on leftist settlements, has not been crossed off the
   agendas of Zionist institutions. However, what particularly hurt

those loyal to tradition was the instituionalization of holidays and ceremonies of the Yishuv's "secular religion," based upon the traditional holidays and ceremonies. See Friedman 1978, pp. 319–320; Don-Yehiya & Liebman 1981.

9. Prior to their reaching an arrangement, relations between them were characterized by conflict over the right to work. See Shefatia 1977, pp. 165–176 and comments to bibliography.

10. The Bnei Akiva Yeshiva at Kfar Haroeh was indeed founded in 1939, but until 1950 it was not a yeshiva high school and its students were not trained for taking matriculation examinations. See extended discussion in Bar-Lev 1977, pp. 116–128.

11. R. Kook did not favor change in pronunciation of prayers. See Kook 1962, p. 243 (Letter 719).

12. The NRP newspaper, *Hatzofe* has instituted a self-imposed censorship of cinema advertisements over the past few years.

13. Research by Raanan (1981) is indeed an important study of this topic but still does not answer several fundamental questions. The study by Sprinzak (1981) considers the connection between Gush Emunim and youth in yeshiva high schools, but I do not believe that it sufficiently clarifies the nature, essence and roots of this link.

14. Good examples of this are the Sephardic and Ashkenazic communities of Venice, Hamburg, Amsterdam and London.

15. This was one of the reasons that these immigrants were not accepted in Agudat Israel, whose traditional Ashkenazic culture was dominant and whose spoken language was Yiddish.

16. This problem has recently been given increased attention. See Egozi 1975; Hen, Levi & Adler 1978; Schwartzwald 1978. pp. 107–122.

BIBLIOGRAPHY

Bar-Lev, M.

1977   "Yeshiva High School Graduates in Israel: Between Tradition and Renewal." Unpublished doctoral dissertation, Bar-Ilan University, Ramat Gan, Israel (Hebrew).

in press (a)   "And These Are the Generations — Fifty Chapters of Action." *Bimeshoch Hayovel* (Jubilee publication of Bnei Akiva — 1929-1979) (Hebrew).

in press (b)   "Bnei Akiva's Educational Institutions: The Yeshiva, *Ulpana* and *Yeshivat Hesder*," ibid. (Hebrew).

Bat-Yehuda (Raphael), G.
1979   *R. Maimon in his Generation.* Jerusalem, pp. 420-423. (Hebrew).

Deshen, S.
1978   "Israeli Judaism: Introduction to the Major Patterns." : Mossad Harav Kook, *International Journal of Middle Eastern Studies* 9, pp. 141–169.

Don-Yehiya, A.
1980   "Stability and Change in a Camp Party — the NRP and the Youth Revolt." *Medina Mimshal Vihasim Benleumiyyim* (State, Government and International Relations) 14, pp. 25-52 (Hebrew).
      & Liebman, C.S.
1981   "The Symbol System of Zionism-Socialism: An Aspect of Israeli Civil Religion." *Modern Judaism* 1, pp. 1-28.

Egozi, M.
1975   "Elementary School Pupils, by Origin and Size of Family — 1975 vs. 1972." Jerusalem: Ministry of Education and Culture, Planning Department, 1975 (Hebrew

Hen, M., Levi, A. & Adler, H.
1978   "Process and Result in Education: An Evaluation of the Contribution of Junior High Schools to the Educational System." Jerusalem: Ministry of Education and Culture (Hebrew).

Katz, Y.
1979   "Traditional Society and Modern Society." *Jewish Nationalism.* Jerusalem, pp. 155–166 (Hebrew).

Fishman, A.
1979   *Hapoel Hamizrachi: 1921-1935.* Tel Aviv: Teudot (Tel Aviv University) (Hebrew).

Friedman, M.
1974   "The Social Significance of the Sabbatical Year Debate." *Shalem* A, Jerusalem, pp. 455–480. (Hebrew).

1978   *Society and Religion.* Jerusalem: Yad Itzhak Ben-Zvi (Hebrew).

1982   "From the Trauma of Erosion to a Feeling of
            Confidence and Supremacy." *Migvan* (Spectrum)
            63, pp. 9—14 (Hebrew).
Kook, Rabbi A.I.
1961   *Letters.* Jerusalem: Mossad Harav Kook (Hebrew).
Raanan, Z.
1981   *Gush   Emunim.*   Tel   Aviv: Sifriyat   Poalim
            (Hebrew).
Schwartzwald, Y.
1978   "As a Foreign Implant? Concerning the Oriental
            Religious Student in Well-Run Junior High
            Schools." *Iyunim Behinukh* (Topics in Educa-
            tion 19, pp. 107—122 (Hebrew).
Shefatia, D.
1977   "Hapoel Hamizrachi's Initial Battle for the Right
            to Work." *Sefer Hazionut Hadatit* (The Book of
            Religious Zionism) B, Jerusalem, pp. 165—176
            (Hebrew).
Sprinzak, A.
1981   "Gush Emunim — The Iceberg Model of Political
            Extremism." *Medina   Mimshal   Vihasim   Ben-
            leumiyyim* (State, Government and Internation-
            al Relations) 14, pp. 25-52 (Hebrew).

7

THE ARAB VOTE

*Jacob M. Landau**

Introduction

The fact that the enfranchised Israeli Arabs (including the Druzes) numbered no less than 10% of the potential electorate, on the one hand, and that every vote counted, on the other hand, ensured as intensive an electoral campaign among Arabs as among Jews in Israel. The larger parties, as well as several of the smaller groupings, dispatched activists to address the public and canvass the Arabs in their homes. Speeches were delivered on the radio and television, advertisements published in the press and hand-bills were passed around and posted on billboards. Special attention was paid to aspects of significance and interest to the Arabs. Self-praise by candidates and slates, along with vituperation of opponents and competitors, were increasingly evident as election-day approached. In other words, the electoral campaign among Israeli Arabs constituted a fascinating amalgam of an old-fashioned personal approach by family elders and other traditional leaders and a modernized campaign based upon mass communication. While the all-Arab slates resorted mostly to the former and the smaller Jewish parties to the latter, Israel's two major lists and the Hadash (Communist) Party attempted to use both.

As a result of the 30th June 1981 voting, five Arabs were elected to the Knesset (as compared with seven, in 1977): Two Muslims from the Alignment, a Muslim and a Christian on Hadash's list and a Druze on the Likud's. An examination of the electoral behavior of Arabs, largely responsible for their election, can be carried out profitably on two levels: comparison with previous Arab electoral behavior and with

*Professor of Political Science, The Hebrew University of Jerusalem

that of the Jewish majority in 1981, respectively. In both respects, there appears to be sufficient similarities and differences to warrant some tentative conclusions.

Poor Voter Turnout

On the first level, the two most striking phenomena were the poor turnout among the Arab voters and the change in their voting trends.

Thanks to the precise, detailed listing of election results by polling station (Central Bureau of Statistics 1981), one may ascertain the degree of participation according to national group or religious community, although an element of uncertainty remains concerning those few polls in "mixed" cities, i.e. those where both Jews and Arabs voted. Out of the estimated 648,600 Arabs living in Israel (including East Jerusalem) at election time, 242,748 had the right to vote (Central Bureau of Statistics 1981a, page 5, Table B/1); of these, about 76% were Muslims, 15% Christians and 9% Druzes. This discrepancy is explained by the sizable ratio of under-age children, on the one hand, and on the other by the considerable number of residents in annexed East Jerusalem who refused to opt for Israeli citizenship (as in many other states, only citizens may vote in parliamentary elections, while all Israeli residents may do so in local ones). There were, at the time, approximately 520,000 Arabs who were Israeli citizens, virtually all within the pre-June 1967 "Green Line," about 1,800 in East Jerusalem and hardly any in the administered territories — which in consequence will not be considered herein.

Table 1: Arab Participation in Knesset Elections

Year	1949	1951	1955	1959	1961	1965	1969	1973	1977	1981
% of Arab participation	79.3	85.5	92.1	88.9	85.6	87.8	85.8	80.0	76.3	69.7

Some 69.7% of enfranchized Arabs exercised their right to vote on 30th June 1981 resulting in 164,862 valid votes. This was their lowest participation in all of Israel's parliamentary election, as shown in Table 1 (Rubinstein 1979, p. 193).

Despite the abstention in 1981 of three-tenths of the Arab electorate, their participation was still higher than that of their counterparts in all other multi-party parliamentary states with free democratic elections in the Middle East (Landau *et al.* 1980). However, it was remarkable nonetheless in comparison with their own past record in Israel. The steady decline in participation may be linked — at least in part — with the P.L.O.'s persistent call to Israeli Arabs to demonstrate a 'protest abstention' in Knesset voting — an appeal intensified in each of the last three electoral campaigns. Several groups of local Arabs have adopted this appeal, arguing that the very act of voting means legitimization of the State of Israel. Most vocal among these were the *Abna' al-Balad* (Sons of the Village), a small group of youths, active since 1973, largely in municipal and local politics (Landau 1981, p. 206), in a nationalist vein, bordering upon open support of the P.L.O. Also active were the equally radical "Progressive National Movement" and extreme Islamic groups, reflecting contemporary political revivalism in Muslim countries. One wonders how many of the more than forty thousand young Arabs registered on the voter rolls since 1977 (Toledano 1981) were influenced by these appeals.

Another explanation of the poor participation of Israeli Arabs in the 1981 parliamentary elections may be found in an entirely different context. In the past, parliamentary and local elections took place simultaneously; in recent years, however, they have been held separately. Consequently, in both 1977 and 1981, interest in the Knesset voting has flagged among Arabs primarily concerned with their own local affairs — some of whom may have voted earlier in parliamentary elections only because they were held simultaneously with local ones. Others frankly confessed their overall disappointment with the Knesset and what they considered its too modest efforts to promote the special interests of the Arab sector in any meaningful way. This was particularly applicable to several Arab groups which did not have "their own" candidates running; for example, participation in 1981 among Negev Beduins was 14% lower than in 1977 (when one of them had competed for a seat). Lastly, the fact that the 1981 elections were held in late June, at the height of the agricultural season (previous elections had usually been set for the autumn), may also have accounted for the high rate of abstention.

In any event, the manner in which the other 70% *did* vote surely merits analysis. Theoretically, Israeli Arabs could vote for any of the competing slates; their votes were indeed distributed over nearly all of them, as evidenced by the vote count at polls in exclusively Arab localities. Barring rare lunatic fringe votes, however, one notices method to their mass voting, which appears rather pertinent to their attitudes and interests. We shall briefly consider how these related to several of the lists competing for Arab electoral support.

Contenders for the Arab Vote

a)   Hadash, organized and headed by the Rakah, a Communist party running (as in 1977) as a 'Democratic Front,' had a no less ambivalent standing among Israeli Arabs. Since it had never been a member of government coalitions, its credit was rather poor in terms of the benefits it could deliver — except in places where it had a majority in the local council. In addition, its record as the only full-fledged anti-Zionist party in Israel made it a natural refuge for the alienated, particularly those refusing to share in a national consensus in Israel — even though some Arabs were reluctant to adopt such an extreme stand. However, these very attitudes served to increase Hadash's appeal to those who hold grudges against the Establishment and desire change. As it was truly an activist Arab-Jewish party, some Arabs felt that they could best express their political views and desires through it. Few were avowed Communists, although not every one perceived that Hadash was indeed a Communist party in nationalist garb. Many considered it as a safety valve for their frustrations, while some aspired to the scholarships which the party arranged for the children of its stalwarts at universities in the Eastern Bloc, averaging sixty annually in recent years (Levy 1982) — thus, incidentally, establishing future cadres as well. Hadash's platform stressed full equality, on all counts, for Israeli Arabs, with emphasis on employment opportunities, higher education, agricultural land for the landless, housing, improvement of public services at government expense and eliminating the compulsory military service for the Druzes. The above and other arguments were repeatedly voiced in Hadash's Arabic bi-weekly *al-Ittihad.* Another important demand was the establishment of a Palestinian State, along-side of Israel (Schenker 1981, pp. 10—11), with the "Egyptian option" proclaimed "dead." This could well be interpreted as support for Arab nationalism. We recall, moreover, that in earlier Knesset elections, the P.L.O. had called upon Israeli Arabs to vote for Rakah/Hadash (Ben-Dor 1980, p. 178), as it did just before the 1981 elections in its organ *Filastin al-Thawra* (Khuri 1981b, p. 40; Zayd 1981a): This call had been broadcast by the P.L.O.'s "Voice of Palestine" in Lebanon and reprinted in Hadash's *al-Ittihad* the day before Election Day. Furthermore, in recent years, Hadash has developed an impressively successful record among Israeli Arabs in trade union (Landau 1973, p. 31ff.; Lustick 1980, p. 224), municipal (Landau 1976, pp. 547—548) and parliamentary elections: after an all-time low share of 11% of the Arab vote in 1959 (Landau 1962), the Israel Communist Party had doubled its share of this vote to 22% in 1961 (Czudnowski & Landau 1965), this rose further to 23% in 1965, 29% in 1969 (Landau 1972), 38% in 1973 (Greilsammer 1978) and 49% in 1977. While *al-Ittihad* and Hadash's other organs attacked all competitors in 1981 (Said 1981), the main thrust of this party's electoral propaganda was directed against the Alignment, whom it accused of fostering unfounded hopes among Israeli Arabs (Mantsur 1981), equating it with the Likud on all counts (Zayd 1981a). In contrast, Hadash presented itself as the sole true representative and promoter of Israeli Arab interests (Abdallah 1981), as well as the only organization capable of "securing their rights" (Jubran 1981). Lastly, it placed three Arabs — Christians and Muslims — among the first five names on its candidates' slate in 1981, thereby appealing to those communities (particularly to the Christians who were not represented in any "safe" place on the slates of the Likud and Alignment).

b) The Alignment, too, was in a somewhat ambivalent position insofar as the Arab electorate was concerned. On the one hand, it was remembered by some as a Zionist party, not essentially different from the Likud in the eyes of those Arabs who felt that the Alignment had not done enough for them during the twenty-nine years it had been at the State's helm. Furthermore, it was now in the Opposition, unable to offer many meaningful inducements. As such, however, it could not be blamed for any of the present government's missteps, either. Moreover, the Alignment did present a real alternative to the Likud Government; its platform, prepared with the help of some of its Arab members (of whom there were about 18,000 in 1981) emphasized its intention to preserve the Arabs' particular characteristics, while integrating them into the party and the State. Through the Alignment, it was claimed, Israeli Arabs would get the best chance of fully participating in all political and social affairs in Israel and in exercising real impact upon local government, employment, education, welfare and health services, housing, agriculture, industry and crafts — all matters of prime importance to them. These arguments were reiterated by the Alignment's emissaries in its newly established offices in the Arab sector. (Khuri 1981b, p. 42). The main thrust, directed at Hadash, was essentially as follows: Hadash cannot provide any of the services promised: furthermore, a vote for Hadash means a vote for the Likud, since the former's radicalism can only breed similar extremism in the latter — and any brand of extremism would affect Arabs adversely (Meridor 1981). Lastly, the inclusion of two Muslim candidates — Muhammad Watad, an experienced Mapam member from the village of Jatt, in the Little Triangle (Tsur 1981), and Hamad Hala'ila, a Labor member from the village of Sakhneyn in Galilee — in "safe" places on the Alignment's slate attracted electoral support in both areas (the Little Triangle and Galilee are the principal concentrations of Muslims, Israel's largest religious minority). It is of particular interest that both Watad and Hala'ila were relatively young Muslims, unrepresentative of traditional Arab politicians who had been promoted by the Alignment — chiefly by its Labor component — in earlier Knesset elections (such conservative Arab politicians as Sayf al-Din al-Zu'bi and Jabr Mu'addi ran independently in 1981 and were not at all affiliated with the Alignment then).

c) Equally relevant were the Arab slates of candidates. There had been such slates in all the previous electoral contests; in most cases, they had been affiliated to a large party, such as Mapai and subsequently to the Alignment. Independent Arab slates had consistently lost in the past (Landau 1969, pp. 108—155). In 1981, the parties which had formerly supported such slates preferred to include Arab candidates directly on their own lists. Although deprived of such support, three independent Arab groupings did run in 1981 nonetheless: 1) The United Arab List, headed by a Nazareth Muslim, Sayf al-Din al-Zu'bi and a Druze, Jabr Mu'addi — both erstwhile Members of the Knesset (affiliated with Mapai) — appealing mostly to conservative Muslims and Druzes. 2) The Arab Brotherhood, headed by a Christian, Hanna Haddad, a retired police officer living in the Galilee village of Tur'an, and a Muslim, Salih Diyab, residing in the Galilee village Tamra; it appealed chiefly to Christians (unrepresented in other slates, except for Hadash). 3) The Arab citizens in Israel, headed by a Negev Beduin living in Lod, Nuri al-'Ukbi, appealing mainly to Beduins (Khuri 1981), although it used nationalist slogans to attract additional Arab votes. All competed with other parties and groups, some of them more experienced in electioneering and equipped with greater financial resources. Moreover, the three Arab slates had adopted platforms which, even when promising everything to everyone, were geared to narrow objectives (Kasim 1981). Their main strength indeed lay in their personal canvassing, based upon family relationships, religious community, local interests and direct acquaintance.

d) The Likud was not too attractive to most Arab voters, due to its avowed strongly-nationalist Zionist ideology, which could hardly appeal to them. However, it was then the ruling party with considerable clout in determining the apportionment of resources and benefits. Furthermore, the *laissez-faire* economic policy of the Likud Government — with liberal emphasis on private initiative — undoubtedly appealed to those middle-class circles which benefited from it, among Arabs no less than Jews. Lastly, the inclusion of a Druze candidate, Amal Nasr al-Din, a Likud M.K. in the outgoing Knesset, residing in the village Daliyat al-Karmil, near Haifa, in a "safe" place on the Likud's slate, attracted votes from

the Druze community which, although smaller than that of
the Muslims or Christians, was no less involved in national
politics (Ben-Dor 1979). Other Jewish slates of candidates
had a rather limited appeal for the Arab electorate, with the
possible exception of the NRP, whose ideology was relevant
to the pious and whose hold on such key Ministries as the
Interior and Religious Affairs may have aroused some hopes
of economic and other inducements. For example, in 1981,
there were 124 mosques in all of Israel (within the "Green
Line"), of which no fewer than 30 were being repaired or en-
larged, while another 23 were in various stages of construction;
the Ministry for Religious Affairs is also responsible for
numerous churches and Druze holy places (Mantsur 1982).
However, the NRP was then in some disarray, thanks to the
recession of some of its Sephardic personalities.

Results of Arab Voting

The results of the 1981 elections, insofar as the Arab vote
was concerned, were essentially as follows:

a) Hadash's Arab vote was one of the great surprises of the
1981 elections. The party still obtained the bulk of its
electoral support from Israeli Arabs. However, despite all pre-
dictions to the contrary, the upward trend of this vote was
interrupted for the first time in twenty years. Hadash, which
had obtained 71,718 Arab votes or roughly 49% of the total
Arab vote in 1977, received in 1981 only 60,397 Arab votes
or nearly 37% of the total Arab vote — retreating to its 1973
level (or even slightly less) of Arab electoral support. Al-

NOTES TO TABLE 2

a) Golan Heights residents participated in Knesset elections for the first time in 1981.

b) Nearly all Arab inhabitants in the Golan Heights and Mount Carmel are Druzes, as are many in Central Galilee.

c) All Arabs in the little Triangle are Muslims, as are all Beduins.

d) There are six cities in Israel with mixed Jewish-Arab populations: Jerusalem, Lod, Ramla, Tel Aviv-Jaffa, Haifa and Acre.

e) The United Arab slate was affiliated with the Alignment in 1977, but was one of three independent Arab slates in 1981.

Table 2: Arab Vote for the Ninth Knesset, 1977

Place	Total Vote	Participation	Hadash Vote	%	Alignment Vote	%	United Arab Slate Vote	%	Others Vote	%
Nazareth	15,080	74%	10,497	70	981	6	2,166	14	1,436	10
Eastern Galilee	18,902	80%	11,013	58	1,117	6	3,232	17	3,540	19
Western Galilee	31,756	76%	21,251	65	2,213	8	2,303	8	5,989	19
Central Galilee	12,968	75%	3,633	28	1,123	9	3,563	27	4,649	36
Mount Carmel	4,361	75%	567	13	1,088	25	711	16	1,995	46
Little Triangle, North	17,915	71%	8,015	45	1,628	9	2,509	14	5,763	32
Little Triangle, South and Central	13,232	70%	8,289	63	866	7	1,378	10	2,699	20
Galilee Beduin	5,668	64%	1,262	22	1,237	22	1,532	27	1,637	29
Negev Beduin	8,099	61%	651	8	918	11	4,873	60	1,657	21
Mixed Cities	17,316	73%	6,540	38	5,156	30	1,315	8	4,305	24
Total	145,297		71,718	49	16,327	11	23,582	16	33,670	23

Source: Arab Department, Israel Labor Party, Results of the Elections to the Tenth Knesset, 30.6.1981, in the Arab Sector, *mimeographed. (Hebrew).*

178 *Jacob M. Landau*

Table 3: Arab Vote for the Tenth Knesset, 1981

Place	Total Vote	Participation	Hadash Vote	%	Alignment Vote	%	Three Independent Arab Slates Vote	%	Others Vote	%
Nazareth	15,435	67%	8,215	53	3,003	20	2,918	19	1,299	7
Eastern Galilee	20,688	73%	9,245	45	4,853	24	2,697	12	3,893	19
Western Galilee	35,941	71%	18,521	52	7,975	22	3,959	11	5,486	16
Central Galilee	15,690	77%	2,444	16	2,540	16	5,366	34	5,340	34
Mount Carmel	5,414	77%	242	5	961	18	1,408	26	2,803	51
Golan Heights	498	88%	—	—	202	41	14	3	282	56
Little Triangle, North	18,938	61%	6,602	35	6,953	37	536	3	4,847	25
Little Triangle, South and Centre	14,516	63%	7,201	48	3,266	24	225	2	3,824	26
Galilee Beduin	6,664	64%	777	12	3,267	49	184	2	2,436	37
Negev Beduin	7,693	48%	369	5	4,019	52	1,350	17	1,955	26
Mixed Cities	23,385	73%	6,781	29	10,340	44	1,933	8	4,331	18
Total	164,862		60,397	37	47,379	29	20,590	12	36,496	22

though Hadash maintained its position as the leading electoral factor among Israeli Arabs, the 12% decline (equaling a proportionate loss of more than a quarter of its Arab support) was even more meaningful against the background of this party's down-trend in a number of Arab localities. In the 1977 Knesset elections, Hadash had obtained a majority of between 50% and 80% in 41 large Arab localities, while in 1981, it remained first only in 21 of them — and with a diminished majority in most. For example, in the only two purely Arab towns, its majority dropped from 69% to 54% in Nazareth and from 75% to 50% in Shafa 'Amr. This phenomenon was particularly striking in the former town, as Nazareth has had a Communist Arab mayor (Tawfik Ziyad, also an M.K.), supported by a Town Council with a Communist majority. This was probably due to disappointment with Hadash's failure to improve municipal conditions (Montsur 1982). The same downward trend was visible among almost all Beduin tribes (Stendel 1981, p. 143). Nevertheless, the party's electoral strength continued to be manifested (despite its setback) in the larger Arab localities, those with more than 2,000 inhabitants and primarily with a Muslim or Christian majority — presumably since its activities had focused upon such areas. The decline in Hadash's electoral support among Israeli Arabs may be explained in several ways. As in certain other countries, it is related in part to the policies and prestige of the Soviet Union. On this occasion, the Soviet Union's intervention in Afghanistan, a Muslim country, and the decline of its influence in the Middle East could hardly pass unnoticed. However, Hadash's decline may be better understood in terms of local developments. It may have been partly an outcome of the abstention of a sizable number of potential voters, who had formerly cast their votes for Rakah/Hadash on nationalist Arab premises. Furthermore, Hadash repeated the same slogans and maintained virtually the same slate of candidates (Khuri 1981a) — making the party's appeal rather lackluster. Rakah/Hadash's original position in national politics — effectively condemning it to a political wilderness in Israel — accorded it very few significant achievements, except in those Arab localities where it was predominant — where it indeed received a proportionately impressive vote in the 1981 parliamentary election.

b)   The Alignment's Arab vote in 1981 was another surprise to many political observers, although less so than Hadash's decline. The Alignment obtained 47,379 Arab votes or almost 29% of their valid votes. At first glance, this compares very favorably with its 16,327 Arab votes in 1977 — merely 11% of the total Arab vote then. However, in 1977, a United Arab List affiliated to the Alignment ran separately and obtained some 24,000 votes,[1] or about 16% of the afore-mentioned total. Adding this 16% to the Alignment's own Arab vote in 1977, one arrives at 27% of the Arab vote. Hence the Alignment's success does not lie primarily in its relatively modest advance from 27% of the Arab vote in 1977 to 29% in 1981, but rather in its ability to persuade Arab voters to transfer their electoral support to the Alignment's own slate of candidates. Naturally, Arab slates (mostly independent ones) attracted a share of the vote, more so in 1981 (20,590 votes) than in 1977 (6,780 votes). (Central Bureau of Statistics 1977, p. 4, Table 1). Moreover, an up-ward trend in the electoral support for the Alignment may be perceived in various Arab localities throughout Israel, especial-ly those localities where the Muslims — represented on the Alignment's slate primarily by Beduins — constituted a majority. Indeed, close to 70% of the votes of the Negev Beduins (about 3,600 votes) went to the Alignment (Zayd 1981). However, the bulk of the Druze vote went to other slates on which Druze candidates had been listed. Christian Arabs, too, displayed some reservations towards the Alignment, presumably since it had failed to include even one Christian candidate in a "safe" place on its slate (Mantsur 1981a). From a broader point of view, the Alignment's advance in Israeli Arab voting may have been a part of its overall electoral gains in 1981, largely recouping its electoral defeat in 1977 — at least partly thanks to tenacious efforts in persistent campaigning among both Jews and Arabs. The frequently repeated slogans of "Likud or Alignment" probably persuaded many Arab voters, just as they did numerous Jewish ones, to support one of the two major parties, in preference to smaller groups, on the reasonably certain assumption that one of the two would form the next government. In other words, not a few Arab voters, critical of the Likud's policies, must have considered the Alignment, rather than Hadash, as the only feasible alternative (Tadmor 1981). Many of these Arabs also preferred the Alignment to the Likud since the former had a better record of attending to their specific needs.

c) The United Arab List obtained 11,590 votes, the Arab Brotherhood 8,304 and the Arab Citizens in Israel 2,596 (Central Bureau of Statistics 1981, 11, Table 3).[2] These represented, respectively, 0.6%, 0.4% and 0.1% of the total number of valid votes cast, which did not suffice even for a single Knesset seat. It is safe to assume that virtually all votes cast for these three slates were Arab ones. One may speculate that had all the Arab politicians heading these slates joined forces, their combined efforts might well have succeeded in gaining a Knesset mandate. The trouble lay less in ideological differences than in their mutual bickering and personal inability to agree as to who would head such a joint slate. As a result, these slates remained with a rather narrow base — personal, regional or religious — unable to atract votes throughout Israel. In a parallel manner, the inclusion of Muslim, Christian and Druze candidates in "safe" places on other slates attracted numerous Arab votes in 1981, as indicated below. Conversely, however, many of the 20,590 votes (or about 12% of the valid Arab votes) attracted by the three independent Arab slates were forfeited by competing slates — chiefly the Alignment and Hadash — which could presumably have garnered part of them. For example, the Arab Brotherhood appears to have attracted Christian Arab votes, which might have gone to Hadash, in such Christian villages as Kafr Yasif, Tur'an, Ma'iliya, Fassuta, 'Ilabun and I'blin: in all six villages, the percentages of votes for the Arab Brotherhood are nearly identical to Hadash's losses (Stendel 1981, p. 144). Political commentators have surmised that these results which continued and emphasized trends noticeable in earlier elections, spelled out the end of independent Arab slates running in future parliamentary elections in Israel. This is possible but unlikely, considering the boundless optimism frequently engendered by political ambitions.

d) All other competing groups— The Alignment and Hadash excepted — obtained about 34,500 Arab votes, that is approximately 21% of the valid Arab votes. Three of these figures merit comment: The centrist Shinui party obtained 6,516 Arab votes, a crucial share (more than a fifth) of its total 29,837 votes. This was probably due to its moderate political and socio-economic program and — no less — to its placing Zaydan 'Atshah, a Druze, in what appeared to be a "safe" third place on its slate of candidates. The Likud's 10,765 Arab votes cannot be considered a setback (Toledano 1981a), as it represents a marked advance over the 4,450 votes it had received in 1977. This was mostly due to a natural desire to support the party in power and — no less — a result of the Likud's placing a Druze in a "safe" place on its slate of candidates. Indeed, no less than a third of the Likud's Arab vote came from the relatively small Druze community. The NRP declined somewhat in its Arab support from 6,512 votes in 1977 to 5,552 in 1981, a possible reflection of its overall loss of votes in the latter case. The fact that it did not lose more Arab votes may well have been due to the consistent presence of its emissaries in the Arab sector and their continuous involvement in Arab affairs. Other groups received less than 3,000 Arab votes each — including the list headed by Moshe Dayan, despite his assumed popularity among Israeli Arabs.

A comparison of the overall Arab vote in 1981 to that of 1977 reveals several prominent characteristics:

a) The total number of Arab valid votes increased by only slightly more than 8,000, due to the much higher rate of abstention in 1981.

b) In both elections, most of the Arab vote went to Hadash, the Alignment, Alignment-affiliated Arab slates and independent Arab slates.

c) Hadash's Arab support declined by about a quarter, proportionately (49% to 37%) as expressed throughout the country. Even so, Rakah/Hadash maintained its foremost position among Israeli Arabs.

d) The Alignment succeeded in drawing votes previously cast for its affiliated slates and in increasing its overall share of the Arab vote, second only to Hadash.

e) All Arab slates declined in popularity and failed to win any seats in the Knesset.

f) Only about one-fifth of the total Arab vote, in both elections, went to all other Jewish slates combined. The rise from 19% to 21%, along with the direct support of the Alignment, may well indicate a trend in Israeli Arab voting.

g) All the above may lead one to perceive "a conservative trend ... among Israeli Arab voters" (Peretz & Smooha 1981, p. 524). This is a debatable point, however, considering the 37% vote of Israeli Arabs for Hadash and the abstention of another 30%, many of whom presumably maintained reservations about the Establishment.

Comparison of Arab and Jewish Electoral Behavior

In 1981, approximately 19,000 votes were required for a Knesset seat. Had all Arab valid votes gone to Arab candidates, eight to nine would have been elected. As only five Arabs entered the Tenth Knesset, one may ask to whose vote their election was due and whom the Arabs' own votes did send to the Knesset. The answers differ: Hadash won four seats, two Arabs and two Jews, meaning that many Arab votes went to elect its Jewish MK's; this occurred frequently in the past as well and some Arab supporters of Hadash have expressed their resentment. The Alignment, with two Arabs

Table 4: Breakdown of the Arab Vote, 1977–1981

Slate	1977		1981	
	Votes	%	Votes	%
Hadash	71,718	49	60,397	37
Alignment	16,327	11	47,379	29
Arab Slates Affiliated with the Alignment	23,582	16	—	—
Other Arab Lists	6,780	4	20,590	12
All Other Jewish Lists	26,890	19	36,496	22
Grand Total	145,297	99	164,862	100

Sources: Central Bureau of Statistics, Results of Elections to the Tenth Knesset 30.6.1981 *and Arab Department, Israel Labor Party,* Results of the Elections to the Tenth Knesset, 30.6.1981, in the Arab Sector *(Hebrew).*

among its MK's, owed two-and-a-half of its seats to Arab votes. The Knesset contigent of the Likud, on the other hand, included a Druze, elected in part by Jewish votes. In contrast, all other Jewish slates, particularly Shinui and the NRP, owed part of one Knesset seat to Arab votes. In other words, the Likud alone "invested" Jewish votes in 1981 in a Druze candidate, while in practically all other slates, Arab votes helped to elect Jewish candidates.

Comparing the Arab to the Jewish vote in 1981, we note that similarities abound. In recent years, the participation rate has declined visibly in both sectors. Many of the Arabs who did vote in 1981 appear to have patterned their vote on the general trend supporting the two major parties as the only political entities capable of forming a government. In many respects, the independent Arab slates greatly resembled the *ad hoc* Jewish slates set up for the 1981 elections: their platforms, although claiming to be ideological and embrace a wide spectrum of political and socio-economic desiderata, focused upon ethnic, local or personal issues — with the common denominator of constituting basically *ad-hoc* groups standing behind a single range of issues or supporting a single leader (or at most a narrowly-based leadership).

Voter mobility in Knesset elections has increasingly characterized political behavior among Arabs and Jews alike. The details of this mobility and its motivation, however, are largely a matter of speculation, especially among Israeli Arabs, due to the non-availability of quantitative public opinion polls among them (and, of course, due to the strict secrecy of voting). It is more than likely that the shift in vote was affected by the increased break-down of traditional social structures and the growing impact of modernization among the younger Arab generation — at least partly under the influence of their Jewish peers. Compared with the possibly conservative vote of the older generation, that of the younger Arabs in Israel appears conditioned by "rational" considerations and evaluations of interests, along with the obvious attraction of Arab nationalism.

In this context, while there were evident differences of style in electoral propaganda among Jews and Arabs in Israel, as well as variety in their preferences, as expressed at the polls, the basic dissimilarity in their voting referred, respectively, to the relatively high support of the Arabs for Hadash versus the equally high vote of Jews for the Likud. However, in this case, as well, one may argue that essentially the same atmosphere induced both groups to cast about 37% of their valid votes for Hadash and the Likud, respectively. Disregarding the obvious impact of socio-economic factors in Israeli voting, if one considers the politico-nationalist aspect as paramount, one may better grasp the large Arab vote for Hadash, with roughly the same proportion of the Jewish vote going to the Likud — both of which respectively strove to foster strongly nationalist images among Arabs and Jews in Israel.

The two nationalisms evidently compete with one another, which is probably why merely 4,521 Jews voted for Hadash and only 10,765 Arabs for the Likud. The fact that they did reminds us, however, that nationalist premises were just one component of voter motivation. The decline in Israeli Arab support of Hadash, on the one hand, and the increase in their support for the Alignment and other essentially Jewish parties, on the other, points to other electoral motivations, such as "votes for services," as against nationalist sentiments, and perhaps a moderate increase in the accommodation of Israeli Arabs with the State of Israel. In other words, the growing resemblance of Jews and Arabs in Israel in such characteristics as education, urbanization, income and behavior indicates trends of socialization which exerts a similar (although not identical) influence upon the voting preferences of both sectors and demonstrates a growing symmetry in their political behavior.

NOTES

[1] Here, again, one notes a slight discrepancy: the Central Bureau of Statistics lists 24,185 votes, the Arab Department of the Israel Labor Party 23,582. The reason may be, in both the following footnote and the present case, that the Party knows of some Jews who had voted for the Arab slate and subtracted their number from the total figures of the Central Bureau of Statistics. In any event, the present reported attempts by the United Arab Lists, in both 1977 and 1981, to obtain Jewish votes (Dar 1981).
[2] The overall figure of the Central Bureau of Statistics for the combined vote for the three independent Arab slates in 1981, viz., 22,490, is higher than that calculated by the Arab Department of the Israel Labor Party (See above, Table 4).

BIBLIOGRAPHY

Abdallah, F.
　　1981　　"The Arab Masses Will Express Their Conscience and Interests by Voting for the Front," *al-Ittihad,* June 6, 1981 (Arabic).

Amnon, K.
　　1981　　"There Are Illusions in the Territories," *'Al Hamishmar,* June 26, 1981 (Hebrew).

Ben-Dor, G.
　　1979　　*The Druzes in Israel: A Political Study.* Jerusalem: Magnes Press.

　　1980　　"Electoral Politics and Ethnic Polarization: Israeli Arabs in the 1977 Election," in: Arian, A. (ed.), *The Elections in Israel 1977,* Jerusalem: Academic Press, pp. 171–185.

Central Bureau of Statistics
　　1977　　*Results of Elections to the Ninth Knesset, May 17, 1977.* Jerusalem.

　　1981a　　*Results of Elections to the Tenth Knesset, June 30, 1981.* Jerusalem.

　　1981b　　*Monthly Bulletin of Statistics* (Jerusalem), **32** (7), July 1981.

Czudnowski, M.M. & Landau, J.M.
  1965   *The Israeli Communist Party and the Elections to the Fifth Knesset, 1961.* Stanford, CA.: The Hoover Institution on War, Revolution and Peace.
Dar, Y.
  1981   "Jabr Mu'addi Attempts to Recruit Jewish Votes," *Davar,* June 4, 1981 (Hebrew).
Greilsammer, A.
  1978   *Les Communistes israéliens.* Paris: Presses de la Fondation Nationale des Sciences Politiques.
Jubran, S.
  1981   "The Way of the Front — The Way of Securing Rights!" *al-Ittihad,* June 19, 1981 (Arabic).
Kasim, K.
  1981   "Where Is the System?," *al-Anba',* June 26, 1981 (Arabic).
Khuri, T.
  1981   "Rushing the Arab Voter" *Yediot Aharonot,* June 1, 1981 (Hebrew).

  1981a   "What Caused 'The Arab Reversal'?," *Yediot Aharonot,* July 3, 1981 (Hebrew).

  1981b   "The Reversal in the Arab Sector" *Migvan* (Spectrum) 62, pp. 40-42 (Hebrew).
Landau, J.M.
  1962   "Les Arabes israéliens et les élections à la quatrième Knesset," *International Review of Social History* (Amsterdam), 7, pp. 1-32 (English translation in: Landau, J.M., *Middle Eastern Themes: Papers in History and Politics,* London: Frank Cass, 1973, pp. 198-227).

  1969   *The Arabs in Israel: A Political Study.* London: Oxford University Press.

  1972   "The Arab Vote," in: Arian, A. (ed.), *The Elections in Israel 1969,* Jerusalem: Academic Press, pp. 253—263.

  1973   "The Arabs and the Histadrut," in: Avrech, I. & Giladi, D. (eds.), *Labor and Society in Israel:*

A Selection of Studies, Tel-Aviv: Dept. of Labor, Tel Aviv University and Dept. of Higher Education, Histadrut, pp. 24-38.

1976   "Israel," *Yearbook on International Communist Affairs, 1976* (Stanford, CA.), pp. 546-550.

1981   "Alienation and Tensions in Political Behavior" (in Hebrew), in: Layish, A. (ed.), *The Arabs in Israel: Continuity and Change* (in Hebrew), Jerusalem: Magnes Press, pp. 197-212.

& Others
1980   *Electoral Politics in the Middle East: Issues, Voters and Elites.* London: Croom Helm & Stanford CA: Hoover Institution Press.

Levy, G.
1982   "Doctors in Red," *Haaretz,* December 17, 1982, Supplement (Hebrew).

Lustick, I.
1980   *Arabs in the Jewish State: Israel's Control of a National Minority.* Austin, Texas: University of Texas Press.

Mantsur, A.
1981   "The Competition for the Arab Vote," *Haaretz,* June 2, 1981 (Hebrew).

1981a   "The Arab Reversal," *ibid.,* July 3, 1981 (Hebrew).

1982   "The Seclusion of Israeli Arabs," *ibid.,* October 18, 1982 (Hebrew).

Meridor, Y.
1981   "Peres at A Mass-Meeting in Nazareth: Voting for Rakah Ultimately Strengthens the Likud," *Davar,* June 28, 1981 (Hebrew).

Peretz, D. & Smooha, S.
1981   "Israel's Tenth Knesset Elections," *The Middle East Journal* (Washington, D.C.), 35 (4), pp. 506-526.

Rubinstein, E.
1979   "The Lesser Parties in the Israeli Elections of
            1977," in: Penniman, H.R. (ed.), *Israel at the
            Polls: The Knesset Elections of 1977,* Washington,
            D.C.: American Enterprise Institute for Public
            Policy Research, pp. 173-197.

Sa'd, A.
1981   "The Propaganda of the Zionist Parties Contra-
            dicts Their Moral, Political and Public Bank-
            ruptcy," *al-Ittihad,* June 2 & 5, 1981 (Arabic).

Schenker, H.
1981   "The Party Platforms," *New Outlook,* June
            1981, pp. 6-11.

Stendel, O.
1981   "Trends in the Voting for the Tenth Knesset
            Among Israel's Arabs," *Hamizrah Hehadash*
            (Jerusalem), 30 (1-4), pp. 138-148 (Hebrew).

Toledano, S.
1981a   "The Arabs of Israel: Wrong Estimates,"*Haaretz,*
            September 4, 1981 (Hebrew).

1981b   "The Meaning of the Arab Vote." *ibid.,* Sept-
            ember 7, 1981 (Hebrew).

Tsur, Y.
1981   "From Jatt to Jerusalem," *'Al Hamishmar,* June
            19, 1981 (Hebrew).

Zayd, K.
1981a   "An Impressive Achievement of the Alignment
            Among the Negev Beduin," *'Al Hamishmar,*
            July 3, 1981 (Hebrew).

1981b   "Friends in Need," *ibid.,* July 7, 1981 (Hebrew).

8

Coexistence or Hegemony?
Shifts in the Israeli Security Concept

*Yoram Peri**

Security constitutes a key feature of the Israeli experience; nevertheless, Israel's security doctrine has remained latent: not a close-knit, well-formulated aggregate of security principles, but rather a series of essentials reflected in the behavior of her military-political elite. In this respect, some prefer not to utilize the term "doctrine" at all, replacing it with "security concept."[1] The non-consolidated nature of these principles and the latency of the security concept have created certain problems for researchers, such as the difficulty in discerning "main line policy" from amid the wealth of often contradictory principles expressed by various members of the elite, or in determining the significant transition points of the security concept, which is dynamic by nature.[2]

Notwithstanding these difficulties, it is possible to define the fundamental principles of the concept, note the contributions of various members of the elite to its formation and follow its "main line." In this respect, the events of 1981 are most surprising: all at once, the traditional security concept was confronted by a new and different approach, not a marginal addition to the old concept, not a change in a single principle alone, but an all-inclusive alternative set. Moreover, even before this new approach was accorded professional-military or public-political consideration, it was put to a practical test. Only a few days after Israeli troops invaded Lebanon in June 1982, it emerged that this war differed from Israel's previous wars and that it was guided by the new system of principles.

*Lecturer in Political Science, Tel Aviv University.

The longer the war lasted, the clearer it became that the lack of national consensus did not stem solely from the depth of the political rift in Israeli society but also from the fact that the war was being conducted according to a policy which differed from Israel's traditional security concept, which apparently had not undergone any change prior to that time, despite the Likud's rise to power in May 1977.

The new security policy resulted from the mutual efforts of Prime Minister Menachem Begin, Defense Minister Ariel ("Arik") Sharon and Chief-of-Staff Lieut.-Gen. Rafael ("Raful") Eitan who, despite their lofty official positions, were unable to erase traditional policies overnight. It was during the Begin government's second term, which commenced in summer 1981, that a confrontation took place between Israel's traditional security conception and the security policies of the political-military leadership.

This paper will consider the difference between the two policy lines and attempt to explain the nature of the change and the causes thereof. Our main assertion is that Israel's traditional security conception was one of coexistence, whereas the new security policy aspires to realize Israeli hegemony within the sphere of regional influence. We commence by examining the components of the traditional concept.[3]

The Rivals

The Israel-Arab conflict, the key element shaping Israel's security concept, comprises three concentric circles: the innermost is the conflict between the Zionist and Palestinian National Movements over recognition of national-political rights and the territorial struggle over *Eretz Israel*/Palestine; the middle one constitutes the policy of "politicide" by Arab states towards Israel, while in the outermost circle, the Arabs and Israel serve as representatives of two rival camps in the East-West struggle.

Each of these spheres of conflict had its own differential weight in Israel's traditional security concept. There was a tendency to underestimate the value of the innermost circle and consider it to be a function of the central one; acts of sabotage and terror were considered a nuisance rather than an existential threat, creating "current" rather than "basic" security problems.[4] The outermost circle was likewise perceived as secondary and Soviet-Israel relations were considered a function of the main conflict between Israel and the Arab states.

In 1948, when the State of Israel was established, the Soviet Union aided the young country both politically and militarily. In fact, a primary foreign policy principle determined by Israel's first cabinet called for "friendship with freedom-loving nations, especially the United States and the Soviet Union."[5] "With the lessening of independence between various regional subsystems of the global international system," the Soviet Union became Israel's adversary (Evron 1973, p. 79). However, neither then, during the 1950s, nor later was she perceived by the Israeli political-military leadership as a direct enemy but rather as an indirect one alone, as one which, motivated by global interests, aids the enemies of the Jewish State. Thus, during the mid-1960s, the Prime Minister and Defense Minister could claim that "Israel does not take part in what is termed the 'Cold War.'"[6] During the height of the War of Attrition at the Suez Canal, Israel continued to signal to the Soviet Union that she wishes to avoid reaching the threshold of provocation, even though Israeli Air Force pilots downed five MiG-21 planes flown by Soviet pilots on June 30, 1970. The essential conception was that "only a nation or regime which defines itself actively as an enemy of Israel will be perceived as an enemy" and the Soviet Union was not included in this category.[7]

The Defensive Approach

The Israel-Arab conflict is essentially asymmetric; from 1948 on, Arab policy was perceived by those who molded Israel's security concept as strongly revisionist in nature: "liquidation of the state, destruction of the Jewish people in Israel and annihilation of all hope of its national renewal" (Allon 1968, p. 228). In contrast, Israel's main line security policymakers were far from adopting parallel objectives, considering the consolidation of the state as a primary political objective.

Some did entertain ambitions for territorial expansion, such as members of the Herut Movement, but these were to be found outside the determining elite. In contrast, revisionist-oriented members of the military-political establishment agreed that the only condition for changing the territorial *status quo* would be if the Arab states initiate open warfare against Israel.[8]

There was some connection between the asymmetry in ambitions of the respective sides and readiness to implement them. The Arab states believed that their overall superiority would enable military resolution of the conflict on the battle-field, which would in itself also constitute the final political victory. Eventually, however, it became clear that the road to comprehensive resolution is a long one; thus, since 1967, the Arabs have restricted themselves to limited military operations for attainment of limited objectives.

Israel's leaders, in contrast, estimated that the IDF's military determinations, successful though they may be, are always necessarily temporary and local. Since the 1956 Sinai Campaign, Israel's security concept had always accepted the assumption that Israel cannot enforce her will upon the Arab world by military means, owing to her inferior geostrategic and geopolitical positions. Israel's objective was therefore preservation of the *status quo,* preventing the Arabs from a possibility of realizing their national aims regarding the fate of the State of Israel, not allowing them to harm her integrity or sovereignty. This was in essence a negatively-oriented defensive, preventive concept, although it was designed to lead to the ultimate achievement of a positive objective — Arab acceptance of Israel's existence.

This defensive character influenced the various dimensions of Israel's security concept: "Since Israel cannot resolve the Jewish-Arab conflict in war, however great her victory may be, we must avoid any war which is not essential. A war which cannot be prevented must be brief and inexpensive, etc."[9] This conception accorded a qualitative dimension to the time factor, which we will consider only briefly hereunder.

The Arabs strive for change in the *status quo,* while Israel seeks to compel them to adjust to reality. It thus emerges that the longer the *status quo* continues, the greater the Israeli "victory." In this context, Israel's leaders attributed positive value to the time factor: the more that time passes and the longer the *status quo* continues, the "closer" the Arabs will come to realizing that "the solution to the conflict is not to be found on the battlefield but rather at the conference table" (Barlev 1978, pp. 3–4). The time element is so important that even territorial concessions, within the framework of interim agreements, were perceived as a trade-off, in which land was exchanged for a gain of time. The goal of buying time has always been an important component of Israel's security concept.[10]

Deterrence as Prevention and Punishment

Since the Sinai Campaign, the defensive nature of the security concept has also accorded great importance to deterrence as a key component of Israeli strategy, "intended to stabilize the *status quo* in terms of both territory and the 'rules of the game' in Israel-ARab relations" (Horowitz 1975, p. 244). Over the years, and especially since 1967 — there has been some debate within the Israel military-political elite regarding the success of this policy of deterrence. It has been noted, for example, that deterrence failed to prevent the Six-Day War in 1967 (Hendel 1973, pp. 49–50). Furthermore, it was claimed that military ability to thwart Arab achievements, even by surprise, necessarily entails a decrease in the value of deterrence (Oz-Hen 1981). The concept of absorbing the first blow, adopted during the period 1967–1973, was said to have supplanted deterrence.

A distinction was made among various types of deterrence: the prevailing opinion was that in the long run, Israel had indeed preserved her general deterrence ability — to neutralize or eliminate the potential military threat — but she did not succeed concomittantly in developing concomitant immediate deterrent ability, primarily aimed at annulling a specific type of threat.[11] This may be the essential reason behind the change in concept of deterrence, which had a primarily preventive nature in the 1950s but acquired the additional punitive attribute in the 1970s, i.e. raising the price which the adversary was to pay for his deeds.[12]

The Crisis-Management Approach

One key component of Israel's security concept was that the conflict would end only when the Arabs desire its conclusion. No Israeli act can bring about a solution to the conflict before a radical change occurs in Arab political conceptions. Further - more, such change does not appear imminent, as the source of Arab enmity towards Israel apparently extends·beyond the political sphere, stemming from deep rooted inter-cultural, inter-religious and ethno-national conflict (Vital 1971). Since change in the conflict is contingent upon a shift in Arab orientation, there is no reason to undertake overall political strategic planning to resolve it.

Thus Israel's leaders justified their decision to reject an approach of "conflict resolution" in favor of "extinguishing conflagrations" or "crisis-management." This approach indeed largely characterized the operative code of Israeli authorities. Within the elite, there is a tendency to favor political consensus over long-range solutions, thereby avoiding conflict over molding the future. The Israeli political elite generally prefers methods of improvisation and intuitive policy-making to long-range factually-based planning. "The preferred policy is 'We'll cross that bridge when we come to it' " (Akzin & Dror 1966).

The conflagration-extinguishing approach has several characteristic manifestations: it led to adoption of a responsive security policy, both on the structural level — the build-up of the IDF forces in response to Arab expansion — and in terms of the annual work plan — as an estimate of the enemy's short-range intentions. The same was true in terms of operative military activity: a policy of reprisals, and even on the political level, resulting, since 1967, in a policy of immobilism.

The conflagration-extinguishing approach engendered an effort to reduce and contain the dimensions of each conflagration and to lower the profile of every crisis as it occurred through shortening the duration of combat, limiting the scope and number of fronts and, wherever possible, sealing off the regional subsystem from superpower intervention (Evron 1973, p. 116). From this approach stemmed the tendency to conclude each crisis with return to an improved *status quo ante,* wherein the improvement expresses the extent of Israeli success in battle and provides bargaining cards for the political negotiations. Finally, there is a highly evident preference for pragmatism, flexibility and non-committalism, or, in Caiden's words: "Don't be irrevocably committed. Leave room to maneuver out of every situation. . . treat every problem separately and seek specific solutions. . . "[13]

The Legitimacy of War

The legitimacy of war as an instrument for attaining national objectives has been the focus of a pointed debate among the political movements which struggled for Israel's independence. The Labor Movement, which dominates the local political arena and therefore also the military organization of the Zionist Movement, had a clearly-defined conception: war in itself is bad and immoral and should be considered a necessary evil. Hence maximum efforts should be exerted to avoid the use of military force for attainment of national objectives.

Itzhak Sadeh, one of the military leaders of the Labor Movement's Hagana Organization, declared that "We must protect youth from. . . placing the rifle at the center of our lives. . . anyone who takes such weapons in hand must remember that they are necessary instruments of emergency, a last resort." In contrast, Zeev Jabotinsky, leader of the Revisionist Movement and forefather of Herut, had changed the words to the anthem of Betar — the movement's youth organization — from "I will prepare to defend my nation and only raise my hand in defense" to "I will prepare to defend my nation and conquer my homeland."[14]

During the period following the establishment of the State of Israel, this concept, which stems from pragmatic political considerations as well as moral ideological beliefs, was gradually integrated into the concept of the *status quo:* war was considered legitimate only when defensive. Initially, the outcome of the War of Independence strengthened the hand of those who favored war as a means of attaining national objectives: the Israel Defense Forces' victory added 6,400 sq. km. to the 14,400 granted the Jewish State according to the 1947 UN Partition Plan. It is therefore hardly surprising that in the early 1950s, there were Labor and right-wing personalities alike who called for "concluding the War of Independence" with regard to the West Bank.[15] However, the Russian-American ultimatum which led to a withdrawal from Sinai at the end of the Sinai Campaign proved the difficulty in changing the territorial *status quo* by military means and bolstered the concept of war as a legitimate policy only when defensive in nature, i.e. a war which protects the *status quo*.

The dispute now concerned the definition of "infringement of the *status quo*": Did it mean only actual infringement, the threat of infringement or perhaps also long-range potential adverse effects? The possible answers to these questions constitute a continuum:

Types of Legitimate Wars

A	B	C	D
Responsive Counterstrike	Preemptive Strike	Preventive War	Instrument for Attaining National Objectives

The types of war are distinguished by two dimensions: one relating to the question of whether or not the *status quo* has been harmed and the second to the dimension of time. Case (A) posits that the enemy did cause an infringement of the *status quo*. In Case (B), it is eminently clear that the enemy is about to wreak such a change within an extremely short time. In (C), there is indeed no change but it is estimated that one will occur within a longer period of time. In Case (D), in contrast, there is no change whatsoever in the *status quo*, nor is change foreseen within any reasonable amount of time.

The heterogeneity which pervaded the question of legitimacy of war among the Israeli military-political elite has disappeared since the Sinai Campaign. At that time, conceptions (A) and (D) were discarded and consensus focused upon (B), along with partial and provisional support for approach (C).[16] It is precisely because of this desire not to be drawn into a preventive war (C) that Israel defined a number of processes or events in determining a *casus belli*, namely a change in the *status quo* to an extent which demands military action for restoration of the *status quo ante*.[17]

In Israel, the conception of a war of defense was termed "a war of no choice." When war does break out, the IDF need not limit itself to prevention of an Arab attack; it may indeed determine additional objectives of war. Nevertheless, Israel will not initiate war to achieve political goals (Barlev 1978). This defensive war concept was a sociological mechanism which enabled maximum mobilization of civilian manpower for the war effort and a very high effective rate of peripheral recruitment for collective needs even between wars. The concept of a "war of survival" also fostered the integration of a society with rather deep social and political cleavages.

Power Diplomacy

A sixth component of Israel's security concept is connected with the question of legitimacy of war, namely the relation between military power and diplomacy in foreign and defense policy. During the pre-State period, a heated debate took place within the Zionist Movement, similar to the dispute on the legitimacy of war, concerning the affinity between these two components of national security. The names ascribed to the different Zionist schools of thought attested to their underlying approach: "Military Zionism" at one extreme and "Political Zionism" at the other.

The dominant elite in the Zionist Movement supported a combined, integrative approach which comprised three components: political, practical and military. This approach, of which Ben-Gurion was a chief spokesman, declared that "Zionism will succeed only when it incorporates three elements: a strong social and economic infrastructure in the Land of Israel, strategic might and a network of political ties and support (Avineri 1980, pp. 231–233). This approach also characterized the military-political elite after the establishment of the state.

Differences of opinion persisted within the elite, especially during the 1950s, between the activist school and the more dovish view, brought about by the identification of Ben-Gurion with the first, power-based outlook. However, a meticulous examination of his political behavior, as distinguished from rhetoric, indicates that Ben-Gurion and his colleagues accorded much consideration to the system of international exigencies whenever they sought to employ military force for purpose of foreign policy.[18] This approach also continued after Ben-Gurion's having bowed out of the political scene.

The Upheaval — 1981

Although Israel's security concept has changed somewhat since the establishment of the state, its main guidelines have largely been preserved despite differences in conditions and key manpower. There was a significant turning point, however, during the early 1980s. While an upheaval had been predicted as early as 1977, upon the rise of the Likud to power after 35 years in opposition, it did not in fact occur at that time. The new Prime Minister, Menachem Begin, was aware of prevailing suspicions both in Israel and abroad concerning his rise to power; hence he exerted a determined, systematic effort to display continuity in government policy in terms of content and the rules of the game. He therefore sought to incorporate into his government representatives of the previous elite, headed by Moshe Dayan.

The process which all had predicted at the onset of the electoral upheaval actually commenced only after the Likud government had secured control and obtained some experience in handling the affairs of state. The government was made more homogeneous with the resignation of partners from the old regime — i.e. the DMC members, headed by Deputy Prime Minister Yigael Yadin, and Dayan. There were changes in the balance of forces within the Likud, such that Herut obtained key cabinet positions. Even within Herut itself, there was a weakening of the dovish sector, headed by Ezer Weizman. It was then that the security conception changed as well.

The stages of transition from the defensive security approach to the new one may be discerned clearly within the top-echelon military-political elite. In 1978, Lieut.-Gen. Rafael Eitan was appointed Chief-of-Staff and differences in approach emerged between him and the Defense Minister, Ezer Weizman, resulting from the former's opposition to a policy of appeasing the Arabs. However, it was only upon Weizman's resignation from the cabinet in March 1980 and the transfer of the Defense portfolio to Menachem Begin himself did Eitan attain maximum influence.[19] The even earlier resignation of Dayan in September 1979, together with that of Weizman, left Minister of Agriculture Ariel Sharon, then head of the Ministerial Committee for Settlement, as a senior minister with a military background and a dominant force in determining defense policy. Following the 1981 elections, he was indeed appointed Minister of Defense.

It was then that a new strategic leadership, with much in common, assumed its place officially, rather than merely on an interim basis: Begin, former commander of the Irgun; Sharon, a founder of Commando Unit 101 and the Paratroopers and Eitan, erstwhile commander of that unit. These personalities represented a political and political-military *Weltanschauung* which largely conflicted with the traditional security concept that had characterized Israel's military-political elite.[20]

The extent of upheaval in the new leadership's security concept stems from its very point of departure, which demands elimination of asymmetry in the Israel-Arab conflict: no longer a situation wherein only Israel is threatened and the Arabs know that there is no danger of any Israeli military action unless they themselves provoke one, but rather a situation of mutual threat, not theoretical but tangible. The traditional concept that solution of the Israel-Arab conflict is not based upon war but upon the conference table gave way to an alternative view,[21] according to which military force may lead to partial solution of the conflict: radical solution within the innermost circle, where the wrestling match with the Palestinian National Movement takes place, and neutralization of the dispute with Arab states in the middle circle through creation of a "new political order" in the Middle East.[22]

This strategic concept demands the basic assumption that Israel has the military power not only to protect itself but also to dictate a military solution. While this may have been a moot question in the past, the signing of the Peace Treaty with Egypt in April 1979 transformed the perceived situation into reality. Israel continues to note the imbalance in national-economic power ratios between her and the Arab world, but the history of the Israel-Arab military conflict is not that of a conflict between two overall powers, as the Arab power potential was never actually exercised.

Furthermore, since the establishment of the State, Israel has declared that it would preserve a ratio of 1:3 between its regular troops and those of Arab armies. In reality, however, the military power ratio is not reflected in the number of troops alone, but rather is expressed as superiority in combined military ability, including weapons systems, fire power, maneuverability and the ability to operate complex systems. Since 1967, Israel has indeed enjoyed absolute superiority in overall fire power (Tal 1978) and her ratio of forces in the battlefield was better than 1:3.

In the Yom Kippur War, Israel was taken by surprise on two fronts and did not succeed in mobilizing her militia-like reserve forces in time. The ultimate ratio of forces was 1:2.3 in number of formations, 1:2.5 for tanks and 1:2.3 for fighter planes. With the withdrawal of the Egyptian Army from the cycle of hostilities in 1979, the IDF enjoyed an unprecedented ratio compared with the combined forces of the eastern front confrontation states and the expeditionary states: 1:2.5 in divisions, 1:1.7 in tanks and 1:1.8 in fighter planes. Egypt's absence from the foreseen theater of battle transformed Israel into a truly dominant power. The essence of the new security policy indeed recommends utilizing this military might in the political arena as well.

The War of Choice

The feeling that Israel possesses a war machine which can impose a military solution upon her enemies led to an essential change in the concept of the fundamental objectives of national security. Once again, the primary objective was not one of thwarting Arab intentions to harm Israel and preservation of the *status quo* until the Arabs accept and recognize the State of Israel, but rather a fundamental modification of the *status quo* and the enforcement of an Israeli solution upon the Arabs either by peaceable means or through creating a new political order in the Middle East which will significantly and radically weaken Arab ability.[23]

Military superiority is a necessary but not a sufficient condition for the flourishing of such a concept, which also requires an additional ideological element, namely a new definition of the essence of legitimate war. Since 1981, the political-military leadership (Begin-Sharon-Eitan) has indeed defined legitimate war in a manner different from the traditional concept of the Israeli military-political elite. General Beni Peled, former Commander of the Israel Air Force, was the first to come out in public against the traditional concept of legitimate war, claiming that Israel must determine her political objectives according to military abilities, define her desired borders and attain them through her army.[24] In other words, Peled declared that the war can and even must be an instrument for attaining national objectives and interests and not solely for preventing and thwarting enemy intentions.

Peled's words were public and strong but the concept was essentially adopted by the new military-political leadership, whose institutional status constrained it to use more prudent language. Prime Minister Menachem Begin publicly renounced the conception of responsive or preemptive counterattacks and granted his seal of legitimacy to the deliberately-initated preventive war, which he defined as a "war of choice".[25] Defense Minister Sharon likewise supported Peled's concept, although he avoided identifying with it publicly. However, Chief-of-Staff Rafael Eitan did express such views in 1981, when he recommended going to war against PLO. Among the points he raised was the fact that the war machine which we had developed ought to be put to good use.[26]

The Offensive Approach

The primary significance of the above-described concept is the change in attitude towards war. Up to 1980, war was essentially a limited act, with the clear military significance of eliminating a threat to Israel. Now, it was accorded wider scope and transformed into an instrument which aided in the realization of political objectives — defense gave way to offense. An analyst who has been following Israel's security doctrine for an extended period of time noted that Sharon's main theme is that Israel should acknowledge her strength, should not underestimate herself and should utilize her might upon the appropriate occasion.[27]

This concept was not a personal revolution for the "Triumvirate" which had shaped the new defense policy since 1981. Menachem Begin was a disciple and guiding force of the Zionist Revisionist school, which related thus to war even during the pre-State period. While the idea that "a homeland is not acquired with gold, nor with brute force, but is built with the sweat of one's brow" was typical of the Labor movement school, the Revisionists identified with the concept expressed by the poet Uri Zvi Greenberg, who wrote: "And I say: the land is conquered with blood, and only that which is conquered with blood is sacred to the nation, through the sanctity of blood" (Wagner & Kafkafi 1982, p. 183). The use of military force in the national struggle for liberation was perceived as legitimate not only during the battle for independence but also in the struggle for consolidation of the state in the 1980s.

Defense Minister Sharon and Chief-of-Staff Eitan were not adherents of the Revisionist school, but their miltiary-political socialization had taken place within organizational frameworks which nurtured the offensive approach, even if limited to a tactical level. During the 1940s, Begin and Shamir objected to the Hagana's policy of self-restraint and demanded offensive initiative. Sharon and Eitan advocated the offense-oriented approach in the 1950s, this time within the IDF. The commanders of Commando Unit 101 and the Paratroopers helped mold the fighting spirit of these units, which became an ideal prototype, a model for emulation throughout Israel's armed forces.

However, while the Revisionist concept was political in nature from the outset, the offense-oriented approach held by Sharon and Eitan was tactical alone. Just as the decision during the pre-State period, the 1930s, to supplant passive defense with tactical offensive defense was taken only after heated political and military deliberation, so too did the establishment of Unit 101 and its methods of operation in the 1950s arouse debate within the top military-political echelons. In any event, it was clear that only tactical operational principles were concerned. In 1981, upon their assuming top-level positions within the political-military decision-making elite, the adherents of the offensive approach were able to elevate it from the tactical to the overall strategic level.[28]

Deterrence as Compulsion

Adoption of an offensive-oriented approach demands change in many components of the security concept, most prominent of which is that of deterrence. Horowitz has rightly claimed that realization of the efficacy of military power in conducting policy, even without its actual implementation, was one of the conclusions drawn from the unique situation of the Israel-Arab conflict, that of "no war, no peace." The dominant political elite of the pre-State period "developed a strategy of political deterrence that, without excluding the possible use of force, placed emphasis on the attainment of political objectives by means of accumulation of power rather than by its actual application" (Horowitz 1975, p. 244).

As noted above, deterrence became a key component of Israel's defensive concept since 1948, initially as prevention and subsequently as punishment. Its ultimate objective was to keep the enemy from changing the *status quo*. This device is not compatible with an offensive security policy. Revisionist policies do not require deterrence, as they seek to alter the status quo from the outset. In the summer of 1979, Begin indeed removed the element of deterrence from the conflict's innermost circle, publicly declaring that he would no longer adopt a policy of retaliation as regards the PLO, but would rather implement an offensive approach which does not depend upon PLO activity.[29]

The concept of overall deterrence vis-à-vis the Arab states also acquired a new character: deterrence in the sense of prevention or punishment now took on the meaning of compulsion, constraining the adversary to proceed in accordance with a certain policy. Israel's threat to use military force now related not to a case in which the Arabs attempt to change the *status quo*, but also to one in which they do not accept Israeli dictates for its alteration. For example, various pronouncements and allusions to Israel's ability to hit the oil wells of Saudi Arabia are to be viewed in this light.

The New Adversaries

Up to this point, the characteristics of the new security

policy have related to the ideological and professional background of the new military-political leadership. However, this
factor is only partially responsible for the change in direction.
Another element which must be considered is the process of
change which took place in the regional sub-system: since the
Yom Kippur War, several of the expeditionary states underwent a process transforming them into conflict states. The
most outstanding example is Saudi Arabia, which the IDF
perceives as playing a far more active military role than it had
in the past.[30]

These two explanations for the change in security concept
are also manifested through the new definition of the ad-
versaries: those which stem directly from the attributes of
the military-political elite and those which result from the
new regional configuration. However, beyond the change in
the middle circle, that of the Arab States — namely the departure of Egypt and the coopting of countries which had
previously been defined as expeditionary states alone —
changes occurred in the innermost and outermost circles as
well.

With regard to the first, the PLO is now perceived for the
first time as a strategic danger and not only as nuisance
terror. Hence Israel ceased considering the PLO as a subversive
element alone. The war in Lebanon during the summer of
1982 was in fact the first war which the IDF waged against
the Palestinians. Of no less significance, moreover, is the
change with respect to the Soviet Union. In contrast to the
traditional concept, the Soviet Union was now perceived as a
direct adversary of Israel, even without connection to the
Middle East dispute. Guided by a powerful, long-term anti-
communist ideology, Menachem Begin declared anti-Soviet
emphasis to be a characteristic of Israel's foreign policy. In
the past, it was Soviet aid to Arab countries which led to
questionable relations between Jerusalem and Moscow; now,
however, the new leadership stressed the ideological conflict
between Israel, "the representative of the free world" and
the communist Soviet Union.[31]

This conception reached its peak in Israeli efforts to obtain an agreement of strategic understanding with the United
States and was integrated into US Secretary of State Haig's
attempt to form an anti-Soviet strategic system in the Middle

East. Within this framework, Israel was prepared to undertake operations against the Soviet Union and her allies in the region, as the regional representative of the Western camp. The agreement did not clarify which activities the IDF would have to undertake beyond the boundaries of the state, but the strong public debate which arose in Israel concerning the topic attested to the extent to which the government's commitment was perceived as a radical change from the traditional concept.[32] Furthermore, perception of the Soviet Union as a direct adversary of Israel was also expressed in Israel's weapons development program in the early 1980s.

Transformation of the Soviet Union into a direct adversary of Israel extended the scope of Israel's interests to states which were not directly connected with the Israel-Arab conflict, but rather served as target regions for Soviet expansion. Sharon explicitly defined this area when he indicated that "Israel's sphere of strategic and security interests must be broadened in the 1980s to include countries such as Turkey, Iran and Pakistan, and regions such as the Persian Gulf and Africa, particularly the countries in North and Central Africa."[33]

Even in the past, Israel's security policies did not ignore countries which were outside the sphere of Arab hostility. In the 1960s, a peripheral policy was developed including Turkey, Iran and Ethiopia. However, this was intended to create an outer, pro-Israel circle which would surround the Arabs and harm their strategic position. Now, the definition of an area from Pakistan to Central and Southern Africa was not only a function of the Arab-Israel conflict but also of the direct conflict between the Soviet Union and Israel, which stems from Soviet expansion in the region defined as Israel's sphere of influence.

Conflict Resolution

The new attitude towards Israel's security problems was not adopted in the context of "extinguishing conflagrations" which break out because of external factors. On the contrary, the approach now adopted is an initiated approach of conflict resolution from a broadly inclusive perception, based upon prior planning. This concept suits the style and *modus operandi* of Defense Minister Sharon. One of the first activities he undertook upon his assuming the Defense portfolio in June 1981 was to set up the National Planning Unit and expand significantly the strategic planning team directly responsible to him. He then ordered it to proceed at once in drawing up operative plans for implementation of the first stages of the "new political order" with regard to Lebanon.[34]

In contrast to the conflagration-extinguishing approach, conflict resolution does not strive to limit the dimensions of each crisis; on the contrary, it may indeed intensify them and utilize them as accelerating factors in other processes. A crisis may be initiated or escalated in order to cause a chain reaction. Conflict resolution does not call for conclusion of each crisis with a return to an improved *status quo ante,* but rather seeks to create a new and fundamentally different situation. It essentially seeks to undermine stability and to create a different order, contending that temporary instability, which brings about a more stable structure in the long range, is preferable to a *prima facie* stability whose future is uncertain.

Power Politics

The use of controlled violence is part of the accepted rules of the game in the Israel-Arab conflict — a situation of "no war, no peace" or a "dormant war." However, it is precisely this mercurial situation which impelled the political leadership to emphasize the element of control, i.e. to consider political exigencies in order to prevent reverting to overall violence. Israel's traditional security concept was thus situated between the two coordinates of violence and diplomacy.

From the time the Begin government first revealed its security policies, it appeared that the diplomatic component had decreased in significance: Begin and Sharon not only maintained more hawkish approaches than their predecessors but more power-oriented ones as well. Sharon's advocating that Israel make more use of its "muscles" and Eitan's belief in a military solution to the Palestinian problem are but a few illustrations.[35]

A series of Israeli actions against the Arab world, in the face of severe world reaction anticipated, even from countries friendly to Israel, underscored the subordination of the diplomatic component to that of power, namely: the bombing of the Iraqi reactor and the air raid of PLO headquarters in Beirut in June 1981, the annexation of the Golan Heights in December of that year and subsequently the siege of Beirut in the summer of 1982. Interspersed with and following these activities, Prime Minister Begin issued a number of statements emphasizing the power component in Israel's foreign policy.[36]

Israel's traditional security concept, which considered the diplomatic and military components to be complementary, held that a balance of power prevails in the Middle East. The Arabs have overall superiority, but Israel has military superiority. The ascription of differential weight to the power component as compared with the diplomatic one, a characteristic of the new security policy, necessarily led to consideration of the ratio of power as unbalanced in Israel's favor. The essence of the new policy calls for exploitation of this military advantage to attain hegemony in the regional sphere of influence.[37]

Nuclear Hegemony

The principle of hegemony was first implemented with respect to nuclear power. Israeli governments up to 1977 maintained that nuclearization of the Israel-Arab arena must be postponed for as long as possible; at the same time, however, the nuclear option must be built up in preparation for the future, when the Arabs may possess such weaponry and, of even greater significance, in order to provide Israel with a "final response" to "the most severe situation of all" in a conventional war.[38] The policy of "a bomb in the basement" which developed in the wake of the Six-Day War was well-suited to this line of thought. In the 1970s, another element was added to nuclear policy, as defined by then Defense Minister Shimon Peres: "The danger in this region stems from the fact that Arab nuclear technology progresses hand in hand with their enmity towards Israel. It will be very difficult to prevent development of nuclear technology. Hence the only way to ward off a nuclear catastrophe is to bring about a change in their policies."[39]

The nuclear policy of Sharon-Eitan-Begin was different: it rejected not only nuclear coexistence in the far future but also nuclear technological development in the present, thus demanding a position of nuclear hegemony for Israel. When the pace of nuclear development in Iraq appeared threatening, a decision was taken to bombard the Osirak reactor and even to publicize Israel's responsibility for the action. The very first official announcements made it clear that this was not an extraordinary action, but rather one which stems from an overall concept, from a "doctrine" declaring that "under no circumstances will we allow our enemies to develop weapons of mass destruction against our people."[40]

This subject was again raised in Sharon's important programmatic speech: Sharon's declared political principle for the 1980s was "our firm decision to prevent the confrontation states or potential confrontation states from gaining access to nuclear weapons . . . for us it is not a question of balance of terror but a question of survival. We must prevent such danger at its very outset."[41] The success of the Osirak mission in the nuclear sphere bolstered the intentions of Begin-Sharon-Eitan to implement the concept of hegemony on the conventional level as well; Lebanon was selected as the first target.

The War in Lebanon: Security Policies Versus the Traditional Security Concept

The war in Lebanon was supposed to have been conducted according to the guiding principles of the new policy. It was clearly an offensive war, planned by Sharon since he entered the Defense Ministry and actually recommended a year earlier by the Chief-of-Staff.[42] It was not intended to meet defensive military needs, but was rather undertaken primarily to achieve wider strategic gains: to strike hard at the PLO militarily and politically and thereby enable dictation of the Israeli autonomy plan on the West Bank; to wipe out the Syrian stronghold in Lebanon and weaken Syrian military potential, and even the Assad regime itself; to change the balance of inter-ethnic power in Lebanon, return rule to the Maronites, headed by the new President Bashir Jumayel, and bring about a peace treaty ensuring Israel's hegemonic status in Lebanon.

The war was part of a vast political-military mosaic which was to institute change in the regional system of political forces, according to the concept of "conflict resolution," including the transforming of the Jordanian monarchy into a Palestinian state.[43] The war expressed the transfer of the center of gravity to the power factor, as compared with that of diplomacy, up to a point where relations between Israel and the United States had worsened and various moves were criticized by President Reagan, who intervened by telephoning directly from the United States.

However, the most unique aspect of this war, the sixth of Israel's wars, was the relation between the new security policy according to which the war was conducted, and Israel's traditional security concept. Despite the fact that the new security policy had been presented before the war, from the moment fighting erupted in June 1982, the war was put forth by Begin, Sharon and Eitan as though it were being conducted according to the old concept. For this reason, the first stage of Operation Peace for Galilee enjoyed vast national support. However, once the IDF crossed the 45 km. limit, the true nature of the war was laid bare, triggering an unprecedented public protest, not only among opposition groups but even within the political elite itself, wherein various cabinet ministers felt that they had been misled by the Defense Minister.[44]

The greater the gap between the new policy and the traditional concept, the stronger the criticism concerning the course of war, even within top IDF echelons. This entailed manifestations of refusing orders and rebellion, threatened and actual resignation by officers and protests against the Defense Minister. There were also instances of violations of orders and draft refusal among enlisted men.[45] The rift between the Defense Minister and the IDF High Command was so severe and public criticism of the principles behind the war in Lebanon were so strong that in late 1982 the political-military leadership again attempted to present the war as though it had been conducted according to the traditional security concept — i.e. as a war which is primarily defensive and preventive in nature. Yet, in the same breath, the new system of security principles was being defended.

Upon entering the post-Lebanon era, Israel faced a dilemma of even greater interest to researchers of security doctrine: what will result from this conflict between the new security policy and the traditional security concept? How long can both concepts coexist? How will developments in the make-up of the political and military elite influence the results of this unique conflict in the near future? The answers to these questions will determine whether Israel's security concept in the 1980s will continue to be one of coexistence as in the past, a balance of power within a heterogeneous system, to use Aron's terminology, or instead become a policy in which Israel seeks hegemony in the Middle East region.

The two concepts are incompatible. In the first case, the absence of war "results from the approximate equality of forces prevailing among political units and forbidding any one of them or any coalition to impose its will," while in the other case peace exists because of the "incontestable superiority of one of the units."[46]

This is one of the key decisions which the Israeli political-military elite will have to reach in the near future. It is also a theoretical and intellectual challenge: can a small state like Israel — which is so dependent upon the international system, and particularly upon the United States, become a hegemonic power even in a limited region? The answer to this question is, alas, beyond the scope of this paper.

NOTES

1. Horowitz's contention (1975) is accepted by many researchers of Israel's security doctrine. Confusion generally prevails in terminology such as security policy, strategic concept, military or security doctrine, security theory, etc. See, for example, Lt. Col. Beni M. (1982), p. 76.

2. One of the problems of researching Israeli doctrine stems from the misapplication of concepts taken from a lower level of security theory, which are then applied to a higher level. In this manner, for example, offensive strategy is mistakenly attributed to Israel. See Churba (1977).

3. The summary of Israel's traditional security concept presented herein is based primarily upon Horowitz (1975 and 1982), Tal (1978) and Hendel (1973). Other important studies in this area were undertaken by Safran (1978) and Brecher (1972). With regard to the Israeli military-political elite, see Peri (1983).

4. Differentiation between problems of current security and those of basic defense has long been accepted in Israel and also constitutes part of strategic analysis. See Ben-Gurion, *Divrei Haknesset* 2, January 1956; also Milstein (1982).

5. See basic government guidelines in the *Government Yearbook 5711*, Jerusalem, 1950, p. 50. For an analysis of Israel-Soviet relations during that period, see Brecher (1972).

6. A quotation from Prime Minister Levi Eshkol upon presenting his cabinet to the Knesset on January 12, 1966, published by the Government Press Office, Jerusalem, p. 4.

7. The quotation, taken from Allon (1968), p.16, reflects a wider conception. This approach towards the Soviet Union was especially prominent in the behavior of Moshe Dayan.

8. New details of these 1950s concepts are recorded in Shimon Peres's biography. See Golan, M. *Shimon Peres*. Tel Aviv: Massada, 1982 (Hebrew).

9. Major-General (res.) Moshe Peled at a symposium on the War in Lebanon, organized by Tel Aviv University's Center for Strategic Studies. For a detailed account of the proceedings, see *Al Hamishmar*, December 3, 1982, p. 9.

10. For a discussion of the time component in Israeli strategy, see Gisin (1982).

11. See Gisin (1982), who probably relates to the terminology used by Patrick M. Morgan in *Deterrence: A Conceptual Analysis.* Sage Library of Social Research, vol. 40, Beverly Hills and London, 1977.

12. In this context, Shimon Peres declared that in the future, any Arab state which goes to war against Israel "will have to allocate resources to protect its hinterland." See Williams (1975).

13. See the analysis of characteristics of the administrative and political system in Israel in Caiden (1970), pp. 84—87.

14. For an analysis of the differences in approach between the Labor and Revisionist Movements, see Wagner & Kafkafi *The Root of the Conflict,* 1982, pp. 109—110.

15. Ben-Gurion's Diary: February 13, July 20 and July 23, 1951.

16. Foreign Minister Yigal Allon declared explicitly that "For both theoretical and practical reasons, Israel will never initiate a preventive war." See interview in the Viennese newspaper *Die Presse*, February 6, 1975. Similar statements were also made by Defense Minister Peres and Prime Minister Rabin, who even reprimanded Chief-of-Staff Gur for expressing views in a different vein. See Peres (1978), p. 236 and the article by Yosef Harif in *Ma'ariv*, September 2, 1974.

17. For detailed consideration of this topic, see Horowitz (1975), pp. 245—246 and Hendel (1973), pp. 60—65.

18. Regarding the Sinai Campaign and Ben-Gurion, Dayan himself testified that without Anglo-French assistance, it is highly doubtful whether Israel would have initiated her own campaign. See Dayan (1956), pp. 13—15.

19.   Eitan, for example, influenced Begin to change the policy towards the PLO in Lebanon. See article by Zeev Schiff in *Ha'aretz*, August 29, 1980, as well as Amir Oren, *Davar*, August 29, 1980.

20.   Also included was Itzhak Shamir, former commander of the Stern Group.

21.   See analysis by Perlmutter (1982), undertaken in the shadow of the war in Lebanon.

22.   A key statement in this context was uttered by Chief-of-Staff General Refael Eitan, who declared that "There is a military solution to the problem of the PLO." This statement aroused many public reactions, primary among which is the view that only a diplomatic solution will resolve the Israel-Palestinian conflict. See *Ma'ariv*, May 31, 1982.

23.   For details on the "new order," see Zeev Schiff, *Ha'aretz*, April 7, 1982. In a lecture delivered on December 16, 1982, upon the establishment of the Center for Peace Studies in Tel Aviv, General (res.) Matti Peled claimed that the vast increase in the size of the regular army since 1973 enabled the IDF to go to war in Lebanon for the first time without having to call up the reserves. Thus, the change in IDF structure enabled a change in its *modus operandi*. It is estimated that Israel's regular army increased in size from 70,000 troops in 1973 to 170,000 in 1982. See *Yediot Aharonot*, January 5, 1983.

24.   Peled expressed such opinions frequently since his release from active service following the Yom Kippur War and his involvement in non-partisan public affairs.

25.   Menachem Begin: "A War of No Choice — or a War of Choice?" *Ma'ariv*, August 20, 1982.

26.   Refael Eitan in *Yediot Aharonot*, May 14, 1982 and *Ha'aretz*, May 17, 1982.

27.   Zeev Schiff, *Ha'aretz*, November 24, 1982.

28.   See the interesting analysis by Milstein (1982), pp. 23—24, concerning the gap between the tactical and strategic echelons of the IDF. Regarding Eitan's offense-oriented approaches, see, for example, the interview in *Ma'ariv*, April 16, 1976.

29.   See, for example, *Ha'aretz*, April 24, 1979.

30.   *Ha'aretz*, March 12, 1982.

31.   *Ha'aretz*, November 24, 1981.

32.   "Will Israel become the Cuba of the West? This is not the purpose for which the Israel Defense Forces were established." Yuval Neeman in a Knesset discussion of the issue. The main thrust of criticism was leveled from the left-wing, dovish camps on the political map. See, for example, *Davar*, December 3, 1981.

33.   Sharon's description of Israel's sphere of interests in the 1980s is taken from a key programmatic speech delivered at the Center for Strategic Studies on December 14, 1981. This speech is one of the most comprehensive documents presenting the new security policy with which this article deals. Sharon (1981).

34. *Ha'aretz*, July 23, 1982.
35. See *Ha'aretz*, November 24, 1982; *Ma'ariv*, May 31, 1982 and also Inbar (1982), p. 12.
36. At a Herut Party convention on May 11, 1981, Begin warned the West German Chancellor that Israel will not stand by silently as neo-Nazi activities are perpetrated in Europe, but will act against them on the soil of European countries. See *Hotam*, May 29, 1982. Perlmutter (1982), who has followed Sharon's activities for many years, declares that "Sharon has never precisely understood the meaning of the word 'limited ' " (p. 74).
37. See the series of articles by Martin Woollcott in *The Guardian*, August 31, September 1 and September 2, 1982, written following his visit to Israel.
38. "Israel's Nuclear Arsenal," a report by a Committee of Experts to the UN Secretary General, September 18, 1981. Also: interview with Yigal Allon, September 29, 1977.
39. Interview with Shimon Peres, January 23, 1981.
40. *Ha'aretz*, November 22, 1981.
41. Sharon (1981). Also see the official government announcement regarding the Iraqi nuclear threat (1981).
42. While Eitan's primary concern was the PLO in Lebanon, Sharon added the Syrian dimension to the original plan. See *Ha'aretz*, July 23, 1982.
43. Sharon addressing the Knesset Defense and Foreign Affairs Committee: "There is a lot of sense to striking at Jordan." *Ha'aretz*, June 29, 1982.
44. The Israeli press described these events in great detail during August 1982 — February 1983.
45. See, *inter alia*, two special meetings of IDF officers on September 28 and 29, 1982, at which severe criticism was leveled at the Minister of Defense concerning the resignation of Col. Eli Geva, as well as the criticism of the Minister by Brig.-Gen. Amram Mitzna, O.C. IDF Staff and Command College. See *Yediot Aharonot*, September 24, 1982. For other reactions, see *Ma'ariv*, September 26, 1982.
46. For an elucidation of a heterogeneous system and the balance of forces, see Aron (1966), pp. 100, 151.

BIBLIOGRAPHY

Akzin, B. and Dror, Y.
1966　*Israel: High Pressure Planning.* Syracuse (New York): Syracuse University Press.

Allon Y.
1968　*A Curtain of Sand.* Tel Aviv: Hakibbutz Hameuhad. (Hebrew).

Aron, R.
1966　*Peace and War.* Garden City (New York): Doubleday.

Avineri, S.
1980　*Varieties of Zionist Thought.* Tel Aviv: Am Oved (Hebrew).

Barlev, H.
1978　"The War and Its Aims." *Maarachot* (Battles) **266**, pp. 2-4 (Hebrew).

Begin, M.
1982　"A War of Choice — Or a War of No Choice?" *Maariv,* August 20, 1982 (Hebrew).

Beni, M., Lt.-Col.
1982　"Israel's Defense Strategy — Continuity Or Change?" *Maarachot* 283, pp. 76-77 (Hebrew).

Brecher, M.
1972　*The Foreign Policy System of Israel.* London: Oxford University Press.

Caiden, G.E.
1970　*Israeli Administrative Culture.* Institute of Government Studies, The University of California, Berkeley.

Churba, J.
1977　*The Politics of Defeat.* New York: Cyrco.

Dayan, M.
1956　*Diary of the Sinai Campaign.* London: Weidenfeld and Nicolson.

Evron, Y.
1973　*The Middle East: Nations, Super-Powers and Wars.* London: Elek.

Gisin, R.
1982　"Israel's Defense Strategy — Continuity Or Change?" *Maarachot* 282, pp. 2-8 (Hebrew).

Government of Israel: Ministry of Foreign Affairs and Atomic Energy Commission
    1981   "The Iraqi Nuclear Threat — Why Israel Had to Act. " Jerusalem.
Gur, M.
    1978   "The IDF — Continuity and Innovation." *Maarachot* 281-282, pp. 4-6 (Hebrew).
Harkabi, Y.
    1975   "Surprise in the Yom Kippur War." in: *Arabs, Palestinians and Israel.* Jerusalem: Van Leer Institute (Hebrew).

    1977   *Arab Strategies and Israel's Response.* New York.
Hen, O.
    1981   "Thoughts on Israeli Deterrence." *Maarachot* (Battles) **279-280,** pp. 33-37 (Hebrew).
Hendel, M.I.
    1973   *Israeli Political-Military Doctrine.* Cambridge (Massachusetts): Harvard University Press, Occasional Papers in International Affairs.
Horowitz, D.
    1975   "The Israeli Concept of National Security and the Prospects of Peace in the Middle East." in Sheffer, G. (ed.) *Dynamics of a Conflict.* Jerusalem: Humanities Press.

    1982   *The Stable and the Variable in Israel's Defense Doctrine.* The Leonard Davis Institute for International Relations, The Hebrew University of Jerusalem. (Hebrew).
Inbar, E.
    1982   *Israeli Strategic Thought in the Post-1973 Period.* Israel Research Institute of Contemporary Society, Jerusalem.
Milstein, U.
    1982   "Operation Peace for Galilee — Strategic Continuation Or Upheaval?" *Kivunim* (Guidelines) **16,** pp. 19-28 (Hebrew).
Pail, M.
    1980   "The Yom Kippur War — A Historical View of the Strategic Level." *Maarachot* 276-277, pp. 3-10 (Hebrew).

Peres, S.
1978   *Tomorrow Is Now.* Jerusalem: Mabat (Hebrew).
Peri, Y.
1983   *Between Battles and Ballots: Israeli Military in Politics.* London: Cambridge University Press.
Perlmutter, A.
1982   "Begin's Rhetoric and Sharon's Tactics." *Foreign Affairs* (Fall 1982), pp. 67-83.

Raviv, Y.
1979   *Israeli-Arab Balance of Military Power Following The Peace Treaty with Egypt.* Tel Aviv University, Center for Strategic Studies (Hebrew).

Safran, N.
1978   *Israel, the Embattled Ally.* Cambridge (Massachusetts) and London: The Belknap Press of Harvard University Press.

Sharon, A.
1981   "Israel's Strategic Problems in the 1980s." Address delivered at the International Symposium on Strategic Problems, Tel Aviv University, December 19, 1981.

Tal, I.
1978   "Israel's Defense Doctrine: Background and Dynamics." *Military Review* (March), pp. 23-37.
United Nations General Assembly
1981   *Israeli Nuclear Armament.* Report of the group of experts, September 18, 1981, A 36 431.

Vital, D.
1971   "Israel and the Arab Countries." in: Spiegel, S.L. and Waltz, K.N. (eds.), *Conflict in World Politics.* Cambridge (Massachusetts): Winthrop, pp. 221-239.

Wagner, Y. and Kafkafi, E.
1982   *The Roots of the Conflict.* Tel Aviv: Am Oved (Hebrew).
Williams, L. (ed.)
1975   *Military Aspects of the Israeli-Arab Conflict.* Tel Aviv: University Publishing Projects.

9

THE POLICY FORMATION –
ELECTORAL ECONOMIC CYCLE 1955 – 1981

Alex Radian*

Introduction

Studies of electoral economic cycles (Nordhaus 1975; Frey 1978; Tufte 1978; Ben-Porath 1975) shed light on two important questions. The first one, which generally pre-occupies economists, is: To what extent do election year politics interfere with long-range economic policies? The second question appeals more to political scientists: What is the impact of elections upon responsibility and responsiveness? In other words, to what extent do elections lead policy-makers to prefer popular policies? In both professions, there is a deep concern with the normative aspect of these questions. Elections create a special kind of politics, which may have an adverse effect on public policies. In the politics of elections, power can be won or lost during a short period of time. What a government does or fails to do during an election campaign may have an important and often crucial impact upon voters (Hibbs 1981; Kinder & Kiewiet 1979). Thus if it is true that " . . . as goes economic performance so goes the election" (Tufte 1978, p. 137), then governments may be tempted to spend money they do not have, artifically reduce unemployment, maintain an artificially low rate of exchange on foreign currency, cut taxes, etc. Since some voters may be convinced to vote for a particular party on the grounds of rather simple pocketbook calculations, then " . . . an incumbent administration . . . may manipulate the short-run course of the national economy in order to improve its party's standing in the up-coming elections." [ibid pp. 3—4].

*Lecturer in Political Science, The Hebrew University of Jerusalem. Research for this paper was funded by the Levi Eshkol Institute.

A rather limited number of empirical studies established that a link between electoral politics and macro-economic policy does exist (Ben-Porath 1975; Stein 1969; Lindbeck 1976; Tufte 1978; Frey & Friedrich 1978; Paldam 1979). Longtitudinal and cross-national comparisons yielded evidence showing that a political economic cycle appears in some countries more often than in others, in some, but not in every election campaign within a single country and in some, but not in all elements of economic policy.

As is often the case, the elegancy of abstract models (Nordhaus 1975; Frey 1978) exceeds the quality of the evidence gathered to confirm, reject or improve the hypotheses. Open questions range from why an election policy link appears in some elections and is absent in others, to what precisely should be measured to test the hypothesis and the meaning of links between policy and elections. The discovery that an economic political cycle does exist is itself insufficient for drawing the conclusion that the government intentionally geared policy tools to improve its electoral standing. Democratic governments are not known for their ability to fine-tune policy. To borrow Lindblom's aphorism, governments have thumbs where (delicate) fingers are needed (Lindblom 1977). Harnessing economic policy and directing it toward election goals poses special problems (Golden & Poterba 1980; Lindbeck 1976). Consider the following example: Every policy decision to lower or raise taxes has a symbolic (Edelman 1977) and a pocketbook meaning. The former takes effect immediately after a decision is announced, while the latter — the actual change in tax bills — may take effect only when returns are filed or when the tax is actually paid (which may be months after the decision has been announced). Thus, tax cuts introduced a few months before elections may show up in tax payments after the elections. Tax cuts introduced a full year before an election will result in lower tax bills during the election year, when voters have long forgotten that a policy change was made. When the first strategy is pursued, the symbolic element is maximized and the pocketbook effect limited. The second strategy sacrifices the symbolic element and increases the pocketbook effect. Which strategy would be more effective in winning voters' support? The answer is not immediately obvious (Kinder & Kiewiet 1979).

Linking politics with economics to win elections requires foresight and the ability to make complex plans long in advance of election day, as well as mustering the various components of the policy process to reach and then implement the desired decisions at the right time.

It is quite possible that elections may influence policy formation through government weakness. It is not sophisticated election strategy that is responsible for electoral-economic cycles, but rather the inability to withstand the pressures exerted on office-holders during election campaigns. Governmental institutions may be unwieldy and slow, but they cannot be entirely immune to pressures. A minister of finance is always under pressure to cut taxes or increase deductions for this or that group; elections weaken his ability to resist. The other side of this coin is that decisions to increase taxes would be postponed until after the elections when the government will be in a better position to ignore those who oppose this policy. Governments, like individuals, are very good at postponing unpleasant decisions. As Tufte suggests " . . . austerity measures . . . are less likely to be pursued in election years than in years without elections" (Tufte 1978, p. 60). Indeed, Ben-Porath found that currency devaluations in the period 1952–1973 were introduced at least eighteen months before an upcoming election and the implementation of the decision to introduce a value added tax was postponed until after the 1973 election (Ben Porath 1975).

An incumbent administration can be expected to use every conceivable strategy to improve its electoral position even when its prospects of winning are high. However, manipulating economic policy to increase popularity cannot be attained without cost. If taxes are cut before an election, they would have to be increased after the election to retrieve lost revenues. Therefore, only when the incumbent party expects to lose an election will it be prepared to ignore the costs of post-election year policies. As Frey suggests:

> If a government is confident of winning the next election it would be irrational not to include (at least) the following term into the time horizon. The next legislative period is of no interest only if the government is absolutely sure of losing the next election (Frey 1978, p. 206).

Not all elections are the same: they differ in the intensity of party competition, the balance of power between the competing parties, the state of the economy and the issues that happen to preoccupy the voter's mind. If the context of elections vary, shouldn't the relationship between policy and elections vary as well?

In this article I will investigate the relationship between elections and tax policy in Israel from 1955 to 1980*

Israel offers a particularly rich field for studying election-tax policy cycles. The tax-GNP ratio has gone up from (roughly) 12% in 1950 to 52.9% in 1976 and has last (1980) been calculated at 47.5%. Few other democracies have matched this rate of growth (Goode 1968). This quadrupling of the tax) GNP ratio in twenty-six years could not have been achieved without decisions which are anathema to policy-makers concerned with election year politics. This makes it possible to test Tufte's hypothesis that austerity measures are more likely to be introduced in non-election than in election years.

The growth in Israel's revenues has never been sufficient for development of a surplus. From the first days of independence right up to the present, finance ministers have operated with tight budgets and large deficits (Horowitz 1972). It is therefore reasonable to assume that as soon as taxes were cut (sending revenues down), budget pressures forced a tax increase — a perfect case for observing the ups and downs of a political-economic cycle.

Israel's political situation is also interesting for this study. To begin with, one party (Mapai, later the major component of the Alignment) was at the center of all cabinet coalitions for eight consecutive terms from 1948 to 1977. During most of this period, the party's dominance was practically unchallenged (Shapiro 1980). Would a dominant party manipulate small policy details to make a relatively secure re-election even more so? A dominant party is likely to develop a strong, long-range perspective on policy calculations, hence it would appear reasonable to expect that it would avoid "stop and go" policies. On the other hand, Mapai did possess the means for harnessing policy to political interests: seasoned politicians

*The period from 1948 to 1955 is a very important one, but available statistical data are unreliable and incomplete.

and a well-developed party machine (Medding 1972; Shapiro 1980).

The political scene changed in a way that must have affected both the need and the capability to manipulate policy. In 1965 Ben-Gurion, the party and the nation's most revered leader, left Mapai and ran for office at the head of a new list. Mapai was split, the machine shaken. In the 1965 elections, there was more reason than ever before to use economic policy to safeguard the party's strength. The party machine, as Shapiro informs us, was quickly rehabilitated by Pinhas Sapir well before the elections and " . . . when Sapir became head of the machine, he used his control of the Ministry of Finance to restore the machine's ability to hand out benefits" (Shapiro 1980, p. 32). The 1965 election should stand out as a campaign in which the incumbent administration initiated popular changes in tax policy. As it turned out, Mapai won the election and Ben-Gurion's party joined a long list of splinter parties which could be invited to join a coalition but would not be in a position to form one.

Though Mapai retained its electoral dominance, the party was weakened. The machine was dealt a final blow when Mapai united with two smaller parties (Rafi and Ahdut Haavoda) to form the Israel Labor Party. According to Shapiro, the 1973 elections are the landmark for the machine's final disappearance. The machine was an essential political apparatus for keeping in touch with party supporters at the grass roots level and hence an important source of information and support for policy maneuvers. The party was further weakened by the leadership crisis ignited by the events of the 1973 war. Veteran Mapai leaders were discredited and forced to resign (Gutmann 1980). A complete overhaul in party leadership brought in newcomers who had little or no tutoring in performing as cabinet ministers. The newcomers were a heterogenous group and, as, Shapiro put it, "Many of them had no political experience and did not know the workings of the political machinery . . . " (Shapiro 1980, p. 33). Governmental decision-making processes must have been affected by these upheavals. Gutmann summarizes the change thus: "The accession of the cabinet formed by Itzhak Rabin in June 1974 after Golda Meir's resignation denoted at the time the final political demise of the first generation of the

Founding Fathers . . . it also meant the displacement of most of those who constituted the second or intermediary political generation . . . " (Gutmann 1980, p. 274).

Though the transfer of power was smooth and orderly, the new government was soon rocked by disclosures of scandals. The machine was no longer at the leaders' disposal to prevent leakage of embarrassing information. The combination of these factors — a disintegrated machine, discredited veteran leaders and inexperienced persons in cabinet posts — would make it most difficult to initiate any strategy that requires fine tuning of complex legislative procedures. The party would not be in a position to take proper care of its interests during an election campaign.

The 1977 election was perhaps the most dramatic political event in Israel's history. The Alignment lost and the Likud came out of three decades in opposition to form the governing coalition (Arian 1980). Insofar as the present analysis is concerned, it is essential that we ascertain whether this result was expected by party leaders. According to Arian, the Alignment campaign strategy was based on the assumption that it would return to power. In his own words:

> While the direction of the 1977 election was no surprise, the timing and the intensity of the Likud's victory were unexpected . . . It was widely believed by pollsters, politicians, reporters and the man in the street that the end would *not* come in 1977 . . . observers tended to analyze events in terms of their preconceptions, being selective with the data and insensitive to what was taking place (Arian, *"The Israeli Electorate 1977"* in Arian (ed.) 1980, p. 255).

Polls taken shortly before the election indicated that the Likud would win, but this shocking news came too late to launch preventive measures. Thus, despite the dramatic nature of the election results, we should expect to find nothing out of the ordinary in policy initiatives.

The first three years of the new Likud government were troubled, ripe with in-house intense conflicts, policy bumbling, frequent resignations and reshuffles at cabinet level (Sharkansky & Radian 1981). The Likud coalition appeared to be unable to govern. Public opinion polls taken as early as two years before the elections (scheduled for 1981) revealed that the Likud would most certainly be defeated. The alarm was sounded early enough to harness economic policy to an election strategy. The pattern of policy initiatives introduced in 1981 should therefore compare favorably with that of 1965.

Political change should be reflected in the political-economic cycle. In times of political turmoil, economic policies can be expected to fluctuate wildly. A strong dominant party, on the other hand, would be capable of maintaining a stable policy over a long period of time, making adjustments in a gradual, incremental fashion.

The timing of elections is another variable to be considered. Fixed dates facilitate the planning and implementation of election strategies. When the election date can be changed at short notice, there may not be enough time to shift policy in the desired direction. Tufte found that "The cycle appeared with nearly equal frequency in countries with flexible election dates and in countries with fixed dates" (Tufte 1978, p. 14). This does not appear reasonable: Suppose an election is held two years and not merely a few months before the end of a term. When this happens, as it did in 1951 and again in 1961, the incumbent administration might be caught with the post-election side of the policy cycle during a pre-election period. In other words, had the government introduced tax increases after the elections in 1949 and 1959, it would have been forced to face the voters in the 1951 and 1961 elections with the costs rather than the benefits of an election year, a sobering lesson which might cure the temptation to tamper with policy. The normal parliamentary term in Israel is four years, although elections can be held at any time before the end of the term if the Knesset votes to do so. There are also provisions that allow elections to be held after the end of a term, as in 1973, when elections were postponed as a result of the war.

If elections influnce policy, then their impact should show up in policy initiatives introduced before and after elections as well as in quantitative indicators of policy outcomes. Every tax amendment goes through a lengthy legislative process before it becomes law. Tracing the timing of major policy initiatives will shed light on how the political economic cycle actually works. Is it true that decisions to raise taxes are generally introduced after elections and well before the new round is held, while decisions to cut taxes are introduced within, say, twelve months of election day (owing to the short duration of Israeli political campaigns)?

What constitutes a proper indicator of policy outcome? If we accept the assumption that voters are rational and calculating, then the correct indicator would be the ratio of net tax burden in the GNP or the national income. The net tax burden is calculated by subtracting transfer payments from total tax revenues. Few taxpayers think in these terms; the tax burden for most people is the amount that appears monthly on their payslips and the price tags of goods purchased (for indirect taxes). Assuming that most voters pay attention to the taxes with the highest visibility and rarely make complex calculations to determine the amount of taxes they paid in economic terms, the politically "correct" indicator for policy outcomes should be the crudest — the ratio of tax revenues in national income. A more sophisticated set of indicators could be developed based on the assumption that a significant part of tax politics involves shifting tax burdens from one group to another. Thus, instead of considering a representative voter, we should define voter groups which might be helped or hurt by certain tax policies.

The simple thesis concerning the cyclical pattern of policy outcome is that the ratio of tax revenues would drop before and rise after elections. The effect of elections could also show up as a break in the annual rate of change in the tax-national income ratio. For example, if a rate of annual increase in the ratio slows down during an election year, this could signify the presence of an election effect on policy.

It is necessary to analyze individual policy decisions in addition to macro-policy outcomes. Politically salient decisions which received wide publicity may leave little or no trace on aggregate data. The government may succeed in creating an image of a tax cut even when the real tax burden is going up. It is also quite reasonable to expect that the oucomes of a number of election year policy decisions would collide with one another. When wages and transfer payments are increased, taxpayers are pushed to higher income brackets, where the marginal tax rate is higher. A policy which aims at gaining popularity with voters might have an adverse effect on popularity in other policy areas.

We may now proceed to examine the findings, beginning with the quantitative indicators of policy outcomes. The following section presents an analysis of annual changes in the ratio of tax revenues in national income.

Findings

The ratio of total tax collections in national income displays an overall pattern of increase. At first glance, there does not appear to be any cyclical movement related to election dates. However, a closer look at Figure 1 discloses a number of breaks in the pattern: these disruptions — a drop in the ratio lasting one year — occurred in 1956, 1965, 1968, 1972, 1975, 1977, 1978, 1980 and in 1981; of these 1965, 1977 and 1981 are election years.

Two of these elections were critical in the sense that the incumbent party was confronted with a serious possibility of losing. Nevertheless, four election campaigns had no effect on the ratio's upward crawl. The "total tax" indicator examined above represents an aggregate of a large number of taxes and compulsory loans; it is therefore quite possible that important cyclical effects in some of these components are washed out when different taxes are combined in one figure. Figure 2 indicates the ratios of direct and indirect taxes. Looking first at indirect taxes, we observe a cyclical movement within the overall trend, whose direction does not generally correspond with the expected timing of "down before, up after." The pattern of increase in the ratio is disturbed for the first time in 1956, a post-election year. In 1961, the ratio changes direction and begins to drop, reaching a nadir in 1967. Then, the trend reverses and the ratio begins to rise, reaching a peak in 1976. Two elections (1969, 1973) were held during this period with no effect on the trend. The pattern of annual increase was interrupted twice during this period; in 1970 (a post-election year) and again in 1975 (a mid-term year). Both cases are contrary to the cycle theory; the ratio dropped when it "ought to" have shown a sharp increase. A new policy pattern is established in 1976; from this point

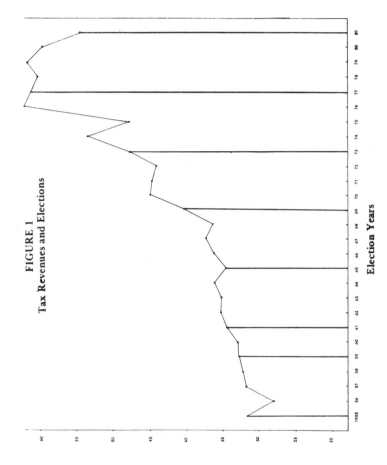

FIGURE 1
Tax Revenues and Elections

Total Tax Revenues/National Income

Election Years

Source: Bank of Israel Annual Reports;
State of Revenue Administration Annual Reports

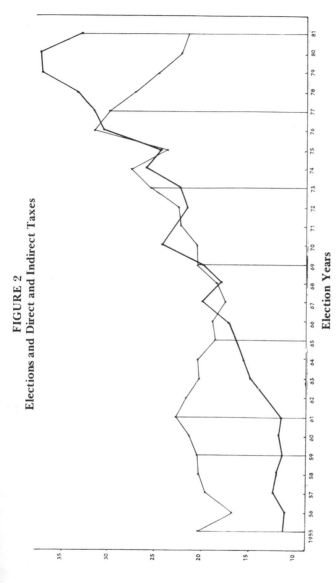

FIGURE 2
Elections and Direct and Indirect Taxes

Taxes/National Income

Election Years

Legend: — Indirect Taxes
          — Direct Taxes

Source: Bank of Israel Annual Reports;
State Revenue Administration Annual Reports

until the end of the period, the ratio of indirect taxes in the national income decreases. The reversal in long-range policy was initiated at a politically convenient time (one year before elections). However, even though the ratio moved downward in 1977 and 1981, we may not attribute this drop to election effects (the ratio is on the decline in non-election years as well as in election years).

The direct tax indicator comprises revenues from income taxes and compulsory loans. A pattern of increase in this ratio is dominant throughout the entire period, broken by several drops and sharp increases. The ratio dropped seven times, of which three cases were in election years (1959, 1961, 1981), two in pre-election years (1968, 1972) and two in mid-term years. Four election campaigns which had no effect on the trend were conducted with rising rather than declining tax ratios. Only one of these campaigns can be explained away as a unique case in which the financing of a major war overpowered election year calculations.

A low ratio was expected for 1965 and 1981, as these were critical elections. The ratio did not drop before, during or shortly after the 1965 election; it therefore appears reasonable to conclude that on the basis of this indicator, the elections did not exert the expected pressure on tax policy. The second critical election did have the expected effect and the tax ratio dropped sharply. One possible explanation is that even this indicator is not sufficiently sharp to measure fine changes in policy. Another possibility is that differences in the respective incumbent parties and the operating personalities are responsible for differences in election strategies.

More conclusive results may be obtained by further disagregating our indicators. Two taxes have been selected for this purpose: income tax collected from wage earners and sales tax. The former is important as the tax is collected through a PAYE (pay as you earn) method; hence lags in collection are negligible. This is not the case, however, regarding companies and self-employed taxpayers, who pay only a portion (often not much more than 50%) of their liability on a current year basis. Thus, the general income tax indicator may be misleading, as it contains tax payments on income earned in previous years.

Figure 3 displays the ratio of income tax paid by wage

FIGURE 3
Elections and Income Tax Collected from Wage Earners

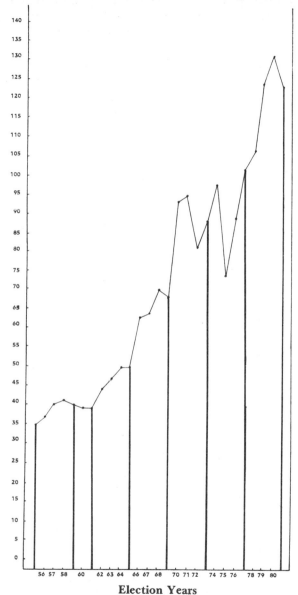

Source: Bank of Israel Annual Reports;
State of Revenue Administration Annual Reports

earners in the national income. This graph is entirely different from the one relating to total income tax collections.

The period extending from 1955 to 1969 is characterized by mild changes from one year to the next. Sharp changes are very frequent in the second period — from 1969 to 1981. The overall trend of increase in the ratio is maintained throughout this period, accompanied by a number of sharp drops followed immediately by equally sharp increases.

The first period may be neatly divided into three subsections, each sharing common characteristics — a four-year period in which the ratio increases followed by one year in which it falls slightly — namely 1955—1959, 1961—1965 and 1965—1969. The years in which the ratio falls (1959, 1965, 1969) are all election years. During a 15-year period, the ratio did not fall even once in a *non-*election year, nor did it *rise* in an election year. It is interesting to note that a different pattern emerges in the three-year period 1959—1961; this is the only case where the upward trend was not resumed in the post election year, nor did it drop in 1961 when an election was held. The 1961 election took place long before the end of the term: the Prime Minister submitted his resignation on January 31, 1961 and elections were held eight months later on August 15. The government was not caught with the wrong side of the policy cycle, even though the election was held in a year that was to be in mid-term. Mapai was then undergoing one of the most intensive political conflicts in the history of the country — the "Lavon Affair" — (Medding 1972; Eisenstadt 1967). This was a period when economic policy was pushed to the back burner.

In conclusion, during this 15-year period, the tax ratio in any non-election year was higher than that of the previous year and those of election years were lower or equal to those of the respective previous years. It is rather unlikely that this connection between low ratio years and elections is accidental. Furthermore, the second phase of an election-economic cycle is present as well: the upward trend was always resumed immediately following elections. Wage earners gained only brief respite from the constant growth in the tax ratios during election years.

The second period does not fit as neatly into this pattern. Only one of the three years in which the ratio dropped —

1972, 1975 and 1981 — was an election year. The decrease in 1972, more than a year before the election, may be interpreted as part of a long-range strategy to boost the government's popularity. Why, then, did it rise during the election year itself? Income tax rates were reduced and personal deductions and minimum taxable income increased early in 1973. Nevertheless, tax revenues went up. According to Bank of Israel analysts, tax revenues soared despite the reductions in rates due to the fact that the government relaxed restraints on incomes. The policy initiatives taken early in 1973 fit well the thesis of the political-economic linkage, even though policy outcomes seem to negate it.

A major income tax reform was introduced in 1975, which may account for the sharp fall in the tax ratio. The reform lowered tax rates, abolished hitherto untaxed fringe benefits and linked tax brackets to the cost-of-living index (Ben-Porath and Bruno 1977). The ratio resumes its ascent in 1976 and continues to climb right through the 1977 election, the only one which had no moderating effect upon the tax ratio's upward crawl. It so happens that 1977 was the first election campaign in which the Alignment was led by a new elite. In the 1981 election, the tax ratio dropped just as it did in all previous elections, albeit at a somewhat sharper rate.

The post-election years fit the "up after" pattern rather well. The ratio shoots up sharply after the 1969 election, attaining its steepest increase of the entire period. A milder increase is found in the years following the 1973 and 1977 elections.

The wage-earners' indicator provided the best evidence yet for the existence of a political-economic cycle in critical as well as "routine" elections. Both elements of the hypothesis are validated: the ratio descends before elections and ascends after elections. Not even once did the descent last for more than a year. Thus, despite the fact that the annual changes in the ratio follow a pattern of increase, we may say that the increase observed in post-election years is at least partly a result of pre-election decisions.

Annual changes in the tax ratio in the period following the 1969 election are more dramatic than in the preceding period. Instability in policy outcomes may be a result of turmoil in government. Note that the period of instability in policy outcomes begins when Mapai's dominance declines. The new elite which came to power in Mapai either could not — or would not — lead policy in the ups and downs of the political cycle. Judging from experience with the 1981 election, it appears that the Likud is both capable and willing to turn the political-economic cycle in the "right" direction.

The sales tax ratio shown in Figure 4 exhibits a pattern of annual changes quite different from the combined "indirect taxes" indicator (see Figure 2). This ratio displays a cyclical movement with sharp peaks and nadirs, although there does not appear to be any "up after-down before" pattern. One interesting observation is that three out of the four drops in the ratio occur after elections; only in one case does the ratio begin a decline in a year preceding an election. the ratio decreased occur after elections; only in one case does the ratio begin a decline in a year preceding an election. The ratio decreased slightly in 1956 (after an election year), then climbed steadily for eight years, slowed down in 1965 (election year) and dropped sharply after the elections. The ratio decreases again in 1970 (1969 was an election year). There is practically no increase during the election year 1973, representing a pronounced deviation from the pattern established in previous years. The ratio begins to rise rather sharply, reaching a peak in 1976, and then declining until the end of the period covered in this study.

This pattern raises suspicions: could there be a time lag effect, so that lower ratios recorded for post-election years are the result of decisions made during the election campaign? The answer may be found by examining policy initiatives introduced in 1955, 1965, and 1976. There was no significant change in sales tax rates in 1955; in 1965, the government introduced a series of deflationary measures, which led to a full-scale recession and massive unemployment (Greenwald 1972). This policy was announced after the election. The recession was responsible for declining sales tax revenues. The government did not take measures to protect this source of revenue, as an increase in sales tax might have worsened the recession (Bank of Israel Annual Report, 1966). Sales tax rates were increased after the elections in 1969, yet the ratio fell nonetheless. In 1976, the government introduced measures for economic restraint, introduced the Value Added

FIGURE 4

Elections and the Sales Tax

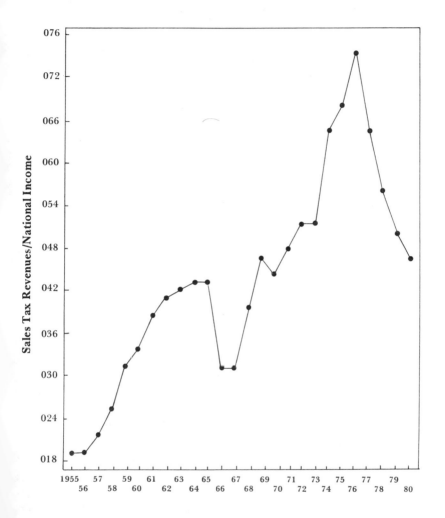

Election Years

Source: Bank of Israel Annual Reports
State Revenue Administration Annual Reports

Tax and abolished a number of sales taxes. This major shift in policy explains the steady and sharp decline in the sales tax ratio which started in 1977.

Thus far, the decline in the ratio recorded for post-election years was a result of unpopular economic decisions initiated after elections. Hence the politics of elections does effect economic policy. One interesting lesson to be learned from this finding is that linkages between policies may cerate unpopular results in one area when popular measures are implemented in another.

Policy Decisions and Elections

Tax policy is hard to pin down and mapping changes therein is even more difficult. Policy comprises legislation, regulations and a horde of administrative rules, few of which remain stable for long, as there is a constant stream of changes, amendments and additions. Tracking down these changes over a period of nearly thirty years has proved to be a mind-boggling task well beyond the boundaries of this paper. To render this task somewhat more manageable, I decided to limit my investigation to principal changes in legislation in income, sales and travel tax. Every change in legislation from 1955 on was marked with a plus or minus sign, indicating direction (increase or decrease), but not magnitude. The condensed data thus produced enables an overview of policy initiatives along a time scale (see Table 1). We may pose the following questions: 1. Are tax cuts clustered in the twelve-months period preceding elections? 2. Are tax increases introduced after elections? 3. Does an election policy cycle exist, i.e. tax cuts before elections and tax increases introduced shortly thereafter?

Most of the changes concerning wage earners involve reductions (exceptions are in 1967, 1968, 1973, 1975, 1978 and 1979). This makes it difficult to attribute tax cuts to elections. The only basis for such a link can be the fact that although tax cuts are distributed across the entire period, they show up in every election year except 1973 and 1977. Exercising extra caution I admit that this may be a coincidence. There is a trend of tax reductions due to the fact

Table 1: Elections and Policy Initiatives

Elections	Year	Income Tax Wage Earner	Income Tax Self-Employed & Companies	Sales Tax	Travel Tax
Jul. 26, 1955	1955[1]	-(4)	+(4)		
	1955[2]				
	1956	-(4)	+(5)	+(5)	+(5)(12)
	1957	-(4)		+(10)	-(6)(8)
	1958	-(4)	-	+	-(4)
Dec. 3, 1959	1959[1]	-(4)		+(9)	
	1959[2]				
	1960	-		+(3)(4)	
Aug. 15, 1961	1961[1]	-(6)	+		
	1961[2]				+(10)
	1962	-		-(2)(4)	+(1)-(2)
	1963				-
	1964	-(1)(5)(10)	+		+(2)
Nov. 2, 1965	1965[1]	-		+(4)	+(9)
	1965[2]				-
	1966		+(4)	+(2)(4)	-
	1967	+(7)		-(8)	-(6)
	1968	+ -(5)(6)	+		-
Oct. 28, 1969	1969[1]	-			-
	1969[2]		+		
	1970		+(4)	+(8)(9)	+
	1971	-	+	+	
	1972	-	+	+	
Dec. 13, 1973	1973[1]	(+)(11)	+(11)	-(4)+(11)	
	1973[2]				
	1974	-	+	+(2)(7)(11)	
	1975	+(6)	+(12)	+(9)	
	1976				+(3)
May 17, 1977	1977[1]				
	1977[2]			-(10)	-(10)
	1978	+(4)-(10)	-		
	1979	+(4)-(10)	-	-(4)(8)	
	1980	-(4)	-		
June 30, 1981	1981[1]	-(3)		-(2)(3)(4)	
	1981[2]				

Legend: ( ) = month; - = descent; + = ascent; 1 = before election; 2 = after election.

that income tax rates were doubled during the War of Independence and rendered steeply progressive. Inflation, economic growth and increase in real wages pushed taxpayers into higher tax brackets and eroded take-home pay (Morag 1967). The government came under intense pressure to lower the tax burden. Tax reductions were required periodically merely to maintain a certain pre-determined tax burden. This accounts for what may appear as a contradiction — a trend of increase in the share of taxes in national income and a trend of tax cuts.

Tax increases (few as they were) were introduced in non-election years; only 1973 stand out as an exception, easily explained by the fact that the Yom Kippur War created economic pressures that forced the government to reverse the course of tax reductions initiated in 1972. The "down-before/up-after" cycle does not exist here, since increases in taxation of wage earners were automatically achieved when tax reductions were not instituted or when reductions were modest compared to the rate of inflation or economic growth.

There is a sharp difference between wage earners and the self-employed, wherein the pattern of change for the latter is one of increase. This pattern was reversed after the Likud came to power in 1977; from then on, reductions were instituted annually. On a number of occasions, income tax was tightened for the self-employed and companies as it was relaxed for wage earners. Furthermore, a number of increases were introduced in election years (1955, 1961 and 1973). Again, exercising caution, we may suggest that Labor governments attempted to placate wage earning voters at the expense of the self-employed and companies. The latter reciprocated by massive evasion (Ben-Porath & Bruno 1977).

The sales tax was increased more often than it was decreased. Decisions to increase the tax were generally introduced after elections (exceptions: 1959, 1965 and 1973). There are almost no tax cuts in pre-election periods. In 1973, sales tax rates were reduced when the government implemented the recommendations of a reform committee to replace sales tax with Value Added Tax. In 1981, the process of shifting from one tax to the other was intensified as significant tax reductions were made. Although these cuts were part of a long-range process initiated earlier by an Alignment government, they were introduced at a politically convenient time — just a few months before the election. The sales tax does not yield the "down-before/up-after" pattern of policy changes because it was used during the 1950s and 1960s as a counter-balance when necessary currency devaluations were postponed.

The travel tax is a sort of "nuisance tax;" changes in its rate would receive wide publicity and win the government popularity, particularly among middle-class voters. Table 1 shows that the majority of changes in this tax were made in non-election years (both increase and decrease); we may therefore declare it free of election effects.

Conclusion

Is there a political economic cycle in tax policy in Israel? A connection between elections and policy has been found, although not of the simple "down-before/up-after" type. The aggregate indicators of policy outcomes show that elections, as a rule, do not interfere with long-range policy trends. Tax ratios were lower in some — but not all — election years. Several of the interruptions in the upward crawl in ratios occurred in election years. More conclusive findings were obtained by disaggregating policy indicators to individual taxes.

Revenues collected at source from wage earners show the greatest sensitivity to elections. Wage earners benefited from every election, but the respite they gained from the constant increase in the tax ratio never went beyond the election year. A similar analysis of the sales tax unveils an inverse political-economic cycle, with revenues dropping in post instead of pre-election years.

The ratio of tax revenues in the GNP and the national income is affected by numerous factors, such as: economic growth, wages and prices, foreign currency exchange rates and a variety of administrative actions. Each of these factors may in turn be affected by the politics of elections, although not in the same direction. Collection and enforcement activities are likely to be less vigorous before elections and become more aggressive once they are over. No one will instruct tax officials to be more tolerant of tax evasion, but seasoned bureaucrats will not embarrass their minister by launching a collection drive in the last months of an election campaign. Thus, revenues may drop before elections and rise shortly afterwards — *as if* by magic — without any corresponding change in policy. Wages are likely to increase in the period before elections, pushing up the ratio of tax revenues collected from wage earners. Economic growth and exchange rate policies will have a similar effect. As the government increases wages, expands credit and postpones a necessary devaluation to create comfortable economic conditions, its tax mechanisms will work in the opposite direction, skimming off part of the resources and channeling them back to the Treasury. Thus, some of the election-induced popular decisions will lose their attractiveness unless steps are taken to protect wages and profits from the tax bite. It is entirely possible that the government outsmarts its voters by taking with its tax arm what it has handed out with the subsidy, wage, currency exchange and credit arms. This could serve as an explanation of an otherwise puzzling finding — rising tax ratios in election years.

The symbolic element in policy decisions played an important role in the elections of 1965, 1973 and 1981. Announcements of tax cuts were made a few months before election day. Nevertheless, the government found ways to make the most out of the pocketbook effect by instituting retroactive reductions or by cutting taxes (such as sales and customs duties) that have an immediate impact upon prices. No evidence was found of long-range planning directed at creating favorable economic conditions during election campaigns, as no one is sufficiently capable of doing so. No conclusive evidence has been found to support the thesis that critical elections have a stronger impact on policy than "routine" elections. Although highly unusual policy changes were introduced in 1965, quantitative indicators do not allow us to single out this particular year from other election years.

Finally, elections in Israel had a moderating effect on the upward crawl in the share of taxes in the GNP and the national income. During the period of political stability, which ended roughly in 1969, annual changes in tax ratios were mild. The government succeeded in maintaining a stable direction in policy, introducing only minor adjustments in election years. Sharp changes in policy direction have been found to characterize the period of political instability. Further research is needed to determine whether the "stop and go" style of economic management is bred by elections as such, or by political weakness/inability to steer policy amidst the multitude of cross-pressures to which it is subjected.

BIBLIOGRAPHY

Arian, A. (ed.)
  1980a   *The Elections in Israel — 1977.* Jerusalem: Academic Press.

  1980b   "The Israeli Electorate, 1977." in: Arian, A. (ed.), 1980a, pp. 253-276.
Ben Porath, Y.
  1975   "The Years of Plenty and the Years of Famine — A Political Cycle?" *Kyklos* 28, pp. 400-403.
    and Bruno, M.
  1977   "The Political Economy of a Tax Reform — Israel 1975." *Journal of Public Economics* 7, pp. 285-307.
Edelman, M.
  1977   *Political Language.* New York: Academic Press.
Eisenstadt, S.N.
  1967.   *Israeli Society.* London: Weidenfeld and Nicolson.
Good, R.
  1968   "The Tax Burden in the United States and Other Countries." *Annals* 379, pp. 85–87.
Gutmann, E.
  1980   "Parliamentary Elites: Israel." in: Landau, J.M. *et al.* (eds.), *Electoral Politics in the Middle East.* London: Croom Helm, pp. 273-297.
Ginsburgh, B. and Michel, P.
  1980   "Random Timing of Elections and the Political Business Cycle." Discussion Paper 8043, Center for Operations Research and Econometrics, Université Catholique de Louvain.
Greenwald, C.S.
  1972   *Recession as a Policy Instrument: Israel 1965– 1969.* London: C. Hurst.

Golden, D.G. and Poterba, J.M.
1980   "The Price of Popularity: The Political Business Cycle Reexamined." *American Journal of Political Science* 24, 4, pp. 203-220.

Frey, B.S.
1978   "Political-Economic Models and Cycles." *Journal of Public Economics* 9, 2, pp. 203-220.
    and Schneider, F.
1978   "An Empirical Study of Politico-Economic Interaction in the United States." *Review of Economics and Statistics* 60.

Hibbs, D.A.
1981   "Economics and Politics in France: Economic Performance and Mass Political Support for Presidents Pompidou and Giscard d'Estaing." *European Journal of Political Research* 9, pp. 113-145.

Horowitz, D.
1972   *The Enigma of Economic Growth: A Case Study of Israel.* New York: Praeger.

Kinder, D.R. and Kiewiet, R.
1979   "Economic Discontent and Political Behavior." *American Journal of Political Science* 23, pp. 495-527.

Lindbeck, A.
1976   "Stabilization Policy in Open Economics with Endogenous Politicians." *American Economic Review* Papers and Proceedings 66, pp. 1-19.

Lindblom, C.E.
1977   *Politics and Markets.* New York: Basic Books.

Medding, P.Y.
1972   *Mapai in Israel.* Cambridge: Cambridge University Press.

Morag, A.
1967.   *Public Finance in Israel.* Jerusalem: Hebrew University Press.

Nordhaus, W.D.
1975   "The Political Business Cycle." *The Review of Economic Studies* 42, pp. 169-190.

Paldam, M.
  1979   "Is There an Election Cycle? A Comparative
            Study of National Accounts." *The Scandinavian
            Journal of Economics* 81, 2, pp. 323-342.
Shapiro, Y.
  1980   "The End of a Dominant Party System." in:
            Arian 1980a, pp. 23-38.
Sharkansky, I. and Radian, A.
  1982   "Changing Domestic Policy: 1977–1981." in:
            Freedman, O.R. (ed.), *Israel In The Begin Era.*
            New York: Praeger.
Stein, H.
  1969   *The Fiscal Revolution in America.* Chicago:
            University of Chicago Press.
Tufte, E.R
  1978   *Political Control of the Economy.* Princeton
            (New Jersey): Princeton University Press.

10

FOLLOWING THE RACE: PROPAGANDA AND
ELECTORAL DECISION

*Dan Caspi**

One of the most outstanding features of the Tenth Knesset election campaign was its high degree of professionalization (Caspi & Eyal 1983). Predictably, this involved a significant increase in expenditures by the various parties in the course of the campaign. Thus the campaign was not only more professional but also more expensive than all its predecessors, a fact also borne out by the State Comptroller's Report of March 15, 1982. This report relates only to the one hundred days which preceded the elections and does not consider lists which did not attain the required minimum votes, nor branch organizations or affiliates which worked on behalf of their respective parties during the campaign. According to this report, the ten relevant parties spent more than IS 180 million (IS 10 = US $1.00) during the designated period of time. Five of them — the Likud, Alignment, Techiya, Telem and Tami — overstepped the legal limit then in effect by more than IS 80 million. This sum is actually even greater if we consider expenses of branch organizations as well (*Haaretz,* March 16, 1982).

The more expensive election campaigns become, the more significant the question of their efficacy and influence — particularly with regard to propaganda — upon voters' electoral intentions. The importance of this issue is also underscored by the fact that since the pioneer research of Lazarsfeld *et al.* (1944), undertaken during the era of radio — a possible reason for its having played down the role of the mass media in shaping electoral preferences — the subject has never ceased

*Lecturer of Political Science and Communications at The Hebrew University of Jerusalem. Data for this article were gathered in a cooperative research effort with Prof. E. Gutmann and Dr. A. Diskin, funded by the Konrad Adenauer Stiftung of Bonn (Federal Republic of Germany).

to be of interest to researchers (Smith 1982) and to produce findings which often contradict one another. Of the eight common approaches to investigating mass media influence (Katz 1980), "uses and gratifications" (Blumler & Katz 1974), is the one most appreciated by electoral researchers in Israel. We too have adopted this approach, not only because it enables comparison of data with findings accumulated in previous election campaigns and location of trends and changes in the Israeli public's exposure patterns but also because this approach — like later ones developed during the television era — restores credit denied to the mass media in earlier studies.

Hence our major concerns will be: Why and to what extent is the public exposed to political party propaganda? Who consents and who refuses to be exposed? Who utilizes electoral propaganda messages and what do voters derive from exposure to them? Did the campaign aid voters in deciding how to vote? Or was the converse the case — did the timing of voters' decisions affect exposure patterns?

Motivations Behind Exposure to Election Propaganda

The answers to the above questions and others considered in this article are based upon a survey undertaken in mid-June 1981, towards the end of the campaign (some two weeks before the elections).[1] These statistics indicate that exposure to party propaganda has increased and that changes have taken place in the motivation behind such exposure. On the other hand, certain doubts are again raised about the efficacy of propaganda — particularly regarding propagandists' ability to focus messages upon desired target populations. Nearly two-thirds (60%) of the respondents admitted that they were indeed interested in the campaign and followed it in the mass media — the press, radio and television (see Table 1). However, the campaign was of special interest to those who had already decided how to vote; about half of the undecided and those who refused to answer, as compared with two-thirds of voters for one of the two major parties — the Likud or the Alignment — declared that they followed the election campaign in the media all or most of the time (Table 1a).

Table 1: Voters' Interest in Mass Media Coverage of the Election Campaign* — By Voting Intentions and Socio-Demographic Background (%)

DEGREE OF INTEREST IN FOLLOWING CAMPAIGN

	Always	Almost Always	Almost Never	Never	N	Sig.
TOTAL**	31	29	27	13	1,111	
a. *Voting Intentions*						
Likud	37	28	24	11	408	.00
Alignment	33	31	29	7	272	
Agudat Israel	25	25	18	32	28	
NRP	19	35	27	19	37	
Undecided	17	31	36	16	140	
No answer	29	21	24	26	80	
b. *Education*						
Up to 8 years	32	23	27	18	218	n.s.
9 −12 years	32	30	27	11	585	
13+ years	29	31	26	15	282	
c. *Age*						
20−29	27	33	30	10	330	.02
30−39	29	29	29	13	252	
40−54	36	28	23	13	247	
55+	34	25	23	18	259	
d. *Religious Observance*						
Religious	33	26	19	23	132	.01
Traditional	32	29	28	11	695	
Non-religious	29	28	29	15	254	
e. *Ethnic Background* (birthplace/ parents' birthplace)						
Israel/Israel	34	31	20	14	70	.02
Israel/Asia-Africa	32	36	25	7	183	
Israel/Europe-America	23	26	36	16	191	
Asia-Africa	35	24	27	14	301	
Europe-America	31	30	24	15	338	
f. *Year of Immigration to Israel*						
Israel-born	28	31	29	12	444	.003
Before 1948	40	19	20	21	156	
1948−1967	32	28	28	12	424	
1968 and later	28	39	20	13	75	

*Question: To what extent do you follow the campaign through the newspapers, radio and television?

**Includes all parties.

Voters for the religious parties also take less of an interest in the campaign, but for different reasons. They are either barely exposed to the mass media at all, as explained below, or maintain a firm predetermined electoral preference and therefore are not especially interested in the overall race. No significant differences have been observed in this respect with regard to level of education (1 b), age (1 c) or number of years in Israel (1 f). Differences were revealed, however, between Israel-born children of European/American-born parents (i.e. those from Christian countries — Ashkenazim) and those of Asian/African parents (Sephardim): 52% of the former and 32% of the latter declared that they take little interest in the campaign. Similar differences were not noted among foreign-born members of the same ethnic groups (1 e).

Doubts regarding propagandists' success in shaping electoral preferences also arise when we examine voters' susceptibility to such influence. More than two-thirds (70%) of the respondents said that the campaigns neither helps nor hinders their choice of whom to support. The remainder are almost equally divided, with a slight tendency favoring the campaign — 17% claim that it helps and 13% that it hinders (Table 2).

In this case as well, we note the paradoxical situation regarding undecided voters and those who refuse to answer: these very people, towards whom the propaganda may well be directed, frequently complain that it hinders their decision (18% and 24%, respectively, as compared with 9% and 16% of Likud and Alignment voters).

Some researchers will undoubtedly interpret these results in a positive light and claim that the undecided complain because the propaganda does not allow them to continue wallowing in their doubts. It disturbs their inner peace and forces them to make a decision. However, this interpretation is disproved when we compare this finding to other survey results, as detailed below, which indicate consistently that it is the undecided — more than any other group of voters — who avoid being exposed to the campaign in general and to propaganda in particular.

Once again, voters for the religious parties, particularly Agudat Israel, are shown to be different from other voters; the vast majority claim that the campaign neither helps nor hinders them, perhaps because their decision has already been made (2 a). Voters who differ in terms of education (2 b), length of time in Israel (2 f) and religious observance (2 d) do not differ appreciably in their susceptibility to the campaign's contribution in shaping electoral preferences. However, such susceptibility is inversely proportional to age (2 c) — that is, more younger voters (21%) than older ones (10% of those aged 55+) appreciate the aid of the campaign. Parents from Islamic countries and their Israel-born children exhibit a greater tendency than their Ashkenazic counterparts to appreciate the aid of the campaign; 24% of voters born in Asia/Africa as compared with 11% of those born in Europe/America expressed a positive evaluation of the election campaign (2 e). Note that this difference is preserved among their children as well (22% vs. 10%, respectively; children of Israel-born parents tend to think like their Oriental peers.

The more positive evaluation of the campaign among young people and Sephardim (parents and children alike) may also explain the varying degrees of readiness among Alignment and Likud voters: 26% of the latter and only 11% of the former estimate that the election campaign aids them (2 a). Likud voters, characterized more by a young age and Oriental ethnic origins (see Peres & Shemer in this volume), rarely complain that the campaign disturbs them (9% vs. 16% for Alignment voters).

The main party propaganda efforts were invested in nightly television propaganda broadcasts. The law allots a certain minimum amount of broadcast time to each party, with additional time in accordance with each party's current representation in the Knesset. Surveys indicated that more than 75% of the voting public watched these broadcasts during the 1981 election campaign, far more than those who did so during the previous (1977) elections (Elizur & Katz 1980). Apparently, the division of broadcasts by the two large parties into three segments each evening prevented selective exposure [2]: only 1% of the respondents indicated that they watched only the messages of the parties they supported and another 1% declared they watched only those of rival parties. Nearly two-thirds claimed that they watched the broadcasts of all parties. This high viewing rate may be the result of the mixed format, the "broadcast cocktail": a Likud spot following an Alignment one and vice versa. Thus viewers could not

Table 2: Voters' Evaluation of the Campaign's Contribution to Their Electoral Decision* — By Voting Intentions and By Voting Intentions and Socio-Demographic Background (%)

	Very Helpful	Helpful	No Help No Hindrance	Hindrance	Considerable Hindrance	N	Sig.
TOTAL**	4	13	70	9	4	1,111	
a. Voting Intentions							
Likud	6	20	66	7	2	384	.00
Alignment	4	7	74	12	4	259	
Agudat Israel	4	—	96	—	—	24	
NRP	0	7	84	10	0	31	
Undecided	0	11	65	15	9	124	
No answer	6	10	67	11	7	73	
b. Education							
Up to 8 years	5	17	68	9	1	198	n.s.
9–12 years	3	13	71	10	4	551	
13+ years	4	11	69	10	6	252	
c. Age							
20–29	5	16	68	10	1	305	.01
30–39	4	13	73	8	3	241	
40–54	4	14	69	10	5	230	
55+	1	9	71	11	7	228	
d. Religious Observance							
Religious	4	12	76	6	2	115	n.s.
Traditional	4	15	69	10	4	657	
Non-religious	3	9	71	12	5	226	

e. Ethnic Background (birthplace/parents' birthplace)

Israel/Israel	2	16	74	5	3	61	.00
Israel/Asia-Africa	6	16	67	10	1	177	
Israel/Europe-America	2	8	77	10	2	176	
Asia-Africa	5	19	66	8	3	279	
Europe-America	2	9	70	12	7	307	

f. Year of Immigration to Israel

Israel-born	4	13	73	9	2	414	.10
Before 1948	3	8	71	9	9	12	
1948–1967	4	15	67	10	4	295	
1968 and later	3	15	68	11	3	66	

*Question: To what extent does the campaign help or hinder you in deciding how to vote?

**Includes all parties.

develop selective exposure to propaganda content; on the contrary, their exposure was extended to propaganda of other parties. Another 17% entirely avoid exposure to propaganda broadcasts and a small minority, 6%, does not watch television at all for ideological and technical reasons (lack of access to a receiver). In any event, the vast majority, nearly two-thirds of all respondents, did watch all broadcasts. The characteristics of this population resemble those determined with respect to overall interest in the campaign, thus explaining the statistical trends which constitute the profile of voters who are and are not exposed to television broadcasts (Table 3).

The difference between the two principal ethnic groups narrowed regarding this issue as well: some 80% of Sephardim and their Israel-born children tended to be somewhat more exposed to all or part of the broadcasts than their Ashkenazic counterparts (3 e), a difference apparently rooted in education. On the one hand, voters with only elementary education exhibit a greater tendency to watch television (3 b), while those with academic education tend more to avoid television and propaganda broadcasts. These differences overlap the educational differential profile of Likud and Alignment supporters, respectively. This time, however, the ethnic and educational differences are not translated into viewing patterns between the two parties, perhaps because there were no clear differences found in viewing habits among the various age groups (3 c) — a key parameter in the sociological profile of the electorate. On the contrary, among Likud and Alignement voters alike, the heavily exposed, selectively exposed and those who avoid exposure were about evenly divided (3 a). The major gap is between voters for the two large parties who are highly exposed to the broadcasts and the undecided and those who refuse to respond, who tend to watch less television and are thus less likely candidates for exposure.

There is a prominent difference — despite the relatively small dimensions of the respective voter populations — between NRP voters — whose viewing habits resemble those of supporters of the two major parties — and Agudat Israel supporters, a difference apparently rooted in the special attitudes of the ultra-Orthodox community to the concept of television. More than 75% of the Aguda supporters in our

Table 3: Patterns of Voters' Exposure to Television Propaganda Broadcasts* — By Voting Intentions and Socio-Demographic Background (%)

ELECTION BROADCASTS WATCHED

	All	Some	None	Don't Watch TV	N	Sig.
TOTAL**	61	15	17	6	1,111	.00
a. *Voting Intentions*						
Likud	65	15	16	5	400	
Alignment	65	16	17	2	268	
Agudat Israel	14	00	10	76	29	
NRP	65	16	11	8	37	
Undecided	54	22	21	3	140	
No answer	57	11	23	9	79	
b. *Education*						
Up to 8 years	62	17	16	6	220	.04
9—12 years	65	14	17	5	576	
13+ years	54	16	21	9	274	
c. *Age*						
20—29	64	15	15	6	322	n.s.
30—39	59	17	19	5	249	
40—54	63	16	14	6	245	
55+	60	12	21	8	257	
d. *Religious Observance*						
Religious	53	5	15	26	131	.00
Traditional	65	16	15	4	691	
Non-religious	55	17	26	3	243	
e. *Ethnic Background* (birthplace/ parents' birthplace)						
Israel/Israel	63	13	16	9	70	.03
Israel/Asia-Africa	68	13	18	1	182	
Israel/Europe-America	52	19	19	10	185	
Asia-Africa	63	17	13	7	297	
Europe-America	61	13	20	6	335	
f. *Year of Immigration to Israel*						
Israel-born	61	16	18	6	437	n.s.
Before 1948	62	7	24	7	135	
1948—1967	61	17	15	7	419	
1968 and later	66	15	15	4	74	

*Question: Do you watch television election propaganda broadcasts?

** Includes all parties.

sample do not watch television at all, as they consider it to be an "unclean" device which adversely affects sacred religious values. Indeed, up to the elections for the Tenth Knesset, Agudat Israel boycotted this medium, trading its allotted propaganda slot to the NRP in return for time on the radio, which is an acceptable medium in Israel's ultra-Orthodox community. This time, however, political needs — i.e. a desire to increase potential support and appeal to voters whose views lie halfway between those of the NRP and of Agudat Israel — compelled leaders of the latter party to utilize that despised device which is banned from the Ortho-dox home. In order to settle internal dissonance, the broad-casts were sponsored by a supporting group affiliated with the party, ABA (Hebrew acronym of "Citizens for Aguda"), which included party loyalists who were not necessarily part of the ultra-Orthodox community. Survey results indicate that a small minority of Aguda supporters do violate the ban and watch television, including election broadcasts, thus justifying — *a posteriori* — the decision to produce them.

The trends noted above with respect to other parameters were in evidence here as well:

Although there is a high degree of exposure to propaganda broadcasts, their effectiveness in determining electoral preference is even more limited than that of the campaign as a whole: 78% of all respondents claimed that television propaganda broadcasts neither help nor hinder them in making their electoral decisions (Table 4).

The trends noted above with respect to other parameters were in evidence here as well:

1. Likud voters again tended to evaluate the contribution of the broadcasts positively — 16% as compared with 5% among Alignment supporters. Religious voters again con-sistently claimed that the broadcasts have no effect; this time, the difference between the NRP and Aguda supporters shrank to 86% vs. 91%, respectively (4 a). The undecided, more than any other group, tend to evaluate the broadcasts negatively.

2. Differences between the parties were again reflected in the socio-demographic profile of the voters. Sephardim of both generations, who tend to support the Likud, are also more inclined to assess the contribution of propaganda broad-casts positively, while the Alignment-leaning foreign-born Ashkenazim tend to express reservations. Their children, as

Table 4: Voters' Evaluations of the Effect of Propaganda Broadcasts Upon Their Electoral Decisions* — By Voting Intentions and Socio-Demographic Background (%)

	Helpful	Not Helpful	Hindrance	N	Sig.
TOTAL**	10	78	12	1,111	
a. *Voting Intentions*					
Likud	16	74	10	391	.00
Alignment	5	81	14	259	
Agudat Israel	4	91	4	23	
NRP	6	86	8	36	
Undecided	9	72	19	132	
No answer	9	79	13	71	
b. *Education*					
Up to 8 years	13	77	10	209	n.s.
9—12 years	11	77	13	555	
13+ years	8	80	13	260	
c. *Age*					
20—29	11	79	11	315	n.s.
30—39	12	77	12	238	
40—54	10	78	12	236	
55+	8	77	15	237	
d. *Religious Observance*					
Religious	10	81	9	118	n.s.
Traditional	11	77	12	671	
Non-religious	7	79	15	230	
e. *Ethnic Background* (birthplace/ parents' birthplace)					
Israel/Israel	7	87	7	60	.02
Israel/Asia-Africa	11	77	12	180	
Israel/Europe-America	6	83	11	175	
Asia-Africa	15	76	9	291	
Europe-America	9	75	17	316	
f. *Year of Immigration to Israel*					
Israel-born	8	81	11	415	.02
Before 1948	5	81	15	123	
1948—1967	12	75	13	410	
1968 and later	19	71	10	70	

*Question: To what extent do the political propaganda broadcasts help or hinder you in deciding how to vote?

**Includes all parties.

well as those of Israel-born parents, adopt a more neutral stand, claiming that broadcasts neither help nor hinder their choice (4 e).

3.   New immigrants tend to assess broadcasts more positively, while veteran settlers either deny their value or are neutral (4 f).

4.   This time, no clear-cut differences were found among the various age, education and religious observance groups.

The widening gap between high exposure to propaganda broadcasts and a modest appraisal of their effectiveness may be rooted in the motivations for exposure — that is, a variety of motivations may impel voters towards exposure to broadcasts and each person may derive a different benefit from them. Our investigation of this phenomenon is based upon accumulated data pertaining to voter gratification and motivation for exposure to propaganda broadcasts over the past four election campaigns.

In the 1969 elections to the Seventh Knesset, the parties used television for the first time to recruit electoral support. At that time, candidates merely stood before the camera and addressed the voters, perhaps because they were still unaware of how to utilize the new medium and had virtually no advisors available to teach them. Gurevitch (1972) investigated viewer gratification by posing two principal questions: one to voters exposed to propaganda broadcasts and one to those who were not, asking each interviewee to explain why he sought or avoided exposure.

During the Eighth Knesset election campaign, which took place both before and after the Yom Kippur War, the parties agreed not to broadcast any specially-produced films and to limit themselves once again — despite the opportunities at their disposal — to speaking before the cameras (Cohen 1976).

The medium of television was only exploited to its fullest potential during the Ninth Knesset Elections of 1977; the two major parties — as well as some smaller ones with appropriate means — hired production companies and advisors to prepare propaganda films and broadcasts (Ansky 1978). Peri (1975) investigated viewer gratification in a manner similar to that of Gurevitch, as did Elizur and Katz (1980) for the Ninth Knesset elections. These questions were repeated in the 1981 survey for sake of comparison. We classified motivations for exposure into four main categories (see Tables 5 and 6): *Informative* — a desire to acquire varied particulars concerning leaders, parties and platforms (5, 1—3); *Reinforcement* of existing opinions (5, 4—5), *Entertainment* (5, 6—7) and *Technical Reasons* — such as "The TV was on anyway" or

Table 5: Reasons for Watching Television Propaganda Broadcasts* (%)

	1969	1973	1977	1981
Informative:				
1. To become familiar with political leaders	19	10	10	4
2. To become familiar with party platforms	18	21	23	19
3. To keep up-to-date on the overall political situation	11	14	11	14
TOTAL Informative	**48**	**45**	**44**	**37**
Reinforcement:				
4. To study the views of the party to which I belong to or support	5	9	10	1
5. To accumulate "ammunition" for political debate	4	2	3	4
TOTAL Reinforcement	**9**	**11**	**13**	**5**
Entertainment:				
6. I enjoy political struggle and debate	9	10	16	33
7. To evaluate the various parties' chances for success	3	3	3	2
TOTAL Entertainment	**12**	**13**	**19**	**35**
8. Clarification of electoral choice	10	9	11	2
9. Incapable of receiving other transmission at the time	21	22	12	22

*Question: Why do you watch election propaganda broadcasts on television?

"No choice, as it's the only station we can pick up," etc. (5,9).

The primary and most outstanding trend in the responses of viewers over the years was the increasing emphasis upon entertainment-related motivations and a decrease in seeking information. Although this trend was noted throughout the four election campaigns studied, there appears to have been a turning point between the last two elections: nearly half of the respondents in the 1969 elections claimed that they watched propaganda broadcasts for "informative" reasons, while only a little more than one-third recorded similar motivations regarding the 1981 campaign (see Table 5). Note that the percentage of respondents who considered the broadcasts as a "guide to voting" was small in all four campaigns studied, although it dropped from 11% in 1977 to only 2% in 1981 (Table 5, 8). This is partly explained by the changes which took place in election propaganda: the more professionalized propaganda becomes and the greater its emphasis upon manipulative and entertaining messages, the greater the proportion of viewers deriving gratification of entertainment-related needs.[3] The increase in the frequency of "entertainment" motives was indeed most noticeable primarily between the 1973 and 1977 elections, when there was a clearly-discernible transition to more professional propaganda broadcasts.

Reasons for non-exposure to broadcasts also changed over time, possibly due to the change in nature of electoral propaganda: 32% of respondents in the 1981 election survey, as compared with 4% to 6% in studies on the three previous ones, indicated their desire to avoid broadcasts or their opposition to them (Table 6, 7—8). The sophisticated character and transparently manipulative aspect of the propaganda apparently aroused increasing opposition to party messages. Furthermore, the drop in indication of "informative" reasons as a motivating factor for viewing apparently stems likewise from changes in propaganda style.

It appears that the few who were exposed to propaganda broadcasts for purposes of guiding and shaping their decisions were primarily those considering themselves to be "undecided": 9% of the undecided as compared with only 1% of Alignment supporters and virtually no other voters watched propaganda for this purpose. Likud voters tend more to

Table 6: Reasons for Avoiding Television Propaganda Broadcasts* (%)

	1969	1973	1977	1981
Lack of Interest:				
1. Uninterested in politics	22	18	13	5
2. Prefer entertainment	15	7	9	18
TOTAL Lack of Interest	37	25	22	23
Mistrust of Politics:				
3. Don't believe party claims	11	18	11	7
4. Some candidates don't take the public seriously	4	6	11	7
5. Broadcasts say nothing new	13	17	18	11
6. It's often difficult to understand what candidates want to say	2	6	5	3
TOTAL Mistrust	30	47	45	28
Objection to Propaganda:				
7. Don't like it when politicians try to fool me	3	4	5	23
8. Don't want to open my home to political propaganda	1	2	1	9
TOTAL Objection	4	6	6	32
9. Already decided and have no need for broadcasts	29	21	27	18

Question: Why don't you watch election propaganda broadcasts on television?

indicate informative and entertainment reasons (Table 7 a), while Alignment supporters more commonly indicated reinforcement and technical reasons. The differences in voter motivation stem once again from the sociological profile. Indeed, Asian-African-born voters record informative reasons more than others (7 e), as do little educated voters (7 b) and new immigrants who arrived in Israel after 1967 (7 f). This time, Israel-born voters and younger voters in general, whatever their extraction, resembled one another in their higher

Table 7: Reasons for Watching Election Propaganda Broadcasts* — By Voting Intentions and Socio-Demographic Background (%)

	Informative	Reinforcement	Guidance	Entertainment	Technical	N	Sig.
TOTAL**	37	5	2	35	22	870	
a. *Voting Intentions*							.00
Likud	40	4	0	37	18	322	
Alignment	36	8	1	30	25	218	
Agudat Israel	33	0	0	67	0	3	
NRP	47	0	0	30	23	30	
Undecided	35	2	9	31	24	105	
No answer	33	6	0	28	33	54	
b. *Education*							n.s.
Up to 8 years	44	3	2	28	23	169	
9–12 years	36	5	2	35	22	460	
13+ years	33	6	1	39	22	189	
c. *Age*							.00
20–29	34	4	1	40	22	257	
30–39	37	4	1	38	20	191	
40–54	39	4	2	36	19	191	
55+	39	10	4	21	26	182	
d. *Religious Observance*							n.s.
Religious	37	7	4	35	17	81	
Traditional	40	5	2	32	21	558	
Non-religious	27	5	2	41	26	176	

e. *Ethnic Background* (birthplace/parents' birthplace)

Israel/Israel	39	2	0	44	15	52
Israel/Asia-Africa	34	5	1	43	18	150
Israel/Europe-America	28	4	1	43	25	131
Asia-Africa	43	5	2	30	22	240
Europe-America	38	7	3	27	24	244

.004

f. *Year of Immigration to Israel*

Israel-born	32	4	1	43	20	333
Before 1948	41	13	1	16	27	92
1948–1967	38	5	2	31	24	328
1968 and later	51	2	7	30	12	61

.00

Question: Why do you watch election propaganda broadcasts on television?

*Includes all parties.

rate of respondents indicating entertainment motivations (in comparison responses recorded) among the parents' generation). The higher the age, the lower the rate of exposure to broadcasts for entertainment reasons. In contrast, voters above age 55 (7 c) with higher education (7 b) and in Israel for a long time (7 f), paralleling the profile of Alignment supporters, admit more to watching propaganda broadcasts in order to reinforce their stand.

Any attempt to sketch the profile of those who avoid exposure to propaganda broadcasts demands a significant methodological compromise, in light of the small number of voters in each category (Table 8). Ignoring this limitation, we might determine that the undecided and those who refuse to answer tend more than any other voters to indicate invulnerability and objection to propaganda broadcasts (8 a), grounded in a lack of interest in politics. About 25% of voters for the major parties claimed that their decisions were firm and that they had no need for broadcasts. Alignment supporters more commonly noted mistrust of politics, while Likud voters recorded a lack of interest therein. Mistrust of politics as the reason for a lack of exposure is indicated more by the religious voters, who also tend not to register a lack of interest in politics (8 d). This is also true of Israel-born Sephardim, who tend to insulate themselves from propaganda out of lack of interest, apparently at the expense of mistrust of politics. In contrast, children of Israel-born parents display the reverse tendency (8 e).

The Election Campaign and Voters' Decisions

One possible common indicator of voter susceptibility to election campaign influence, including propaganda, is the proportion of voters who make their electoral decisions during the course of the campaign itself. At times, this indicator is liable to frustrate those who conduct electoral campaigns, as it emerges that a significant proportion of voters determines its vote even before the campaign and with no connection to it (Katz 1971). Available statistics on the past three campaigns indicate that significant — if differing — percentages of voters decided how to vote during

Table 8: Reasons for Avoiding Election Propaganda Broadcasts* — by Voting Intentions and Socio-Demographic Background (%)

	Mind Made Up: No Need	Lack of Interest	Mis-trust	Object-ion	N	Sig.
TOTAL**	18	23	28	32	241	
a. *Voting Intentions*						
Likud	27	24	23	25	95	.004
Alignment	23	11	39	27	56	
Agudat Israel	0	0	0	100	1	
NRP	0	33	50	17	6	
Undecided	0	31	28	42	36	
No answer	0	32	21	47	19	
b. *Education*						
Up to 8 years	20	26	28	26	50	n.s.
9–12 years	17	23	24	36	123	
13+ years	18	21	32	29	68	
c. *Age*						
20–29	27	28	15	30	67	.02
30–39	17	28	33	22	54	
40–54	15	23	31	31	52	
55+	10	13	33	43	67	
d. *Religious Observance*						
Religious	9	17	44	30	23	n.s.
Traditional	18	22	26	34	137	
Non-religious	19	27	24	30	79	
e. *Ethnic Background* (birthplace/ parents' birthplace)						
Israel/Israel	17	0	42	42	12	.01
Israel/Asia-Africa	20	36	7	38	45	
Israel/Europe–America	17	26	36	21	58	
Asia-Africa	28	21	31	21	58	
Europe-America	11	18	29	42		
f. *Year of Immigration to Israel*						
Israel-born	18	27	23	31	99	n.s.
Before 1948	15	18	25	43	40	
1948–1967	19	22	29	30	86	
1968 and later	8	17	58	17	12	

Question: Why don't you watch election propaganda broadcasts on television?

** Includes all parties.

the campaigns. In 1981, however, the proportion of voters who made their decisions during the latter stages of the campaign was lower than comparable figures for the two previous ones. According to a survey undertaken approximately two weeks before the last elections, only about 20% of voters responded that they had formulated their electoral preference during the three months preceding the elections, as compared with the 55% who indicated that they had decided one month before the 1977 elections and 35% one month before those of 1973 (Elizur & Katz 1980, pp. 235–236). In contrast to apparent high mobility indicated by public opinion polls in the daily press, 58% of the respondents indicated that they had made their electoral decisions "about half a year ago or more." Only 7% said that they formulated their vote before the Histadrut elections, 6% — one month before and 8% two weeks before the elections, i.e. during the final stage. Some 22% of the interviewees were still undecided two weeks before the elections.

Voters for the religious parties were predictably among the most loyal and decisive. Some 89% of NRP voters and virtually all Agudat Israel supporters decided how to vote six months or more before the elections. The Likud succeeded somewhat more than the Alignment in convincing potential voters during the course of the campaign, as proved by the fact that 68% of Likud voters, as compared with 78% of those for the Alignment, had formulated their electoral opinions six months or more before the elections took place.

Apparently, the government's policy of "disarmament" among ministers — who ceased attacking one another in the media — as well as an overall positive electoral climate, fostered an improvement in evaluation of government performance (although this cannot be corroborated in any causal manner). In January 1981, only 14% of respondents approved of the government's handling of then-current problems — a proportion which increased threefold, to 45%, two weeks before the elections. Interestingly, support for the government was still low (20%) in March of that year; only in May and June was there any substantial recovery, with the rate of support rising to 33% and up.

Two explanations are suggested for the change in public evaluation of government functioning. Some attribute the change to the economic policies of Finance Minister Yoram Aridor; others, denying the effects of "Election economics" upon improvement in the evaluation, ascribe the difference to tension in security matters (the Syrian missile affair), the summit conference at Ophira and the bombing of the nuclear reactor in Iraq. It indeed emerges that the proportion of respondents who decided to vote for the Likud about one month before the elections (at the height of the missile affair) exceeded the rate of respondents who decided in favor of the Alignment: 9% vs. 3%, respectively. In any event, Aridor's policies may indeed have had a cumulative influence in returning voters to the Likud no less than did the security-related events which occurred subsequently. At the same time, 27% of Likud and 16% of Alignment voters chose to support their respective parties during the last three months of the campaign (Table 9 a). The differences between the two parties are again explained in terms of ethnic differences. Only 12% of foreignAshkenazim formulated their electoral opinions during the last three months. They and their Israel-born children stand out among the undecided who apparently postponed their decision until the last minute and formulated it as a result of dramatic events which occurred just before the elections (9 e). About 25% of Israel-born voters, irrespective of ethnic origin, formulated their electoral opinions during the campaign. In contrast, veteran settlers made their decisions earliest of all: 69% had done so some six months before the elections (9 f) — perhaps because they had more party commitment and loyalty than others.

Older (age 55+) religious voters and those in Israel for a long time were quick to make their choice. The Israel-born among them were apparently more influenced than others by the bombing of the reactor: some 11% of them reported that they made their decisions upon the basis of this incident. Those with higher education were not as quick to decide; about one-third, the highest percentage among all educational-level groups, were still undecided at the time the survey was undertaken.

Table 9: Timing of Electoral Decision* — By Voting Intentions and Socio-Demographic Background (%)

	Six Months Ago or More	Three Months Ago	One Month Ago	Very Recently	Still Un-decided	N	Sig.
TOTAL**	58	7	6	8	22	1,111	
a. *Voting Intentions*							.00
Likud	68	10	9	8	6	408	
Alignment	78	7	3	6	7	274	
Agudat Israel	97	0	0	0	3	29	
NRP	89	0	0	8	3	37	
Undecided	1	0	1	3	95	139	
No answer	45	8	3	5	39	75	
b. *Education*							.03
Up to 8 years	63	5	3	6	23	214	
9–12 years	59	8	6	7	19	581	
13+ years	52	6	5	9	29	272	
c. *Age*							.00
20–29	54	11	9	9	17	324	
30–39	54	4	6	10	26	251	
40–54	60	6	3	7	24	241	
55+	63	6	2	3	26	254	
d. *Religious Observance*							
Religious	73	3	4	5	15	131	
Traditional	57	8	5	7	23	683	
Non-religious	52	7	7	8	25	249	

e. Ethnic Background (birthplace/ parents' birthplace)						
Israel/Israel	62	9	2	6	21	66	.002
Israel/Asia-Africa	61	9	8	8	14	183
Israel/Europe-America	48	8	7	11	27	189
Asia-Africa	55	7	8	8	23	298
Europe-America	64	5	2	5	25	329
f. Year of Immigration to Israel						
Israel-born	56	9	7	9	20	438	.007
Before 1948	69	8	2	3	18	132
1948–1967	59	5	5	7	25	419
1968 and later	43	6	8	8	35	72

*Question: When did you make your final decision how to vote?

**Includes all parties.

Summary

The Tenth Knesset election campaign more closely resembled the professional electoral campaigns which currently take place in most democratic countries than did any of its predecessors. The characteristics of this "new style" (Agranoff 1972) pertained primarily to the two major, resource-rich parties, the Likud and the Alignment. Hence this study sought to determine whether the efforts of the parties and the propagandists serving them were profitable in terms of the public's exposure to and benefit from political messages in formulating their electoral decisions.

The findings presented in this study point to a number of trends:

a) Although public interest in the election campaign was rather high and many were exposed to and followed the mass media, there was only a modest appraisal of the benefit to be derived therefrom regarding voters' final decisions. A similar trend characterizes exposure to television propaganda broadcasts and evaluation of their contribution to the voter.

b) Voters who were still undecided at the time the survey was undertaken tended to be less interested in and have a lower estimation of the benefits of both the campaign and the broadcasts.

c) Supporters of the two major parties — the Likud and the Alignment — do not differ in terms of their interest in the campaign and broadcasts, but rather in their evaluation of their benefits, which the former appreciate more than the latter.

d) Differences between the two electorates are apparently rooted in the different sociological profiles, which parallel differences between the two major ethnic groups: Sephardim — who identify more with the Likud and who tend to express a higher evaluation of the effects of party propaganda, including television broadcasts — and Ashkenazim, whose estimation of it is somewhat lower.

e) In time, cognitive-informative gratifications give way to entertainment-escapist ones. In comparison with past election campaigns, more people have indicated entertainment as the reasons behind their exposure to propaganda, while fewer seek information about the parties, their candidates and platforms.

f) Likud supporters seek more information and entertainment in the broadcasts, whereas Alignment supporters desire reinforcement of previously-formulated views.

g) Contrary to previous impressions, a high percentage of voters — exceeding that of previous campaigns — decided how to vote during the early stages of the campaign.

h) More voters who made their final decision during the campaign voted for the Likud than for the Alignment.

i) Voters who remained undecided up to the last minute did not ultimately support only a single party. On the one hand, this group included many educated and non-religious persons, features which also characterize Alignment supporters. On the other hand, however, it also comprised new immigrants and Israel-born voters, who are more closely identified with the Likud including those of Ashkenazic origin.

The voter's ability to reach an early decision or — conversely — to hesitate up to the last minute are features of concern to politicians and their attendant propagandists. The fact that these two characteristics are dispersed among various groups prevents them from focusing their messages on any one clearly-defined homogeneous target group. Survey findings, including those reported here, add to the confusion and to the long-standing dispute on the efficacy of propaganda and its benefit in the election campaign. One way or another, there will always be those who seek to derive conclusions — even if rather hasty and unfounded — from such findings.

The Likud's ecstatic praise for the campaign and broadcasts may be interpreted as testimony to its quality and effectiveness; the Likud indeed derived more benefit than the Alignment from the campaign's influence upon voters' decisions. This conclusion, however, ignores the well-known trend of "coming home," i.e. the return of voters to the party they formerly supported, which generally accelerates towards the end of the campaign and near Election Day and was further encouraged by the government's more impressive performance. It is thus virtually impossible to isolate the effect of the campaign from other trends and dramatic events which influence voters' decisions.

Similarly, we have long tended to believe that the current findings will cause both parties in the dispute to cling to their previous contentions, perhaps with even greater vigor. While electoral propaganda researchers will again point to the statistical trends which indicate that undecided voters derive less benefit from the election campaign than do voters who have already formulated their opinions, the politicians and professional propagandists will certainly claim that even if these findings are correct, one should not belittle the relatively small population of undecided voters which is influenced by the campaign and may determine the balance of power on the political map; moreover, voters' testimony as to the efficacy of the campaign does not reflect objective truth or prevailing realities with any degree of certainty.

NOTES

1.   The survey was undertaken by the Israel Institute for Applied Social Research and the Institute of Communications of the Hebrew University of Jerusalem.
2.   The Alignment, too, decided to utilize the method adopted by the Likud in the previous election campaign, in which the broadcasting time allotted was divided into three units each evening. The two large parties thus broadcast three messages of 2–3 minutes' duration every evening. An agreement between the parties determined that an evening which opened with a Likud message would close with an Alignment one and vice versa. Dispersing of propaganda time originates in the parties' desire to create an impression of constant presence on the screen.
3.   The increase in consideration of propaganda as entertainment may well be a result of expansion and variety in the viewing audience. In the elections to the Seventh Knesset, in which television was used for the first time, 35% of interviewees responded that they had no television sets (Gurevitch 1972). Over the years, television sets became more popular and the audience became more varied.

BIBLIOGRAPHY

Agranoff, R.
1972   *The New Style in Election Campaigns.* Boston: Holbrook Press.

Ansky, A.
1978   *The Selling of The Likud.* Tel Aviv: Zmora, Bitan, Modan (Hebrew).

Blumler, J.G. & Katz, E. (eds.)
1974   *The Uses of Mass Communications.* Beverly Hills: Sage.

Caspi, D. & Eyal H.C.
1983   "Professionalization Trends in Israeli Election Propaganda: 1973–1981," in: Arian, A. (ed.), *The Elections in Israel — 1981.* Tel Aviv: Ramot.

Cohen, A.A.
1976   "Radio vs. TV: The Effect of the Medium," *Journal of Communication* 26, 2, pp. 29-35.

Elizur, J. and Katz, E.
1980   "The Media in the Israel Election of 1977," in: Arian, A. (ed.), *The Elections in Israel — 1977.* Jerusalem: Academic Press.

Gurevitch, M.
1972   "Television in the Election Campaign: Its Audience and Functions," in: Arian, A. (ed.), *The Elections in Israel — 1969.* Jerusalem: Academic Press.

Katz, E.
1971   "Platforms and Windows: Reflections on the Role of Broadcasting in Election Campaigns," *Journalism Quarterly* 48, 2, pp. 304-314.

1980   "On Conceptualizing Media Effects," *Studies in Communication* 1, pp. 119-141.

Lazarsfeld, P., Berelson, B. and Gaudet, H.
1944   *The People's Choice: How the Voter Makes Up His Mind in a Presidential Campaign.* New York: Duell, Sloan and Pearce.

Peri, Y.
  1975   "Television in the 1973 Election Campaign," in
            Arian, A. (ed.), *The Elections in Israel—1973.*
            Jerusalem: Academic Press.
Smith, A.
  1982   "Mass Communications," in: Butler, D., Penni-
            man, H.R. and Ranney, A. (eds.), *Democracy at
            the Polls: A Comparative Study of Competitive
            National Elections.* Washington, D.C.: American
            Enterprise Institute, 1981.

11

EVERY DAY IS ELECTION DAY
Press Coverage of Pre-Election Polls

Gabriel Weimann[*]

The diffusion of political polls in the mass media has aroused a growing interest in the effects of their coverage on voters' behavior. The ongoing debate on the direction and magnitude of these effects has almost entirely ignored the changes that have occurred in the form and content of reporting polls in the media.

This paper attempts to examine these changes, suggesting that any study of the impact of polls upon voters must take into account the manner in which polls are covered and reported in the mass media.

The case of Israel is well-suited for this study because during a relatively short period, opinion polling in Israel has mushroomed and the diffusion of polls in the media has undergone significant changes in both form and content.

The Emergence of Mass Media Polls

Newspaper polling can be traced back to 1920, when "straw" polls were conducted to gauge the outcome of the U.S. Presidential election (Fenton 1960, p. 7). Crude and unsophisticated as these "straw" polls were, they served as an informal medium for the expression of voting intentions as well as a pseudo-scientific means of forecasting election results. Newspaper-sponsored "straw" polls, designed to forecast elections, continued to be conducted throughout the nineteenth century and into the twentieth century (for a detailed listing see Robinson 1932; Crespi 1980). The years 1935–1936 witnessed the emergence of syndicated, newspaper-

*Lecturer, in Sociology, University of Haifa.

sponsored polling organizations such as Gallup, Roper and Crossley, which employed newly-developed sampling techniques. The Gallup Poll was syndicated in over 100 newspapers and the correct forecasts of several elections led most of the American press to sponsor, conduct and report polls. The European media soon followed suit: British Gallup, the first organization of its kind in Europe, was founded in 1937 and has been publishing poll results ever since in British dailies (Worchester 1980).

In the beginning, this tendency to report polls is to be explained by their newsworthiness: polls supplied hard data — statistical facts concerning the up-to-date situation of parties and candidates. The obsession to forecast election results was satisfied by polls which chronicled the public's fluctuating voting intentions. However, the last decade, the 1970s, has added a new dimension to the interest of the mass media in conducting and reporting polls. The emergence of "precision journalism," with its stress on the use of systematic research methods (Meyer 1973), has led to a growing acceptance of scientific methodology and findings: "Social Science is now doing what we journalists like to think what we are best at: finding facts, inferring causes . . . " (Meyer 1971, p. 15). Over the past few years, Weaver and McCombs have argued (1980, p. 490) that there is evidence that both journalists and instructors of journalism have heeded Meyer's plea for the increased use of and reliance upon social science methods. Consequently, there has been a marked increase in newspaper polling since 1970: a 1978 survey of 437 daily newspapers in the U.S. (Rippey 1979) revealed that more than half of the 162 polling papers have conducted their first poll since that date. Moreover, even newspapers which have never conducted a poll of their own show an overwhelming acceptance of polling techniques and data.

The newsworthiness of pre-election polls, together with the emergence of a journalistic mode, "precision journalism", have thus led to the recent diffusion of polls in the mass media. Furthermore, the growing interest of the media in political polls has changed the relationships between the media and polling organizations. In the past, newspapers and networks merely bought the rights to print polling results, recently however, they have begun to conduct and commission their own polls. In this manner, the news organizations do not simply report findings but rather create news by their own initiative, shaping it through choice of topics, questions and responses. This development appears to threaten the media with the "feedback loop," whereby the journalistic definition of what constitutes news determines the content and form of polling, which in turn affects the political process which then becomes news . . .

The Disputable "Bandwagon" and "Underdog" Effects

The prevalence of polls in the mass media has stimulated various hypotheses regarding their effects upon voting behavior, which may be classified into two categories: (a) effects on voter turnout and (b) effects on voter preference. Each of these is further divisible into effects which increase the advantage of the leading candidate, according to the polls and those which decrease it and support the trailing candidate. Voter turnout may be affected by defeatism among supporters of the trailing candidate or over-confidence among those who back the presumed leader.

With regard to voters' preferences, it has often been claimed that polls may increase victory margins by inducing voters to cast their ballots for the leading candidate, a process known as the bandwagon effect. However, empirical research has not provided substantial evidence in support of this claim. In his review of studies on bandwagon effects, Klapper concludes: " . . . there is no absolute conclusive evidence . . . that publication of poll results does or does not affect the subsequent votes. The existing literature provides considerable reason to believe that the publication of poll results does *not* produce any bandwagon or underdog effect of any significant magnitude among the electorate" (Klapper 1964, p. 55). Several studies and reviewers of public opinion research concur (Mendelsohn & Grespi 1970; Roll & Cantril 1972; Atkin 1969; Roshwald & Resnicoff 1971 and Oskamp 1971 to name only a few). Moreover, Mendelsohn and Crespi ask: if bandwagon or underdog effects have proved to be minimal, why has so much attention been paid to this issue?

A recent trend in the study of voting behavior claims that more powerful effects than those mentioned above may be related to the appearance of polls in the media. The "strong effect" proponents support the idea and findings of Noelle-Neuman (1973, 1974) and her call for "a return to the concept of powerful mass media." Noelle-Neumann claims that in the process of opinion formation, a crucial role is played by the "climate of opinion," that is, the individual's perception of which opinions are dominant. The publicized polls may well affect the voters' recognition of such a "climate," causing a spiralling process: "People still clinging to their old faith were afraid of being the only ones who did so, and as they were frightened of isolation, they joined the masses, even if they did not agree with them" (Noelle-Neumann 1973, pp. 90–91). In this manner, the opinions or preferences presented as those of the majority may in turn exert pressure upon the individual to conform to the general, popular preference.

A recent study conducted by Ceci and Kain (1982) has provided evidence for the strong effect, although in the opposite direction. In their experimental study, Ceci and Kain examined the effects which previous polling information on a candidate's standing had had upon voter preference. During the months preceding the Reagan-Carter election in 1980, subjects were provided with one of three types of information concerning current polls (Carter commanding a lead; Reagan commanding a lead; no information) and their preferences were studied before and after exposure to the information. The data accumulated demonstrated that both strength of attitude and candidate preference are influenced by knowledge of previous polling results. The results reveal both "shifting" in attitude (change of strength of one's opinion) and "switching" of preference (from the support of one candidate to either the undecided position or to support of the other). Ceci and Kain argue that the absolute magnitude of the shifts were quite large and that the shifts were typically *away* from the candidate depicted as dominant in the polls. This tendency was most apparent in specific cases: "It is clear from the overall data that the greatest amount of change did in fact occur among the undecided and weak supporters of both candidates" (Ceci & Kain 1982, p. 239).

These findings clearly indicate the existence of the underdog effect, what Ceci and Kain term "oppositional reactivity."

We are faced with inconsistent and even contradictory findings and conclusions regarding the effects of polls on voters. There are various reasons for this lingering debate — the type of population studied, measures of voter preferences and variation in a voter's decision process. We suggest another possible intervening variable: change in the way polls are presented and analysed in the media. We argue that the changes in the independent variable (i.e., the reports of poll results) may be greatly responsible for the inconsistent findings regarding the dependent variable — the effects on the public's preference.

The aim of this study is to document the changes in form, volume and content of pre-election polling coverage in the Israeli press, thereby providing empirical evidence for the necessity of including coverage analysis in the study and comparison of the effects of polls on voters.

Methods

The present study is a secondary analysis of data originally accumulated for a study of polling in Israel 1948—1981 (Weimann 1983). We applied the content analysis method for studying media contents (Gerbner 1969). In order to analyze press coverage of pre-election polls, we studied all polling reports of Israel's eleven dailies during the three months preceding each Israeli election since 1948.[1]

Our coders were instructed to analyze the reports by using pre-set categories (according to the listing provided by Stone & Morrison 1976 and Charlebois 1979). The following components were recorded for each report:

(a) Form: Date, name of newspaper, space allocation (in column-inches), placement (front page or inside pages), sponsorship (by the reporting paper, by another paper, by a political body or unspecified).

(b) Content: Inclusion of information or sample size, definition of population sampled, sampling error, method of interviewing (i.e., in person, by telephone, mail), phrasing of question, refusal rate, timing (dates interviews were conducted), respondents' breakdowns by socio-economic variables, comparison with previous polls, measures of intensity of opinion and identification of pollster.

(c)   Indirect Coverage: Any reference made to polls (besides direct reporting of results) in news stories, feature articles, interviews, campaign calendars, editorials, letters to the editor and so forth.

The coders were trained prior to the investigation and were subjected to a reliability test which yielded inter-coder reliability scores as high as .94 in form, .91 in content and .89 in indirect coverage.

Diffusion of Poll Reports

The early pre-election polls in the Israeli press were rather modest and unimpressive. Only during the election campaign for the Seventh Knesset (1969) did the Israeli press begin to publish the results of polls. None of these were initiated or commissioned by the press; most were "pseudo-scientific" surveys, such as a forecast based on a sample of 500 students, reported in all three leading dailies,[2] or a survey whose sample consisted of fourteen journalists[3]. Most reports published in 1969 were based upon the partial results of polls conducted for political bodies and then leaked to the press.

Table 1 reveals the dramatic change in press coverage of polls since 1969. By any measure, polls have become important news items, gaining more and more attention, space and prominence in the press. Thus, while in 1969 only three dailies reported polling results, the following pre-election periods have witnessed the initiation of polls coverage in other newspapers; by 1981, every newspaper published in Israel included at least one pre-election poll report. The prominence of polls in the press may also be seen in the consistent increase in space allocated to poll reports: our analysis reveals an increase of over 4000% — from 172 column-inches in 1969 to 6,927 in 1981. The increase in number of polls placed on the front page (21% of the reports in 1981) indicates that polls have become important news, as revealed in the

Table 1: The Diffusion of Pre-Election Polls in the Israeli Press

	Aug.-Oct. 1969	Oct.-Dec. 1973	March-May 1977	April-June 1981	% of increase 69/73 to 72/81
(a) Number of newspapers reporting polls	3	6	8	11	211
(b) Number of reports on polls	16	52	109	216	477
(c) Average number of reports per newspaper $\frac{b}{a}$	5.33	8.66	13.62	19.63	237
(d) Space allocated for poll reports (in column — inches)	172	513	1,297	6,927	1,200
(e) Average space allocated for poll reports per newspaper in column — inches $\frac{d}{a}$	57.33	35.50	162.12	629.72	554
(f) Placement: % in front page	7	12	15	21	189
% inside pages	93	88	85	79	−9
(g) Sponsorship: % by the reporting paper	0	9	37	47	933
% by other papers	5	22	28	33	225
% by political bodies	71	49	22	11	−72
% unspecified	24	20	13	9	−50

frequency of reporting as well: the average number of reports per newspaper increased from 5.33 reports per paper in 1969 to 13.62 in 1977 and 19.63 in 1981. This measure comprises different frequencies of reporting, varying significantly from one paper to another. Thus, we find that the major dailies published the results of polls nearly every other day; at times reports on several polls were published in a single day's edition.

The growing interest of the press in polling has induced changes in the relationship between the press and the polling agencies. As journalists become more and more interested in poll forecasting and findings, the press has become more involved in commissioning and conducting polls. *Ha'aretz* was the first newspaper to sponsor private polls (in 1973). Soon, the three major dailies commissioned their own polls, each contracting a different pollster. Table 1 reveals that in 1973, only 9% of the reports covered polls sponsored by the reporting newspaper; this rate increased to 37% in 1977 and 47% in 1981. Moreover, the coverage of press-initiated polls was not confined to self-sponsored projects; all of the newspapers included reports on results and forecasts drawn from polls sponsored by other papers. This trend yielded a growing share of press-commissioned polls which reached a peak in 1981: 80% of the publicized polls were commissioned either by the reporting paper or by other papers.

The decline in reporting of polls sponsored by political parties may be explained by the growing reluctance of politicians to leak such results due to "strategic" considerations[4] or by the growing skepticism of journalists to rely on this type of data.[5]

Selective Enrichment of Polls Reporting

The emergence and prevalence of polls in the Israeli press is manifest not only in the changing form and prominence of poll reports but also in the contents of the reports themselves. The comparisons presented in Table 2 indicate that content elements have changed significantly.

In 1973, press reports of pre-election polls read merely as a short summary of the results. During subsequent pre-election

Table 2: The Changing Contents of Poll Reporting in the Israeli Press

Item	Percent of Reports Including the Item:				
	Oct.-Dec. 1973	March-May 1977	April-June 1981	American Newspapers 1972 — 1979*
1. Sample Size	54	86	92	89
2. Definition of Population	56	68	84	91
3. Sampling Error	0	6	9	31
4. Method of Interviewing	29	32	51	62
5. Wording of Question	14	21	28	71
6. Refusal Rate	63	71	88	—
7. Timing	38	51	64	76
8. Respondents' Breakdown	6	16	28	—
9. Comparison to Previous Polls	17	36	52	—
10. Intensity of Opinion	0	8	11	—
11. Identification of Pollster	75	87	96	—

*Data for this comparison comes from a study of 116 poll reports in the Chicago Tribune, Los Angeles Times and Atlanta Constitution, conducted by Miller and Hurd (1982).

periods, however, the reports have become more richly textured and detailed. Nevertheless, such enrichment has been rather selective and certain items still tend to be omitted.

Comparison in time[6] shows that the reports have become more informative with regard to sample size, definition of population, method of interviewing, refusal rate, pollster identification and timing of data accumulation. To a lesser extent, an increase has also been noted in reports containing information regarding respondents' breakdowns (mostly by ethnic origin, age and education), phrasing of questions and comparisons to previous polls.

The tendency to enrich the reports does not include aspects such as sampling deficiencies,[7] confidence intervals or measures of opinion intensity. Without these items, the reports may impose a distorted interpretation, beyond the scope of the data. The reports are more informative regarding comparisons and breakdowns but not regarding methodological limitations which may alter the conclusion derived from the results. Leo Bogart claims that "public misunderstanding of opinion surveys can be expected to continue as long as the mass media ignore or belittle their technical intricacies" (Bogart 1972, p. 23), while Wheeler argues that "the reader of opinion polls is given no hint that they may not be trustworthy" (Wheeler 1976, pp. XVI–XVII). Going beyond Wheeler, Paletz and his collaborators have found in their study of polls in the American media that "the way methodological information about polling is reported in the media tends more to reassure than alert the audience about the possible defects of poll data" (Paletz *et al.* 1980, p. 506). The situation in Israel appears to be more critical than in the U.S. Comparison of the Israeli data with the findings of Paletz *et al.*, and those of a recent study of 116 poll reports in the American Press (Miller & Hurd 1982) reveals that the Israeli press provides less adequate information about methodological deficiencies than does the American press. While 71% of the American reports include the polling questions, rates, the respective rate in Israel is only 28% (in 1981). Moreover, while 31% of the former include information on sampling errors, only 9% of the latter contain such information. Bearing in mind the findings of Lang and Lang (1980) on the impact of different wording of questions upon respondents' attitudes, we may conclude that the readers are not aware of the existence of this factor which may limit or otherwise change interpretations based upon the frequencies of various responses. The combination of the growing prominence and sophistication of poll coverage and the accompanying lag in reporting methodological intricacies may result in a significant change in the impact these reports have on their readers' evaluation and preferences.

Indirect Coverage of Polls

The last dimension of change examined in our content analysis was indirect coverage, that is, references to pre-election polls in editorial material (besides direct reports of results). Our coders scanned the papers in search of any references made to polling results or forecasts in news columns, editorials, interviews, letters to the editor and so forth.

Table 3: References to Pre-Election Polls in the Israeli Press

	1973	1977	1981
% in news stories	48.9 (21)	42.7 (56)	33.2 (71)
% in editorials	18.6 (8)	23.7 (31)	27.1 (58)
% in interviews with politicians	6.9 (3)	19.8 (26)	23.8 (51)
% in interviews with pollsters	2.3 (1)	6.1 (8)	8.9 (19)
% in others	23.3 (10)	7.6 (10)	7.0 (15)
Total	100 (43)	100 (131)	100 (214)

The comparison in time, as seen in Table 3, reveals the striking infiltration of polling results and forecasts into various journalistic items. More and more editorials contain references to polling data, while interviews with politicians and pollsters add a new arena for quoting, discussing and referring to the polls. The overall growth in volume of indirect coverage (from 43 references in 1973 to 214 in 1981) is a result of the growing diffusion of polls into certain journalistic items, namely editorials and interviews. The data in Table 3 show a decline in time in the number of references to polls in news stories. This may be explained by the concomitant growth in direct coverage (that is, reporting on polls in news columns), as shown in the previous tables.

The diffusion of polls into various contents of the press supports the testimony of Bill Kovach, Washington Editor of the New York Times: "The polling tool has been so completely factored into our decision-making process, especially in political reporting, that I had difficulty remembering how we worked before we had this tool . . . Beyond political reporting, in the broader area of public responses to social or economic changes, the polls have broadened and deepened our understanding and, I hope, our reporting" (Kovach 1980, pp. 567–569).

The diffusion of polls — especially pre-election polls — in the media has inspired several claims concerning the effects of such vast coverage on the public. At this stage, it would be of value to point out and discuss two of these claims: the distorting effect and the change in the public's orientation toward polling.

The Distorting Effect: From Parties to Personalities

The potential distorting effect exerted by polling upon media coverage of elections — and, in turn upon setting the public agenda — is a most popular theme in analyses of the press-polling liaison. The basic claim is that press-conducted or published polls primarily emphasize superficial aspects of public opinion — such as focusing on what is termed "horse-racing journalism" in election coverage. "The kinds of data obtained by public opinion research and disseminated in the mass media seem designed more to entertain than to inform. The quality of the information conveyed seems not much different from that conveyed in the sports page, or, better yet, the daily racing form" (Rokeach 1968). Broh (1980) provides empirical evidence that elections are rendered shallow by the popular use of the horse-race metaphor: "for journalists, the horse-race metaphor provides a framework for analysis. A horse is judged not by its absolute speed or skill but in comparison to the speed of other horses and especially by its wins or losses. Similarly, candidates are pushed to discuss other candidates; events are understood in a context of competition; and picking the winner becomes an important topic. The race — not the winner — is important" (Broh 1980, p. 515). No wonder that expressions like "Poll calls race tied," "Running neck and neck," "Polls show candidate X trailing" or "Holding the lead" are so frequently used in poll reports. However, while this image provides the journalist with an amusing story, it may distort the voter's perception of the political process, encouraging him to focus upon exciting but ultimately irrelevant aspects of a campaign. Issues which are complex, ideological and not hotly debated may be passed over in the search for exciting, newsworthy items.

Coverage of polls in the Israeli press has evidently displayed a consistent trend towards horse-race imagery. The most significant evidence for this is "candidate-centered" polling and reporting. As Fiorina (1980, p. 33) has written, "Candidates would have little incentive to operate campaigns independent of parties if there were no means to apprise the citizenry of their independence. The media provide the means." The decline in salience of political parties is more obvious in Israel, where voters choose among parties and not candidates. However, the rise of candidate centered campaigns (see Wattenberg 1982) is more suited to the horse-race frame of journalistic reference. Thus, we find that more and more polls reported in the media deal with political personalities and not with parties. In 1969, all reports used polls about party references, whereas in 1973 only four included data about the candidates' popularity (i.e. only 7.6% of the published reports). However, the 1977 elections witnessed the expansion of personality popularity polls: out of 109 reports, 24 (22%) dealt with the ratings of various candidates. The most frequent comparison was between Menachem Begin and Shimon Peres, the leaders of the largest parties and hence the candidates for Prime Minister. However, this type of personality rating extended to other governmental positions as well, including candidates for the posts of Minister of Defense, Foreign Affairs and Finance. This type of polls was even more popular during the three months preceeding the 1981 elections: out of 216 press reports of polls, 53 dealt with personalities, thus comprising about one-quarter of all reports.

We are not suggesting that the trend toward personality-centered campaigning has been caused by the media in general or by the compatibility of personal popularity polls with journalistic frames of analysis in particular. Rather, we believe that the expansion of personality polls is an integral part of the political process whose focus is changing from parties to candidates. The main contribution of the media is in cultivating, ritualizing and amplifying this new political trend. The horse-race metaphor has several valuable functions, of which the most important is its enhancement of the public's interest in a process which otherwise tends to be remote and boring: "Because it makes the electoral process appear as exciting and competitive as possible, the horse-race image maintains a vital link between the mass of people and a very few elected officials" (Broh 1980, p. 527). However, the question to be considered is whether such changes in emphasis and frame of analysis are beneficial to the functioning of democracy: "Just as bettors on a race may be misled by the beauty of the horses — voters may be misled by the trivia of the campaign" *ibid.,* p. 528).

The Public's Acquaintance with and Trust in Polls

Several years ago, Biderman scanned the literature on the public's conceptions of polling and concluded: "The public opinion research profession constitutes a notorious case of the barefoot shoemaker" (Biderman 1975, p. 51). Gollin (1980) provides empirical evidence that only a minority of the public (between 15% and 35%) has gained personal knowledge about polling by being interviewed. However, the degree of acquaintance with polls or surveys, largely channeled through the mass media, is fairly widespread: In 1944 Goldman found that 44% of a national sample had never heard or read about pre-election polls (Goldman 1944). Thirty years later, during the 1976 U.S. presidential campaign, only 16% failed to recall hearing something about polls.

The Israeli case provides additional evidence for the relationship between media coverage and public awareness.

The "obsession" to cover polls has led to a greater rate of acquaintance and familiarity with polls by the public at large. A "poll on polls" conducted in Israel during 1981 (Caspi & Eyal 1982) revealed that 44% of a sample of 1,200 respondents reported that they had been interviewed for polls: 21% were interviewed once before, 10% twice and 13% three times or more. Acquaintance with polls or surveys has become very widespread: Goldman found that only 19% of his 1944 national sample said they followed the published polls "regularly." In 1977, Meadows found that 34% of a Kentucky sample claimed to pay attention to the results of polls "very often" (Meadows 1980). The Israeli findings show that only 25% of Caspi and Eyal's sample claim that they are not interested in poll results at all. Moreover, 64% object to the proposition that the publicizing of pre-election polls should be banned because it affects voters' preferences. As for the usefulness of polls to voters, 46% of the Israeli sample argue that polling results reported in the press, radio or television are "very helpful" or "rather helpful" in influencing their electoral choice.

Evidence of the credibility of poll findings is equally impressive: only 25% of the Israeli sample find "most" or "all of the polls" to be unreliable. Three-quarters of the respondents, therefore, trust all or at least some of the reported polls. These levels of reliance and trust are significantly higher in Israel than in the United States, where trust in the results of surveys as being "almost always right" or right "most of the time" was expressed by 40% of respondents in two nationwide surveys (Turner & Krauss 1978, p. 468).

Finally, the vast coverage of polls in the media should be regarded as one of the mass media's instruments of involvement in the reconstruction of the "Climate of Opinion." Noelle-Neumann argues that individual processes of opinion formation are influenced by the individual's perceptions of existing dominant opinions and those about to become dominant (Noelle-Neumann 1973). Hence, public opinion is considered to be the outcome of the interaction between the individual's attitudes and his conception of the majority's attitude: "Mass media are part of the system which the individual uses to gain information about the environment. For all questions outside his personal sphere he is almost totally dependent on mass media for the facts and for his evaluation of the climate of opinion" (Noelle-Neumann 1974, p. 43). Public opinion polls provide the best up-to-date report on the state of dominance of the majority's preference and thus serve as a main factor which elaborates and documents the current climate of opinion. Caspi and Eyal (1982) provide evidence supporting this claim; they found that the public relies mainly on publicized polls to estimate the popularity of parties and also tends to accept the forecasts of the polls pertaining to the outcome of the upcoming election. Respondents were asked to estimate the results of the elections before and after reading the results of a given poll. The result was that the most respondents, after being exposed to a poll forecast, tended to correct their own estimates to fit those supplied by the poll.

Conclusions

Guided by the ongoing debate concerning the political impact of mass media polling, we examined the changes in their presentation and noted significant changes in volume, content and form of reporting pre-election polls in the Israeli press. Over the past twelve years, polls have become an important news item, gaining more and more attention from journalists and consequently from the public at large. Nevertheless, this increased coverage appears rather selective: reports have become more richly textured but have excluded items which may impose severe limitations upon interpretations derived from the data at hand.

Our overall results appear to bear implications for the political system, the involvement of journalism in newsmaking and voters' decision-making processes. To some extent, of course, politicians are captured by events and processes not of their own making. The fact that polls are so widely and frequently covered by the media may exert pressure upon politicians to act in accordance with the polls' results. As a consequence, politicians are led to short-term considerations which may improve their standing in the polls. Insofar as the political involvement of the public is concerned, the prominence of polls in the media does increase voters' interest and familiarity but may also lead them to focus upon trivial considerations, i.e. horse-race imagery and personality contests instead of the more basic and serious questions of ideology, political viewpoints and long-term policies.

Eagerness to conduct and report polls — the "obsession to forecast" — has caused the media to be more involved in the "feedback loop" as they are actually creating the news to be reported. In this sense, polls have often become "pseudo-events." Boorstein (1961) refers to this phenomenon as a synthetic piece of news that is planned, planted or incited specifically in order to be reported, to become news. Nevertheless, the trend towards "precision journalism" has supported the growing acceptance of polls as both important and newsworthy. However, when the trend is not accompanied with increasing ability to understand and criticize the methodological deficiencies of such polls — and when standards for reporting polls are ignored or poorly-observed[8] — the results of such "precision journalism" would emerge as far from accurate.

Finally, from a methodological perspective, our findings call for inclusion of the nature of coverage itself in analysis of its effects on voters' preferences. The disputable "bandwagon" and "underdog" effects — the lack of consensus about the influence of media coverage of pre-election polls upon voters' "shifting" and "switching" their preferences — may be partially overcome through comprehension of the changing character of the media coverage itself. Without such understanding, debate on the impact of mass media polls will undoubtedly persist.

NOTES

1. We focused upon press reports, as Israeli law bans the government radio and T.V. networks (the only ones operating in Israel) from reporting, analyzing or quoting any items of information concerning the election during the month preceding it). Thus, the press is the main medium publishing and supporting pre-election polls.
2. Reported in *Ma'ariv* (October 27, 1969), *Yediot Aharonot* (October 26, 1969) and *Ha'aretz* (October 27, 1969.
3. Reported in *Ma'ariv* (October 23, 1969) and *Ha'aretz* (October 23, 1969).
4. Typical of this reluctance was the case of a pre-election poll con-

ducted during May 1977 for the Likud Party. Likud leaders decided to conceal the poll, whose results forecasted their victory. Its existence was publicized only after the election.

5. This skepticism was encouraged by several cases of false or inaccurate leaking of poll results. The worst case was that of a poll published by *Yediot Aharonot* (February 15, 1974), later discovered to be a hoax and deliberately "planted" by a political body.

6. The 1969 campaign period was dropped from the table due to the low frequency of poll reports.

7. Most samples are drawn from the urban Jewish population, thus misrepresenting non-urban and non-Jewish sectors.

8. Miller and Hurd's (1982) study on the conformity to the American Association for Public Opinion Research (AAPOR) standards in newspaper reporting public opinion polls reveals a dramatic increase in the number of polls reported but not in the level of conformity to standards: methodological information is often omitted from press reports on polling despite the standards of reporting set by AAPOR.

BIBLIOGRAPHY

Atkin, A.
    1969   "The Impact of Political Poll Reports on Candidate and Issue References." *Journalism Quarterly* 46:3, pp. 384-391.

Biderman, D.
    1975   "The Survey Method as an Institution and the Survey Institution as a Method." in: Sinaiko, H. W. and Broedling, L.A. (eds.), *Perspectives on Attitude Assessment: Surveys and Their Alternatives.* Washington D.C.: Smithsonian Institute, pp. 48-63.

Bogart, L.
    1972   *Silent Politics,* New York: Wiley.

Boorstein, D.J.
    1961   *The Image: A Guide to Pseudo-Events in America.* New York: Atheneum.

Broh, A.C.
    1980   "Horse-Race Journalism: Reporting the Polls in the 1976 Presidential Election. *Public Opinion Quarterly* 44, pp. 514-529.

Caspi, D. and Eyal, H.C.
1982 "The Public's Attitude Towards Polls," paper presented at the Annual Meeting of the Israeli Sociological Association, February 1982.

Ceci, S.J. and Kain, E.L.
1982 "Jumping on the Bandwagon with the Underdog." *Public Opinion Quarterly* 46, pp. 228-242.

Charlebois, C.
1979 "Multiple Measures in the Study of Press Response." *Journalism Quarterly* 56, pp.851-856.

Crespi, I.
1980 "Polls as Journalism." *Public Opinion Quarterly* 44, pp. 462-476.

Fenton, J.M.
1960 *In Your Opinion.* Boston: Lillte, Brown and Co.

Fiorina, M.
1980 "The Decline of Collective Responsibility in American Politics." *Daedalus* 109, pp. 25-45.

Gerbner, G.
1969 *The Analysis of Communication Content.* New York: Wiley.

Goldman, E.F.
1944 "Poll on the Polls." *Public Opinion Quarterly* 8, pp. 461-467.

Gollin, A.E.
1980 "Exploring the Liaison Between Polling and the Press." *Public Opinion Quarterly* 44, pp. 445-461.

Klapper, J.T.
1964 *Bandwagon: A Review of the Literature.* Office of Social Research, Columbia Broadcasting System.

Kovach, B.
1980 "A User's View of the Polls." *Public Opinion Quarterly* 44, pp. 567-571.

Lang, G. and Lang, K.
1980 "Polling on Watergate: The Battle for Public Opinion." *Public Opinion Quarterly* 44, pp. 530-547.

Mendelsohn, H. and Crespi, I.
1970   *Polls, Television and the New Politics.* Scranton, Pa.: Chandler.
Meyer, Ph.
1971   "The Limits of Intuition." *Columbia Journalism Review* (July-August 1971), pp. 15-20.

1973   *Precision Journalism: A Reporter's Introduction to Social Science Methods.* Bloomington: Indiana University Press.
Miller, M. M. and Hurd, R.
1982   "Conformity to AAPOR Standards in Newspaper Reporting of Public Opinion Polls." *Public Opinion Quarterly* 46, pp. 243-249.
Noelle-Neuman, E.
1973   "Return to the Concept of Powerful Mass Media." *Studies of Broadcasting* 9, pp. 67-112.

1974   "Spiral of Silence." *Journal of Communication* 24, pp. 43-51.
Oskamp, S.
1971   *Attitudes and Opinions.* Englewood Cliffs, New Jersey.
Paletz, D. et al.
1980   "Polls in the Media: Content, Credibility and Consequences." *Public Opinion Quarterly* 44, pp. 495-513.
Rippey, J.N.
1979   "Use of Opinion Polls as a Reporting Tool." unpublished manuscript, Pennsylvania State University.
Robinson, C.E.
1932   *Straw Polls.* New York: Columbia University Press.
Rokeach, M.
1968   "The Role of Values in Public Opinion Research." *Public Opinion Quarterly* 32, pp. 547-559.
Roll, C.W. and Cantril, A.H.
1972   *Polls, Their Use and Misuse in Politics.* New York: Basic Books.

Roshwald, I. and Resnicoff, L.
1971 "The Impact of Endorsement and Published Polls on the 1970 New York Sensational Elections." *Public Opinion Quarterly* 35, pp. 410-414.

Stone, G.C. and Morrison, J.
1976 "Content as a Key to Purpose of Community Newspapers." *Journalism Quarterly,* 53, pp. 488-494.

Turner, C. F. and Krauss, E.
1978 "Fallible Indicators of the Subjective State of the Nation." *American Psychologist* 33, pp. 456-470.

Wattenberg, M.P.
1982 "From Parties to Candidate: Examining the Role of the Media," *Public Opinion Quarterly* 46, 216-227.

Weaver, D. and McCombs, M.
1980 "Journalism and Social Science: A New Relationship?," *Public Opinion Quarterly* 44, pp 478-492.

Weimann, Gabriel.
1983 "The Obsession to Forecast," *Journalism Quarterly* (forthcoming)

Wheeler, M.
1976 *Lies, Damn Lies and Statistics.* New York: Liveright.

Worchester, R.M.
1980 "Pollsters, the Press and Political Polling in Britain." *Public Opinion Quarterly* 44, pp. 548-566.

INDEX